METAPHYSICS

OR THE

PHILOSOPHY OF CONSCIOUSNESS

PHENOMENAL AND REAL

BY

HENRY LONGUEVILLE MANSEL, B.D.

ISBN: 979-8-89096-433-5

Printed: August 2023

Published and Distributed By:
Lushena Books
607 Country Club Drive, Unit E
Bensenville, IL 60106
www.lushenabks.com

ISBN: 979-8-89096-433-5

THE present volume differs only in a few verbal corrections from the article "METAPHYSICS," as originally published in the last edition of the *Encyclopædia Britannica*. In estimating its character, with reference both to what it omits and to what it attempts to perform, it will be necessary to bear in mind that it is but a reprint of an article written under specified conditions, as a portion of a larger work, and not as an independent treatise. The plan of the article, embracing Metaphysics in the most comprehensive sense, together with the limited space allotted to its execution, rendered it necessary to attempt a general outline of a wide and in some degree ambiguous subject, which, in some respects, might perhaps have been more satisfactorily discussed by means of separate treatises on its subordinate parts. Some matters have thus been entirely omitted, and others very cursorily touched upon, which, under other circumstances, might have had a claim to insertion or fuller treatment. Thus, with the exception of some very slight notices of the modern German philosophy, no attempt has been made to furnish any historical account of the progress and various phases of metaphysical speculation ; a task which, as far as the Encyclopædia was concerned, had in a great measure been already performed in Stewart's Preliminary Dissertation ; and which, besides, could not have been added to the present treatise without exceeding the reasonable limits of an article. And in what has actually been attempted, many important questions, especially in the latter part of the work, have been indicated rather than discussed : some hints have been given to stimulate and direct further inquiry; but little has been done to satisfy it. Some of these deficiencies it would probably be out of my power to remedy; others, which I would gladly have attempted to supply, had I had leisure and opportunity for a complete revision, must at any rate be left as they are for the present. Nevertheless, though fully conscious of the imperfections of the work, I venture to hope that it may be of some service in giving English readers a clearer apprehension of a subject which, in this country, has been much neglected and misunderstood, and which, into whatever errors and extravagances it may at times have fallen, yet has its foundation in some of the deepest needs of human nature, and its superstructure in some of the noblest monuments of human thought.

CONTENTS.

CONTENTS.

METAPHYSICS.

INTRODUCTION.

AMONG the various changes which the language of philosophy has undergone in the gradual progress of human knowledge, there is none more remarkable than the different significations which, in ancient and modern times, have been assigned to the term METAPHYSICS—a term at first sight almost equally indefinite in its etymological signification and in its actual use. As regards the origin of the name, the most recent discussions appear on the whole to confirm the commonly-received opinion, according to which the term *Metaphysics*, though originally employed to designate a treatise of Aristotle, was probably unknown to that philosopher himself. It is true that the oldest and best of the extant commentators on Aristotle refers the inscription of the treatise to the Stagirite ;* but in the extant writings of Aristotle himself, though the work and its subject are frequently referred to under the titles of

---

* Alexander *in Arist. Metaph.* B. (p. 127, ed. Bonitz).

B

First Philosophy, or *Theology*, or *Wisdom*,* no authority is found for the later and more popular appellation. On the whole, the weight of evidence appears to be in favour of the supposition which attributes the inscription τὰ μετὰ τὰ φυσικά to Andronicus Rhodius, the first editor of Aristotle's collected works.   The title, as given to the writings on the first philosophy, probably indicates only their place in the collection, as coming *after the physical treatises* of the author.†   In this respect, the term *Metaphysics* has been aptly compared to that of *Postils;* both names signifying nothing more than the fact of something else having preceded.‡

The title, thus indefinite in its etymological signification, does not at first sight appear to admit of more precision with reference to its actual application.   Mr. Stewart, towards the end of his dissertation on the progress of metaphysical and ethical philosophy,§ notices "the extraordinary change which has gradually and insensibly taken place, since the publication of Locke's

---

* Asclepius, apud Brandis, *Scholia*, p. 519, b. 19.   Bonitz *in Arist. Metaph.* p. 5.

† "Titulum vulgatum τὰ μετὰ τὰ φυσικά non ab ipso esse Aristotele his libris inscriptum, adeo est verisimile ut pro certo haberi possit. . . Ad ordinem librorum hanc inscriptionem referri, ut libri de prima philosophia excipere significentur libros physicos, communis fere est ac verissima interpretum Græcorum sententia " (Bonitz *ad Arist. Metaph.* pp. 3, 5). M. Ravaisson, on the other hand, is of opinion that the name should be referred to Aristotle himself, or to one of his immediate disciples.

‡ Cardwell's preface to Taverner's *Postils.*

§ See *Encyclopædia Britannica*, 8th edition, vol. i. p. 227.

Essay, in the meaning of the word *Metaphysics*—a word formerly appropriated to the ontology and pneumatology of the schools, but now understood as equally applicable to all those inquiries which have for their object to trace the various branches of human knowledge to their first principles in the constitution of our nature." "This change," he continues, "can be accounted for only by a change in the philosophical pursuits of Locke's successors—a change from the idle abstractions and subtleties of the dark ages, to studies subservient to the culture of the understanding ; to the successful exercise of its faculties and powers ; and to a knowledge of the great ends and purposes of our being. It may be regarded, therefore, as a palpable and incontrovertible proof of a corresponding progress of reason in this part of the world."

This change in the pursuits, and consequently in the language, of philosophy had been noticed shortly before by a philosopher of another country in a very different spirit. Hegel, in 1816, introduced his lectures on the history of philosophy in the following words :—" In the other countries of Europe, in which the sciences and the cultivation of the understanding have been prosecuted with zeal and credit, every remembrance and trace of philosophy, the name only excepted, has perished and disappeared. Among the Germans alone it has maintained itself as a national possession. We have received from nature the higher mission to be the preservers of this sacred fire, as the Eumolpidæ of Athens were intrusted with the preservation of the Eleusinian mysteries."* Between these opposite conceptions of Metaphysics or Philosophy (for in the language of Hegel the two terms may be regarded as synonymous), it is not easy for an expositor to select his point of view. A definition of Metaphysics which would include both would be defective philosophically from its vagueness ; one which would exclude either would be defective historically from its incompleteness. To omit the view indicated by Hegel would be to neglect the whole of the ancient and a great part of the modern history of the science. To omit the view indicated by Stewart would be to overlook almost entirely the important share which the writers of our own country have contributed towards

---

* Hegel's *Werke*, vol. xiii. p. 4. English philosophy, name and thing, is especially honoured with the contempt of this critic. "The natural sciences," he says, "are in England denominated Philosophy, An English *Philosophical Journal* treats of chemistry, agriculture, and manure, of housekeeping and professional knowledge, and communicates discoveries in these departments. The English call physical instruments, such as the barometer and thermometer, philosophical instruments. Theories, especially in morals and moral sciences, which are derived from the feelings of the human heart or from experience, are called Philosophy, as well as those which contain principles of political economy. Thus the name at least of Philosophy is honoured in England" (*Ibid.* p. 72 ; see also vol. vi. p. 13). In the same spirit are dictated his criticisms on Bacon, Locke, and Newton ; the latter of whom, he says, has exhibited in his Optics a perfect specimen of the manner in which experiment and reasoning should not be conducted.

the solution of the great problem of philosophy. Yet the reader who has perused a few pages of Aristotle's *Metaphysics* or the later works of a cognate character, on the one hand, and of Locke's *Essay* or Stewart's *Elements*, on the other, will probably be at a loss to conjecture what possible common notion can be found to unite together works so utterly distinct in their aim and method. A few preliminary observations on this point may, it is hoped, in some degree assist in throwing light on this obscure and almost imperceptible link of connection.

Speculative Philosophy is divided by Aristotle into three branches—Physics, Mathematics, and Theology. The first investigates the special attributes of this or that body as such : the second considers the properties of bodily figures abstracted from their material accompaniments : the third contemplates pure existence, apart from the sensible accidents of matter or figure.* This division, however, is one which could not have been made until after philosophy had attained to some considerable development. In the earlier stages of its history, philosophy in general would naturally be identified with one or other of the above branches only, according as its first cultivators sought to explain the

* *Metaph.* v. 1. See also *De Anima*, i. 1. The distinction may be ustrated by an example. Suppose the object of contemplation to be a wooden square ; the physical philosopher considers it *quâ* wooden ; the mathematician, *quâ* square ; the theologian or metaphysician, *quâ* something which exists.

principles and causes of things by means of this or that fundamental assumption. Hence it is, that while the history of *Philosophy* in its widest sense opens with inquiries identical in their aim with those afterwards pursued by the metaphysician, the history of *Metaphysics* proper can hardly be said to have commenced until the progress of thought, and the failure of previous speculations, led men to attempt the solution of the general problem of philosophy in a particular manner.

Philosophy in general may be defined, as nearly as a conception so vague admits of a definition, as an inquiry into the principles and causes of things.* Metaphysics has been defined by Aristotle (and the definition may be for the present provisionally accepted) as the science which contemplates being as being, and the attributes which belong to it as such.† The latter definition, while verbally resembling the former, exhibits, in fact, an important modification of it ; for it implies that the progress of philosophy had necessitated the division of things in general into beings, or things as they are, and phenomena, or things as they appear. The material principles assumed by the Ionians, and the mathematical relations of the Pythagoreans, were

---

* Arist. *Metaph.* i. 1. Τὴν ὀνομαζομένην σοφίαν περὶ τὰ πρῶτα αἴτια καὶ τὰς ἀρχὰς ὑπολαμβάνουσι πάντες. See also Hobbes, *Computatio sive Logica.* chap. 1, sect. 2.

† *Metaph.* iii. 1. Ἔστιν ἐπιστήμη τις ἣ θεωρεῖ τὸ ὂν ᾗ ὂν καὶ τὰ τούτῳ ὑπάρχοντα καθ᾽ αὑτό.

INTRODUCTION.

theories of the universe, falling under the general conception of Philosophy ; but the origin of Metaphysics must rather be dated from the period when the Eleatics denied the reality of the sensible world, and confined the region of truth to the supersensible unity which can be obtained only by contemplation.*

Philosophy becomes synonymous with Metaphysics in the view of those philosophers who regard thought alone as the channel by which men can attain to reality and truth—a point of view which predominates in the speculations and language of ancient Greece and of modern Germany. Our own countrymen have for the most part erred in the other extreme, and limited the province of philosophy too exclusively to the investigation of the phenomena of sense. And the result has been that, while in Britain the name of *Metaphysics* has been rescued from contempt only by an abuse of language which identifies it with a branch of inductive science, in Germany it is not unusual to represent the country of Bacon, Newton, and Locke, as one which has produced no philosophy.

The first step towards a definite conception of Metaphysics was attained by regarding it as *the science of real existence.* But this conception, like the wider one

* Arist. *Metaph.* v. i. Εἰ μὲν οὖν μὴ ἐστί τις ἐτέρα οὐσία παρὰ τὰς φύσει συνεστηκυίας, ἡ φυσικὴ ἂν εἴη πρώτη ἐπιστήμη · εἰ δ' ἐστί τις οὐσία ἀκίνητος, αὕτη προτέρα καὶ φιλοσοφία πρώτη.

of Philosophy in general, becomes in its subsequent process developed from different and even contradictory points of view, till the resulting systems appear to have nothing in common but the name. The notion of *being*, as distinguished from *phenomenon*, corresponds in its original signification with that which the mind conceives as permanent and unchangeable, in opposition to that which is regarded as transitory and fluctuating. Such an object of inquiry may be approached from two opposite sides. It is the real in itself, and it is contemplated by the mind as such. The problem has thus a twofold aspect, as related to the conditions of being and to the conditions of thought ; and its solution may be attempted from the one or the other starting-point. We may commence with abstract principles of being in general, and endeavour to deduce *à priori* the essential characteristics of existence *per se ;* or we may commence with an examination of the actual constitution of the human mind, and endeavour to ascertain empirically how the conception of reality is formed, and what is its consequent value. And either of these methods of inquiry may be so conducted as in the end to lose sight of the original relation which binds them together ; and each may thus present an aspect of irreconcilable antagonism, in place of the mutual pursuit of a common object. The *à priori* reasoner may pervert his conception of absolute being into a form which finds no counterpart

in the human consciousness, and, confident in the infal-
libility of his own process, may condemn as worthless
the mirror which refuses to reflect back the distorted
image. And the investigator of the facts of consciousness, when his imperfect analysis has failed to discover
the hidden element of reality, may proclaim reality itself
to be a dream and a delusion, and the mind and all that
it contains a mere aggregate of phenomena. Deceived by
the apparent parallelism of the distant rays, the opposing theorists forget that those rays must converge some-
where in a common centre : they forget that philosophy
itself is but the articulate development of consciousness ;
that from consciousness all inquiries set out, and to consciousness they must all return.

And such, history tells us, has been the actual fate
of Metaphysics. The clue to its distant mazes, lost
almost at the outset of the journey, became more and
more irrecoverable as the paths diverged more and more
from their common centre ; till its latest expositors on
both sides were unconscious of its existence. If Aristotle for a moment grasped the important truth, that the
laws of things and the laws of thought were alike objects of metaphysical inquiry,* the conviction produced
hardly any result in the details of his treatment: his

---

* *Metaph.* iii. 3. Ὅτι μὲν οὖν τοῦ φιλοσόφου καὶ τοῦ περὶ πάσης τῆς
οὐσίας θεωροῦντος ᾗ πέφυκεν, καὶ περὶ τῶν συλλογιστικῶν ἀρχῶν ἐστὶν ἐπι-
σκέψασθαι, δῆλον.

psychology allied itself chiefly to physics : his metaphysics, after its introductory chapter, deserted the track
of psychology.   If Locke laid the foundation of a better
method of metaphysical inquiry, when he declared, that
"before we set ourselves on inquiries of this nature, it
was necessary to examine our own abilities, and see
what objects our understandings were or were not
fitted to deal with,"* he prematurely excluded the very
question which his method was required to solve, by
asserting that we have no ideas of body or spirit as
substances, but merely suppose an unknown substratum to our external or internal ideas.† The barrier
thus interposed between the sister streams of thought
was widened as each flowed on : the ontological philosophers of modern Germany gloried in being not merely
independent of, but even contradictory to, the testimony
of consciousness, while the psychological teachers of
France and Britain confined themselves more and more
within the charmed circle of phenomena, till D'Alembert
declared that the office of metaphysics was to prove
that all our ideas come from sensation ;‡ and Stewart
denounced the inquiries of ontology as "the most idle
and absurd speculation that ever employed the human

---

* *Essay*, Epistle to the Reader.   † *Essay*, b. ii. ch. 23.

‡ "La métaphysique a pour but d'examiner la génération de nos
idées, et de prouver qu'elles viennent toutes de nos sensations" (*Elém.
de Philos.* p. 143 ; *Mélanges*, vol. iv., quoted in Sir W. Hamilton's
edition of Stewart's Works, vol. i. p. 404).

faculties."* But the principle on which this conclusion logically rests is, as regards the Scottish philosophy, an excrescence rather than an integral portion of the system. We may refuse to admit the unproved dogma which denies to the human mind any conception of substance, and yet avail ourselves of the psychological researches of Reid and Stewart, as a valuable, if an incomplete contribution to the philosophy of consciousness, and, through that, to the solution of those fundamental problems of metaphysics to which consciousness gives rise.

As the metaphysical writings of Aristotle and his followers are likely to be but little known to the majority of modern readers, it may be useful to add a brief account of the ancient method of treating the subject, which will serve at the same time to exhibit more clearly the chasm which separates the earlier conception of the science from that of the modern disciple of Locke or Stewart. "There is a certain science," says Aristotle, " which contemplates Being in so far as it is Being, and the attributes that belong to it essentially as such. This science is not the same with any of those which are called particular sciences ; for none of these inquiries generally concerning Being as Being, but each selects some separate portion of Being, and contemplates the properties of that alone ; as, for example, mathematics. But since we are seeking for the principles and highest

* *Philosophical Essays*, Preliminary Dissertation, ch. i.

causes of things, it is clear that these must have some
nature to which they properly belong.   We must therefore take as the object of our inquiry the first causes of
Being as Being."*

A similar conception of the great problem of philosophy had been previously exhibited by Plato in his
sketch of the office of Dialectic—a science which, though
differing in name and method, is in its purpose and aim
identical with the First Philosophy or Theology of Aristotle.   In the sciences of geometry and arithmetic, he
tells us, certain principles of numbers and figures are
assumed by hypothesis as self-evident, but not investi-
gated by any process of reasoning; and from these
assumptions the proposed questions are demonstrated.
But in dialectic the same hypotheses are employed, not
as first principles, but as stepping-stones to some higher
truth and absolutely first principle, which is grasped by
the intellect without hypothesis, as that on which all
other reasoning ultimately depends.†

The problem of Metaphysics, as conceived by both
these philosophers, may be perhaps more clearly stated
in modern language as follows :—" To determine the
relation that exists between the subjective necessities
of thought and the objective necessities of things."   In

* *Metaph.* iii. 1.   The same view is also exhibited more fully in
v. 1, in a passage too long for quotation.

† *Republic*, vi. p. 510.

mathematical demonstration, for example, we start from certain axiomatic principles, of which, as mathematicians, we can give no other account than that they are *self-evident;* that is to say, that we are compelled by the constitution of our minds to admit them. But this opens a further question. What is the relation of self-evidence to reality? Is the necessity, of which I am conscious, of thinking in a certain manner, any sure guarantee of a corresponding relation in the objects about which I think? In other words, are the laws of thought also laws of things; or, at least, do they furnish evidence by which the laws of things can be ascertained? Is thought identical with being, so that every mode of the one is at the same time a mode of the other? Is thought an exact copy of being, so that every mode of the one is an adequate representative of some corresponding mode of the other? Or, finally, is thought altogether distinct from being, so that we cannot issue from the circle of our ideas, to seize the realities which those ideas are supposed to represent? Does anything exist beyond the phenomena of our own consciousness? and, if it does exist, what is the path by which it is to be reached?

The ancient and mediæval metaphysicians adopted almost unanimously the *à priori* method of reasoning downwards from the assumption of abstract principles of Being,—as the moderns have laid the foundation of the inverse method of reasoning upwards from the

phenomena of Thought.   A short analysis of the principal
subjects treated of in the *Metaphysics* of Aristotle will
serve to exhibit the details of the former method, as far
as our present limits will permit.   In the order of the
books we shall follow the common arrangement, which,
though far from unexceptionable, is perhaps not more
liable to objection than others which have been proposed
in its place.

The first book comprises a psychological account of
the nature of science and its origin in the human mind,
followed by a history of the researches of previous
philosophers into the principles and causes of things.
To this is subjoined a kind of appendix (the book
known as *A minor*), containing an argument in favour
of the existence of a first principle of things, and
consequently of the possibility of attaining to a knowledge of it; with a caution concerning the method
to be pursued, and the necessity of accommodating the
mode of reasoning to the nature of the object.

The second book commences with a list of questions,
which are to be answered in the course of the treatise,
and which may be regarded as furnishing a sort of table
of contents to the rest of the work.*   They may be
briefly summed up as follows :—1. Do the principles of

---

* The correspondence, however, is by no means exact.   Michelet observes :—"En général, il faut remarquer ici que l'énumération et le dé-
veloppement des problèmes contenus dans ce livre ne répondent pas

being and those of demonstration belong to the same or to different sciences, to one science or to many? 2. Are there other substances besides objects of sense ; and, if so, of how many kinds? 3. To what science does it belong to take cognisance of identity and difference, similarity and dissimilarity, priority and posteriority, and such like? 4. Are the principles of things to be sought in their genera, or in the material elements of individuals, or does there exist a cause or causes other than matter, and separable from it? 5. Are there the same principles of things perishable and imperishable, and are all principles themselves imperishable? 6. Are being and unity the essence of all things, or must other elements be added? 7. Are the principles of things universal or individual, potential or actual, active or passive? 8. Are numbers, lines, figures, and points substances or not ; and, if substances, do they exist separate from the objects of sense? A further development of the difficulties involved in these questions occupies the remainder of this book.

The third book is occupied with the sketch of a

exactement à leurs solutions données dans les autres livres. Car beaucoup de problèmes sont transposés ; quelques-uns n'y sont qu'effleurés ; plusieurs y sont réunis, à cause de l'affinité qu'il y a entre eux ; d'autres enfin sont traités en différents endroits " (*Exam. Critique*, p. 131). The division of the questions themselves admits of considerable variety. Michelet and Ravaisson enumerate as many as seventeen. Mr. Maurice (*Moral and Metaphysical Philosophy*, p. 183) reduces them to six.

Science of Being as such, which has for its object both the principles of things and the laws of reasoning. In it the philosopher maintains the truth of the logical principles of contradiction and excluded middle, against the objections of Heraclitus, Anaxagoras, and others, and establishes the distinction between being and appearance, and consequently between truth and error.

The fourth book is an explanation of the various significations of several philosophical terms. The terms defined are,—principle, cause, element, nature, necessity, unity, being, substance, identity, distinctness and diversity, similarity and dissimilarity, opposition and contrariety, priority and posteriority, power, quantity, quality, relation, perfection, limitation, in respect of and in itself (καθ' ὅ and καθ' αὐτό), disposition, habit, passion, privation, possession, derivation, part, whole, imperfection, genus, falsehood, accident.

The fifth book continues the sketch of a Science of Being which was commenced in the third. This science (called by Aristotle *Theology*, and afterwards known as *Metaphysics*) is distinguished from Physics and Mathematics. Being *per se*, the proper object of Metaphysics, is distinguished from other senses of the term,—such as accidental existence, which is not an object of science, and truth in judgments, which belongs to thought and not to things.

The sixth book is a continuation of the same subject.

Being, in the highest sense of the term, is identified with Substance, to the exclusion of the other categories. But *substance*, again, is a term used in various senses; sometimes for the essence of a thing, sometimes for its universal attributes, sometimes for the genus, sometimes for the subject of attributes, or the individual. A discussion of these different senses, and of the philosophical theories connected with them, occupies the remainder of the book.

The seventh book continues the discussion of Substance. The essence of sensible things may be considered in two points of view,—as regards the *matter* or potential essence, and as regards the *form* or actual essence, corresponding to the genus and difference in a definition. The unity of such objects must be sought for in the principle which unites these two. Intelligible objects, which have no matter, are one by virtue of their form.

In the eighth book the distinction between matter and form, or potential and actual existence, is further discussed. The distinction between the potential and the actual is defended against objections. The actual is prior to the potential in the order of nature and of reason, and, in one sense, in that of time also. It is prior in the order of reason; for power has no meaning but in relation to performance. It is prior, too, in the · order of time in the species, though not in the individual;

for the powers of anything are produced by its efficient cause, and the cause, as such, is in action. Hence it follows, that the distinction between the potential and the actual exists only in relation to things perishable; for that which is eternal cannot have become what it is, and therefore can never be potentially that which it is not actually. In other words, there is a cause of change which itself acts unchangeably, and which is prior to all change. The chief good and highest principle is thus ever active, and there is no eternal principle of evil; for actual evil is a corruption posterior to the possibility of evil. The book concludes with a discussion of the nature of truth and falsehood; the latter of which can have no place in relation to first principles, which must either be absolutely known or absolutely unknown.

The ninth book is a digression, treating of the opposition between the one and the many. The various senses of unity enumerated in the fourth book are now reduced to four,—the continuous, the whole, the individual, and the universal. Unity is identified with existence, and declared in opposition to the Pythagoreans and Platonists, to be not a substance, but an universal notion predicable of every kind of subject in the several categories. The opposition between unity and plurality is shown to be not one of contrariety, but of relation. The book concludes with a further digression

on some points connected with the opposition of con-
traries.

In the tenth book, as well as in the ninth, the connection of the argument is somewhat interrupted. This
book, in fact, contains little more than a recapitulation
of matters treated of in some of the earlier books. The
concluding chapters of this book are an abridgment of
a portion of the *Physics* of Aristotle, and appear altogether out of place in their present position.

The eleventh book is the most important of all ; and
though apparently incomplete in itself and in its connection with its predecessors, may be regarded as containing an outline of Aristotle's views on the profoundest
problems of metaphysical philosophy. In this book,
after some preliminary remarks on the nature of substance, change, and causation, the philosopher resumes
his inquiry into the nature of the first cause—the unchanging principle of all change and motion. Sensible
substances, the objects of physical science, are subject to
change ; and all change implies a progress of the same
subject from one of two opposite states to the other ;
from not-being to being, or the reverse. Hence change
implies three elements : the form, the privation, and the
matter potentially susceptible of both. But change itself must take place in consequence of some cause ; we
must therefore add a fourth principle to the three elements. We are thus led to the notion of a substance

which is the efficient cause of change, and this substance
must be eternal; for even change and time are conceived
as imperishable, and these depend upon a substance.
The cause of change must therefore be a being eternally
acting, and which, consequently, cannot be conceived as
having a power to act prior to the exercise of that power.
In other words, the first cause (as was said before in the
eighth book) can never be potentially that which it is
not actually. The first cause is thus active without
being passive; it moves all things without being
itself moved. The action of an unmoved cause of
motion may be regarded as analogous to that of an
object of desire on the appetite, or of an object
of contemplation on the intellect; for these excite
to action without being themselves acted upon. Thus
the principle of change may be conceived both as
first cause and as final cause or chief good, which all
things desire, and by the desire of which they are
moved.* This first cause is God, who, as the highest
object of intellectual contemplation, must himself be
conceived as Intellect, as ever active, as living (for the
activity of intellect is life), as immaterial, having neither
finite nor infinite extension, and consequently no parts,
as impassive and unchangeable. To this sublime theology are appended some curious astronomical speculations, apparently intended to reconcile the unity of the

* Κινεῖ δὲ ὡς ἐρώμενον. *Metaph.* xi. 7.

Divine Mover with the seeming variety in the celestial motions. To these speculations, which are chiefly derived from previously existing astronomical theories, the philosopher himself does not appear to attach much importance. Resuming the theological argument, he maintains that the Deity, as an ever-active and unchanging Intellect, must have an unchanging object of contemplation, and as there is no other such object, he must contemplate himself. The book concludes with a criticism of previous philosophers, whose opinions, as he considers, are irreconcilable with the existence of one supreme Ruler of the Universe.

The two last books must be considered either as an introduction to the eleventh, which most modern commentators regard as the conclusion of the whole treatise, or as a controversial appendix, intended to fortify the positions which that book had established. The controversy is chiefly directed against the Pythagorean and Platonic philosophies, which sought the eternal principle of the universe, the one in the theory of numbers and geometrical magnitudes, the other in that of ideas. The details of this controversy, part of which is little more than a repetition of the arguments of the first book, are chiefly valuable in a historical point of view, as throwing light on the Pythagorean and Platonic doctrines ; but they contribute little to the elucidation of Aristotle's own conception of Metaphysics.

The Aristotelian First Philosophy, as exhibited in the above sketch, has certainly little enough in common with an inductive science of the human mind; and its speculations will probably appear to a modern reader sufficiently vague and barren. But they have a value, historical and philosophical, far beyond their apparent significance to a superficial inspector. They have a historical value, as representing the course of metaphysical inquiry which was pursued, with scarcely an exception, for nearly twenty centuries, and which even now exercises a legitimate influence over the minds of men hardly less extensive than its former absolute dominion. And they have a philosophical value, of which their historical position is the index. However wide may be the gulf that separates the ancient and modern systems of philosophy, they have this at least in common, that both are the product of human minds, thinking under the same laws, and impelled to speculation by the same irresistible motive of yearnings unsatisfied, and doubts unsolved. Each seeks to comply with the requirements of the same nature : each sets out from the ground of that common consciousness which, in intellect no less than in affection, makes the whole world kin. "Homo sum; humani nihil a me alienum puto," is a maxim no less applicable to the most abstruse speculations of philosophy than to the affairs of our every-day life. Philosophy, in all its aspects, is a contribution to the history of humanity; an attempt, successful or unsuccessful, to carry out the great end and purpose of man's existence. The study of the master-minds of the human race is almost equally instructive in what they achieved and in what they failed to achieve; and speculations which are far from solving the riddle of existence have their use in teaching us why it is insoluble.

Thus it appears that the term METAPHYSICS has been at different times used in two principal senses: 1. As synonymous with Ontology, to denote that branch of philosophy which investigates the nature and properties of *Being* or *Reality,* as distinguished from *Phenomenon* or *Appearance.* 2. As synonymous with Psychology, to denote that branch of philosophy which investigates the *faculties, operations, and laws of the human mind.* These two sciences may be regarded, as has been already observed, as investigations of the same problem from opposite points of view; but this feature of relation has been practically overlooked by the majority of writers on either side; and the link which is to connect the actual contents of each remains still to be pointed out. One, indeed, but hardly definite enough, has been indicated by Dugald Stewart. "On comparing together," says that distinguished philosopher, "the multifarious studies now classed together under the title of Metaphysics, it will be found difficult to trace any common circumstance but this—that they all require the same sort of mental exertion for their prosecution ; the exercise, I mean, of that power (called by Locke *reflection*) by which the mind turns its attention inwards upon its own operations, and the subject of its own consciousness." This passage seems to point out a closer connection between the different senses of the term *Metaphysics* than that which it actually expresses. For it refers us not merely to a common method of inquiry, in the process of *reflection*, but also to a common object, in the *facts of our own consciousness*. But to exhibit this connection clearly, the latter term must be extended to a somewhat wider signification than that sanctioned by Stewart's use of it.

On this term, Sir William Hamilton remarks : " Aristotle, Descartes, Locke, and philosophers in general, have regarded consciousness, not as a particular faculty, but as the universal condition of intelligence. Reid, on the contrary, following probably Hutcheson, and followed by Stewart, Royer-Collard, and others, has classed consciousness as a co-ordinate faculty with the other intellectual powers, distinguished from them, not as the species from the individual, but as the individual from the individual. And as the particular faculties have each their peculiar object, so the peculiar object of consciousness is *the operations of the other faculties themselves, to the exclusion of the objects* about which those operations are conversant.

"This analysis we regard as false. For it is impossible, in the *first* place, to discriminate consciousness from all the other cognitive faculties, or to discriminate any one of these from consciousness ; and, in the *second*, to conceive a faculty cognisant of the various mental operations, without being also cognisant of their several objects.

" *We know ;* and *we know that we know :*—these propositions, *logically* distinct, are *really* identical ; each implies the other. We *know* (*i.e.* feel, perceive, imagine, remember, etc.) only as we *know that we thus know ;* and we *know that we know,* only as we know in *some particular manner* (*i.e. feel, perceive,* etc.) So true is the scholastic brocard :—' *Non sentimus nisi sentiamus nos sentire ; non sentimus nos sentire nisi sentiamus.*' The attempt to analyse the cognition *I know,* and the cognition *I know that I know,* into the separate energies of distinct faculties, is therefore vain.

" But the vice of Reid's analysis is further manifested in his arbitrary limitation of the sphere of consciousness ; proposing to it the various intellectual operations, but excluding their objects. . . . The assertion that we can be conscious of an act of knowledge, without being conscious of its object, is virtually suicidal. A mental operation is only what it is, by relation to its object ; the object at once determining its existence, and specifying the character of its existence.

But if a relation cannot be comprehended in one of its terms, so we cannot be conscious of an operation without being conscious of the object to which it exists only as correlative. For example, We are conscious of a perception, says Reid, but are not conscious of its object. Yet how can we be conscious of a *perception*, that is, how can we *know* that a perception exists,—that it is a perception, and not another mental state, and that it is the perception of the rose, and of nothing but a rose,— unless this *consciousness* involve a knowledge (or consciousness) of the object, which at once determines the existence of the act, specifies its kind, and distinguishes its individuality ? Annihilate the object, you annihilate the operation ; annihilate the consciousness of the object, you annihilate the consciousness of the operation."*

Extending the term *facts of consciousness*, in accordance with the principle of the above criticism, to denote all those phenomena of mind whose existence in a definite form, as operations of a particular kind, and the knowledge of that existence, are identical ; we may find in these facts an adequate object for the investigations of *Metaphysics* in the most general sense of the term ; and in this sense, accordingly, we would define the science of which we are treating, as " Metaphysics, or the Philosophy of the Facts of Consciousness, considered subjectively, in relation to the mind knowing, and

* *Discussions*, p. 47.

objectively, in relation to the things known." Meta-physics will thus naturally divide itself into two branches,—PSYCHOLOGY, or the science of the facts of consciousness as such ; and ONTOLOGY, or the science of the same facts considered in their relation to realities existing without the mind.

Neither of these two branches of Metaphysics, thus treated, can be considered as exhausting the senses in which their respective names have been used. Psycho-logy, both in its earliest and in some of its latest develop-ments, has been treated in connection with physiology, and thus extended to phenomena beyond the range of the facts of consciousness properly so called. Aristotle, the first systematic expositor of the science, enumerates, in conjunction with the threefold division of the facts of consciousness into those of sensation, thought, and voli-tion,* a fourth function of nutriment and growth, the existence of which cannot be identified with the con-sciousness of it. *I perceive*, and *I know that I perceive ; I think*, and *I know that I think ; I will*, and *I know that I will :*—these propositions are severally equivalent to each other ; but not so *I digest*, and *I know that I di-gest*. Modern writers on psychology have treated it with

---

* I have ventured to use the term *volition*, as nearly equivalent to the *motive principle* of Aristotle ; though the connection of the latter with the will is but imperfectly exhibited in his treatise, owing to the want of a strict distinction between the phenomena of human conscious-ness and those of animal life.

a similar extension to physiological phenomena. Ontology, in like manner, has, in modern times especially,
sought a foundation for its speculations beyond the domain of consciousness, and even contradictory to it ;
nearly the whole of the systems of German metaphysicians since Kant being a series of attempts, more or less
plausible, to account for the origin of the facts of consciousness themselves, by postulating a principle of which
we are not and cannot be conscious. Neither of these
extensions of the field of inquiry will be adopted in the
present treatise. We shall, indeed, have to borrow largely
from physiology in illustration of the bodily conditions
on which mental consciousness depends ; but the two
sciences will be considered as distinct branches of
inquiry, though the conclusions of the one may throw
some collateral light on the researches of the other.*
On the other hand, the transcendental method, which
seeks to found a Philosophy of Being in a point above
consciousness, will be rejected, from a conviction of its
utter inability to furnish any reliable or even intelligible results. All such theories are open to two fundamental objections:—they cannot be communicated, and
they cannot be verified. They cannot be communicated ;

---

* The limits of psychology and physiology are defined in an excellent
essay by M. Jouffroy, *Nouveaux Mélanges Philosophiques*, p. 222. The
phenomena of consciousness, which are known only as affections of
myself, belong to the former science ; those of animal life, which can
be discerned by observation of foreign bodies, belong to the latter.

for the communication must be made by words ; and the
meaning of those words must be understood; and the
understanding is a form of consciousness, and subject to
the laws of consciousness. They cannot be verified ;
for, to verify, we must compare the author's experience
with our own ; and such comparison is again an act of
consciousness, and subject to its laws. This consideration must serve as our apology for the neglect of
systems which are indeed entitled by their celebrity to
a prominent place in the history of metaphysical philosophy, but which cannot, except upon the ground of
their truth, claim admission into a treatise on the
science itself.

There is a wide application of the term *consciousness*, in which it is coextensive with the whole cycle of
human knowledge ; for we can know nothing without
being conscious that we know it ; and we can investigate no objects but those whose existence, real or apparent, must be made known to us by consciousness. In
this sense, what is out of consciousness is out of the
field of human knowledge altogether. But this consideration does not affect the definition which assigns
the facts of consciousness as the proper object of metaphysical science. For in other sciences those facts are
considered, necessarily indeed, but secondarily only, as
the means by which the direct objects of such sciences
are made known to us. The manner in which con-

sciousness operates as the instrument of the physical sciences is not taken into account by those sciences, nor is the nature and veracity of its testimony called in question. Physical science does not trouble itself with the inquiry, whether the objects which it investigates are real or apparent; qualities of matter or modes of the spectator's own mind; whether they are gained directly or indirectly; by innate or acquired powers; by one faculty òf the mind alone or by the union of many. Its researches are not in any way affected by the adoption of this or that theory of consciousness itself; though consciousness is the means by which its objects are conveyed to it. In metaphysical science, on the other hand, consciousness itself is the direct object of our inquiries; and that in two points of view: 1. In its *phenomenal character*, in relation to the conscious subject; in which we consider the several affections of the human mind in which consciousness consists, and the faculties, operations, and laws, upon which those affections depend. 2. In its *real character*, in relation to the objects of which we are conscious; in which we consider the veracity of its testimony in reference to things without the mind, and the indications which it is supposed to furnish of the actual constitution of those things. Of these two inquiries, the first is preliminary, and auxiliary to the second; both because it is necessary to know what the facts of consciousness are in

themselves, before inquiring into their ulterior relations, and because the light which the former inquiry is
calculated to throw on the laws and limits of human
thought, will be of importance in determining how far
it is possible to obtain a satisfactory answer to the
latter. We commence, then, with the first portion of
our inquiry.

I.

PSYCHOLOGY, OR THE PHILOSOPHY OF THE PHENOMENA OF CONSCIOUSNESS.

CONSCIOUSNESS, in its relation to the subject or person conscious, is of two kinds ; or rather, is composed of two elements—the presentative or intuitive, and the representative or reflective. The phenomena of the former class may be distinguished by the general name of *Intuitions ;* those of the latter by that of *Thoughts.*

Presentative or intuitive consciousness is the consciousness of an *individual object,* be it thing, act, or state of mind, immediately present before me, *here* or *now ;* that is to say, with a definite position in space, or in time, or in both. Representative or reflective consciousness is the consciousness, *primarily* and *directly,* of a *general notion or concept,* indifferently related to any number of possible individuals ; *secondarily* and *indirectly,* of *one or more actual individuals* conceived as exhibiting at the moment, in an unity of representation, the several attributes which the general notion involves. For example, I see a triangle drawn on paper. I need not know that the figure now lying before me is called a triangle. I may be unable to give any definition of it.

D

It is enough that I see a figure, which I did not construct for myself according to any pre-existing notion, but found there already constructed. This is *presentative consciousness,* or *intuition.* The triangle is before me, as an object seen in itself, not necessarily representative of anything else. But, having seen the triangle, I gather a general notion of its figure, indifferently applicable to it or to any other specimen ; and I imagine a particular figure, at another time and in another place, as embodying that notion. This is *representative consciousness,* and in a two-fold manner. First, the general notion is representative of any number of possible triangles, even when none is actually present to the consciousness. Secondly, the same notion is now actually exhibited in an image ; which image represents the original figure from which the notion was derived. The same distinction is applicable to mental as well as to bodily phenomena. I feel an emotion of anger ; I am conscious of its presence now, as a definite state of mind distinguishable from others. This consciousness is *presentative.* When the angry fit is over, I meditate upon my past state, and recall in imagination the emotion which I have experienced. This consciousness is *representative.* Presentative consciousness contains two constituent elements—the conscious subject, and the object of which that subject is conscious. Representative consciousness contains three elements—the subject, the object (*i.e.* the image), and the concept or general notion mediating between them. A fourth element is implied as a condition, though not actually present in consciousness—viz. the original intuition from which the notion was derived, and which the object or image represents.

The ultimate object of all consciousness is thus an *individual;* for all intuitions are directly cognisant of individuals ; and all concepts, to be realised in consciousness, require to be individualised in an image. Without the application of this test, we should not be able to distinguish between the conceivable and the inconceivable ; between signs indicative of notions and signs indicative of no notions at all. I may define a *triangle* as a rectilinear figure of *three* sides ; and I may also define a *biangle* as a rectilinear figure of *two* sides ; and nothing but the attempt to construct the corresponding images can show me that the one term denotes a conceivable object, and that the other is an inconceivable piece of nonsense. The individual is thus the ultimate object of all actual consciousness ; in intuition directly, and in thought indirectly. To complete our explanation, we must therefore determine what is meant by an *individual.*

By the term *an individual* is meant, in psychology, no more than an object occupying a definite position in space or time. It is indifferent, in this point of view, whether the several individuals thus distinguished can or cannot really exist apart from each other ; or whether the portion of space or time which each occupies is distinguished from other portions naturally or arbitrarily. The leaf which I see before me is an individual ; so is the bough ; so is the tree ; so is the forest. Each has its own position in space, which nothing else can occupy along with it. A chain of six feet long is an individual ; whether it exists separately, or only as part of a longer chain. Every link, and every fragment of a link, of the chain is again an individual, in so far as, with or without physical separation, it may be made a distinct object of sight or thought. What space is to material individuals, time is to individual phenomena of mind. I may feel anger or fear many times in succession ; but each has its own peculiar portion of time ; and the passion which I felt yesterday, however similar in other respects, is numerically distinct, as an individual state of mind, from that which I felt the day before yesterday, or that which I am feeling at this moment. We need not at present inquire whether each of these distinct individuals has in reality a separate existence apart from our point of view or not. They may be independent units : they may be fractions of larger units : they may be multiples of smaller units : they may be constituent parts of one only real unit, the universe. They may be modes of my own mind ; or they may be attributes of something distinct from myself. These questions belong to Ontology, not to

Psychology. It is sufficient for our present purpose to state, that whatever occupies a distinct portion of space, however arbitrarily distinguished, is an individual object of external intuition ; and whatever occupies a distinct moment of time, without extension in space, is an individual object of internal intuition.

On the other hand, general notions or concepts, as such, have no definite position in time or space ; though, when realised in an individual act of thought, they *must* have a relation to the former, and *may* have to the latter. The definition of a triangle, as a rectilinear figure of three sides, is indifferently applicable to a triangle in England or to one in America ; to one drawn on paper or to one engraved on stone ; to one conceived yesterday or to-day. But when actually employed in conception it becomes *my present thought about a triangle ;* and this has its definite position in time, and is related to an image conceived as occupying a definite position in space. The verbal description of a particular coin is indifferently representative of all coins struck from the same die ; but two shillings of the same coinage, though they may be undistinguishable in other respects, are yet separate individuals, as occupying distinct portions of space. The general notion is thus *potentially* representative of many individuals ; that is to say, it may, *in different acts of thought*, be employed in relation to any member of a certain class ; but when *actually* so employed, *in any one single act of thought*, it becomes amalgamated with the individual in which its attributes are united, and is only conceived along with the special characteristics of the individual. Thus the notion of a triangle, as such, does not imply that it is equilateral, isosceles, or scalene ; but I can never actually conceive a triangle which is none of these, or all of them at once. I must conceive it as some one of them only. But, *in successive acts of thought*, the same general notion may be represented in the imagination, at one time with three equal sides, at another with two, at another with all unequal. The notion is thus not the adequate and actual representative of any single object, but an inadequate and potential representative of many.

We have thus one characteristic of the concept or general representative notion ; namely, *that it cannot in itself be depicted to sense or imagination ;* though, in every complete act of representation, it forms one element of an image which is so depicted. The mere notion of a triangle, apart from the consideration of the equality or inequality of its sides, is not an object of imagination ; nor the notion of an equilateral triangle, without a given length of the sides ; nor, again, the notion of an equilateral triangle whose sides are each two feet long, without the additional limitation of its occupying a particular position in space ;—under which limitation, it is no longer general, but individual, and can be constructed in the imagination as an object of intuition. A second characteristic of all general notions is, *that they require to be fixed in a representative sign.* The general notion, as such, is not a sensible image, but an intelligible relation ; and such a relation, as far as our experience can testify, cannot be apprehended without the aid of *language—i.e.* of some system of signs, verbal or other. The case of the deaf and dumb is no exception to this rule ; for *language,* in the above sense, is not synonymous with *articulation.* The mental development of the deaf and dumb is effected by the substitution of a system of signs addressed to the eye or the hand, in the place of one addressed to the ear ; and this system performs precisely the same office in relation to them that speech performs in relation to others : it constitutes, in fact, *their language.* Language in this sense appears, as far as experience can inform us, to be necessary, not merely to the communication, but even to the formation of thought. The notion, as such, must be emancipated from all special relation to space or time. The definition of a triangle must not imply where it exists ; nor the definition of anger, when it takes place ; and this emancipation is never completely effected, except by means of symbols, verbal or other, by which the notion is fixed as a relation in the understanding.* We have thus, in the complete exercise of

---

* The distinction between intuition and thought thus corresponds

thought, three successive representations. The sign is representative of the notion ; the notion is representative of the image ; and the image is representative of the object from which the notion was formed.

Presentative and representative consciousness, thus distinguished, must be considered, in their actual exercise, as indicating a logical rather than a real division ; as pointing out the elements of a perfect act of consciousness, which are separable in thought; but not two distinct acts existing separately in practice. In every complete act of consciousness offered to us for analysis, the presentative and representative elements are combined; and without such a combination, it would appear as if consciousness, properly so called, could have no existence. To have a complete consciousness, for example, of any particular object of sense, say of an oak-tree, two conditions are necessary ; first, that certain impressions should be made upon the organ of sensation ; and secondly, that these impressions should be discerned as constituting an object ; i.e. that they should ·be separated from all other objects, and considered by themselves as constituting a whole, which can be compared with and distinguished from other wholes. To the mere sight the oak is presented along

to that noted by Leibnitz between *intuitive* and *symbolical* knowledge. See his *Meditationes de Cognitione Veritate et Ideis*, where, however, the distinction is hardly marked with sufficient precision.

with the surrounding scenery ; but to recognise it as an
oak, the trunk must be considered separately from the
ground from which it springs, and the branches and the
leaves must be discerned as parts of the tree, and separated from the surrounding objects. The reception of
the whole scene presented to the eye is an act of mere
intuition ; but the knowledge of each impression as
being what it is, and the combination of a portion of
such impressions into a separate whole, is an act of
reflection or thought.* Neither of these two elements
alone can constitute a complete act of consciousness.
Let us suppose, for instance, the existence of a being
furnished with human organs of sensation, but with no
power of remembering or reflecting upon the objects
presented to them, and no continuance of any impression
beyond the moment of its actual presence. It is probable that, in such a case, though diverse objects might
be successively presented to the senses, yet there would

---

* Cheselden says of his patient, who had been couched for cataract,—
"He knew not the shape of anything, nor any one thing from another,
however different in shape or magnitude." The language is ambiguous ;
it may mean that he was unable at first to separate the different objects
in the field of vision from each other, or it may mean only that he could
not distinguish them by their right names. Condillac goes beyond the
warrant of the original in rendering, "Il apercevoit tous les objets pêle-
mêle et dans la plus grande confusion" (*Traité des Sensations*, p. iii.
ch. 5). But Cheselden's experiment, besides the want of precision in
the report, is not decisive for other reasons : 1. Because a cataract does
not produce total blindness ; 2. Because the other senses had been
educated before the operation was performed.

be no consciousness of their diversity; for such consciousness requires the juxtaposition of the objects in the mind, and this can only be effected by memory. Animals, trees, and stones, might be successively placed before his eyes. Pleasure and pain and fear and anger might possibly take place within him; but as each departed, he would have no knowledge that it had ever existed, and consequently no power of comparison with anything else. He would thus have no distinct consciousness of each object *as referred to a separate notion:* he could not say, this which I see is a tree or a stone; this which I feel is fear or anger. His consciousness, if consciousness it could be called, would probably be no more than an indefinite sense of uneasiness, a feeling of momentary irritation in the organ affected, but without discerning in what manner it is affected, and without distinguishing the permanent self from its momentary affection.* This is the lowest degree of intelligence, the germ of consciousness, but not itself entitled to the name; as being deficient in the essential conditions of limitation and difference, not having realised the distinction between subject and object, or between one

---

* A state of representation very nearly resembling this is supposed by Leibnitz to exist in his monads. This state he calls perception without apperception or consciousness, and considers it as the characteristic state of existence of simple monads, as distinguished from souls, which are capable of memory and distinct consciousness. (See *Monadologie*, sect. 14, 19.)

object and another.*   But let us go one step further, and
suppose the same being to be capable, not merely of
receiving, but of retaining and associating together,
various impressions, though still destitute of the power
of reflecting upon them.   Let us suppose, that is to say,
that the impression, once made, may continue for a time
in conjunction with others, and spontaneously recur
upon certain occasions ; though the subject of the impression is unable to set it apart as an object of thought,
or to recall it by an effort of his own will.   We have
now a second stage of intelligence—a partial consciousness, embracing a variety of objects and relations of
similarity or dissimilarity between them : we have the
recurrence, moreover, of certain feelings upon the
repetition of the circumstances under which they were
originally excited.   In a word, we have *an association of
intuitions*.   But the conditions of consciousness are not
yet complete ; for memory, at this stage of its development (the μνήμη of Aristotle), though it implies a repetition of phenomena, does not as yet imply a knowledge

---

* If the testimony of Psychology is to be trusted, the sublime intellectual condition in which subject and object are identified, a condition
longed for by mystics of all ages, and proclaimed as the basis of philosophy by modern German metaphysicians, is a degradation of man to the
level, possibly, of a zoophyte.   Yet there have not been wanting philosophers to proclaim this lowest possible manifestation of animal existence
as the exaltation of man to the level of God—as the state of Deity con-
templating himself.

that it is a repetition.   An animal at this stage of intelligence might, for instance, be beaten for a fault, and the recurrence of the fault might naturally suggest an imagination of the pain ; but this imagination need not be consciously regarded as a remembrance of pain felt at a former time.   The reproduction would be spontaneous, not voluntary, and probably not accompanied by any conscious reference to past time.   Let us now assume another step in the scale of intelligence, and suppose our imaginary being to possess, not merely a power of receiving and retaining impressions, but also of recalling them by a voluntary effort (the ἀνάμνησις of Aristotle). This implies that the leading features of the impression remain fixed in the mind, independently of the presence of the object at a particular place or time.   This is the distinctive feature of the concept or general notion, in which, whether by a conscious process or not, the mind abstracts the leading attributes of an object from the condition of limitation in space and time, and is able, under the guidance of those attributes, to recognise the object when presented to it at other times, and, under the same guidance, to reproduce at will the image of the object when absent.   Here we have the co-operation of thought proper, as evidenced by a conscious recognition of objects as such, and of their several relations to the one conscious self, whose permanence and personal identity is necessarily discerned in every act of consciousness properly so called, as the continuous subject of successive modifications. This is the only form of intelligence which can properly be expressed by the judgment, *I know*, or *I know that I know;* and at this stage we have reached the point of true consciousness, in which the existence of a phenomenon is identical with the knowledge of its existence, and the mind, in the act of being affected in any manner, is at the same time cognisant of being so affected.

The above stages must not be regarded as corresponding to a chronological development of the actual phenomena of the human mind. Logically, perhaps, the several elements by whose co-operation consciousness is produced, may be thus analysed; but in the actual progress of the mind by education, the several elements are so mingled together that it is impossible to point out any particular time at which one exists separately from the rest, or to mark the period of each new accession. Classifications, which we are unable to form for ourselves, are, from the earliest dawn of intelligence, given to us, already formed by others. The child, in learning to give names to the objects placed before him, and to repeat those names at each recurrence of the objects, learns, unconsciously to himself, to perform the acts of reminiscence and generalisation, along with that of sensation, and advances by imperceptible degrees to a definite consciousness. To point out each successive stage of the process by which sensibility gives birth to intuition, and intuition to thought, is as impossible as to determine the several moments at which the same child receives each successive increase of his stature, or each successive development of his bodily powers. The mind, like the body, acquires its functions by insensible degrees, "unseen, yet crescive in its faculty," and we find ourselves in the possession and exercise of nature's gifts, without being able to say how we acquired them.

Consciousness proper, as above described, must possess in some degree the attributes of *clearness* and *distinctness*. Using the same term in a wider and less accurate sense, we may distinguish between an *obscure* or an *indistinct*, and a *clear* or a *distinct* consciousness. An act of consciousness, whether presentative or representative, is *clear* when its object as a whole can be distinguished from any other; when this cannot be done, it is *obscure*. An act of consciousness is *distinct* when the several parts constituting its object can be distinguished from each other; when this is not the case, it is *indistinct.** To form a clear or distinct consciousness, an act of reflection must accompany the intuition. An obscure or indistinct consciousness may in some degree be obtained by intuition alone. The latter con-

---

* The difference between *clear* and *obscure, distinct* and *indistinct* or *confused* cognitions is due to Leibnitz. (See his *Meditationes de Cognitione Veritate et Ideis.*)

tains all the materials of the former, though not disposed in the same relations to each other. In an obscure or indistinct intuition we may be dimly aware of the existence of differences of some kind, but be unable to say what they are. In order to obtain this latter knowledge, the first step must be to separate our confused intuition into distinct portions ; and in performing this task we are, as a matter of fact, invariably assisted by the distinctions of language ; that is to say, by a classification already performed by the reflection of others. By learning to recognise under their names the different portions of a confused intuition, we take the first step towards a clear and distinct consciousness of things and thoughts. It is obvious, however, from what has been said before, that the terms *clear* and *distinct* are rather relative than absolute, and that a perfectly obscure consciousness is no consciousness at all in the proper sense of the term.

ORIGIN OF LANGUAGE.

What has been said concerning the relation of thought to language may perhaps suggest two other questions which have often been discussed without any satisfactory answer. It may be asked, in the first place, how we are to account for the origin of language itself, and how the distinctions which language now helps us to make could themselves have been made available in the original imposition of names ; and, in the second place, it may be asked how the different phenomena of consciousness can be distinguished from each other by the lower animals, who have no nomenclature to assist them. Both these questions admit of many ingenious conjectures, but of no scientific answer. And the reason is obvious ; for both relate to states of consciousness which we never have experienced and never can, and which are so utterly unlike our own, that we have no reliable data for examining them. To conceive an inventor of language, we must conceive a man existing in the full maturity of his faculties ; those faculties not having been developed by any of the means that are indispensable now, and consequently not having assumed the same form in their development. Such a being is to us as inconceivable as one of a wholly different mental constitution. His thoughts are not our thoughts ; his conditions of speech are not ours. Our experience is so unlike what his must have been, that it will but mislead us if we reason from it ; and if we conjecture without the aid of experience, we deal in fiction, not in philosophy. Nor is the difficulty lessened if we suppose language to have been of divine origin ; for the real problem is, not to determine how the system of signs came into being, but how man learnt to associate it with his own distinctions of thought; or how, independently of it, he came to have such distinctions at all. The origin of language must ever remain a mystery; but it is a mystery which has its parallel in every other phenomenon of the sensible or intelligible world; for of all, while the existence is undeniable, the generation is inconceivable. That a man living in solitude from his earliest infancy, supposing him to be preserved to animal maturity, or any number of such men brought together into a separate society, apart from other men, could never acquire the mental power to invent a language, seems as nearly certain as such a point can be. Beyond this we have no means of speculating on the origin of language at all. Nor are we much better off in relation to the second question, as to the mental condition of the lower animals. To analyse a dog's consciousness, it is necessary that we should have a dog's consciousness ourselves; and besides this, that we should retain a distinct recollection of it after we have acquired a human one. The dog can distinguish his master from a stranger; that is clear. He can be educated by associations of pain or pleasure; that is clear also. But when conscious of his master's presence, does he recognise him as a being distinct from all other objects—as an object that can be observed or contemplated alone? When he is uneasy at losing him, has he a distinct consciousness of what it is that he wants? When he is educated, does he consciously represent to himself the association between tit-bits and sitting upright? And if he does so, does he do it by the aid of any system of representative signs, which, though unintelligible to us, performs an office analogous to that of human language?* In a word, does his state of intelligence more nearly resemble the second or the third stage of our supposed development of consciousness? Instinct resembles reason in many of its results; does it therefore resemble it in its manner of obtaining them? We may speak positively on these points with all the hardihood of ignorance; but in doing so, we are speculating on the nature of an intelligence different from our own, and whose conditions cannot even be

---

* Mr. Morell states positively the view which we have only ventured to hint interrogatively. "While the brute perceives objects, and acts in reference to them only *instinctively*, either for the satisfaction of its appetites, or for self-preservation; a conscious separation is instantly effected by the *human* faculty between the subject and the object. In this separation lies the first distinctive act of *human intelligence*, an act to which there soon succeeds an apprehension of *qualities* in the external object, totally different from any intelligence that can take place in the case of the lower animals. The animal does not think within itself, I am a dog or a horse, and that is a hare or a corn-field; it is simply impelled *by the force of instinct* towards the object, without any apprehension of its own personality, as distinct from the thing presented to it. On the other hand, the child or the savage, without the least culture whatever, *consciously* separates self from the objective world in the very first distinct act of *perception;* and it is exactly here, in this very act, that the *intellectual* quality of perception is first manifested" (*Elements of Psychology*, p. 141). Compare, for a similar view, Hegel, Encykl. § 24 (*Werke*, vi. p. 47).

conjectured, except by the arbitrary assumption of its partial similarity to our own.

Human consciousness, then, in the only form in which it can be examined and described, is a compound of various elements, of whose separate action, if it ever existed, we retain no remembrance, and therefore no power of reproducing in thought. It is impossible to have a distinct conception of an act of pure sensation— *i.e.* of an affection of the organs of sense only, unaccompanied by reflection upon it ; for such an affection, though possibly the earliest step in our mental development, could not at that time be recognised as such, nor leave traces that could be recognised afterwards. Our personal consciousness, like the air we breathe, comes to us as a compound ; and we can no more be conscious of the actual presence of its several elements than we can inhale an atmosphere of pure azote. Hence it follows, that in distinguishing and describing the several phenomena of consciousness, we must describe them according to their *predominant characteristics as compounds,* not according to their *separate natures as simples.* The phenomena, for example, of sensation, are so called from their prominent feature ; the presence, that is to say, of an object affecting in a certain way the organs of sense ; though the consciousness of the manner of that affection in each case, and consequently its existence as a distinct phenomenon, depend likewise upon the co-operation of other faculties, which play a necessary though a subordinate part. The neglect of this consideration constitutes the weak point in Condillac's celebrated hypothesis of the statue becoming conscious. He starts with the assumption that the possession of a single organ of sense is sufficient for the discernment of distinct sensations as such, for remembrance and comparison of various sensations, for the preference of one to another, for voluntary efforts to recal them, and for self-consciousness throughout. Whereas, in truth, though the existence of the sensation in a perfect state is identical with the consciousness of that existence, yet we are by no means warranted in assuming that either can be brought into that state by the operation of an isolated organ of sense. With this preliminary caution as to the relation of the several faculties and acts of consciousness to each other—a caution which must be carefully borne in mind throughout—we shall now proceed to examine and describe the various phenomena of consciousness separately, so far, at least, as separation in this case is possible.

OF PRESENTATIVE OR INTUITIVE CONSCIOUSNESS.

The distinctive feature of presentative consciousness consists in the fact that it is caused by the actual presence of an individual object, whether thing, act, or state of mind, occupying a definite position in time, or in space, or in both. It is true that this object is not discerned as such, and the consciousness of it, therefore, is not fully realised without the co-operation of the representative faculties ; and it is true also that representative consciousness, when complete, is exhibited in an individual unity of representation ; but as the presence of the individual object is in the one case the principal, in the other only an accessory feature; and as in the one it may be regarded as the cause, in the other as the effect of the accompanying consciousness, it furnishes a sufficient principle of distinction between the two. We shall therefore class under the general denomination of *Intuitions*, all those states of consciousness in which the actual presence of an object, within or without the mind, is the primary fact which leads to its recognition as such, by the subject; and from these will be distinguished, under the name of *Thoughts*, all those states of consciousness in which the presence of the object is the result of a representative act on the part of the subject. In the former case, the presence of the object is involuntary ; in the latter it is voluntary. In both, the presentative and representative faculties act in combination, for this is the condition of all complete consciousness ; but in the former case the object is *given to*, in the latter it is *given by*, the conscious act. For example, while I am in the company of a friend, I have by sight an intuitive consciousness of his presence. I do not cause his presence by any mental effort of my own ; it is *given to me* ; and so long as my eye is turned towards him, I cannot help seeing him. But if I am thinking of an absent person, and endeavour to recal to mind his features, I make a voluntary effort, and thereby bring into consciousness a mental image which becomes internally now present ; but the presentation is one of my own making, constructed by means of the reflective or representative faculty. In adopting the term *presentation* or *intuition*, to express the consciousness of any individual affection of the mind, a writer may be liable to the charge of innovation, in what was at least in the last generation the established language of English philosophy. But in this case necessity has no law. We need a term which shall indifferently express the presence of an individual sight or sound in the eye or ear, and of an individual emotion or volition in the mind ; and if none such exists in current use, there is no resource but to coin one. It may be added, that if such a term had been in use in the days of Locke, his writings need not have been liable to the perpetual misunderstanding which arises from his ambiguous use of the term *reflection*. The same apology must serve for the occasional introduction of other philosophical terms, which, though gradually coming into use, are hardly as yet in general circulation.

Presentative consciousness, thus distinguished, appears, like all consciousness, in the form of a relation between the subject or person conscious, and the object, or that of which he is conscious. These two terms are correlative to each other, and imply each other. The subject is a subject to the object, and the object is an object to the subject.* The subject can only be conscious by knowing itself to be affected in a particular manner by an object; the object can only be known as affecting the subject in a particular manner. Thus the two are given in relation as mutually determining and determined by each other. We are affected in various manners by various objects presented to us. But these objects again exist for us as objects, only in so far as they are discerned by our faculties of consciousness. The subject and the object are thus only cognisable as existing in and affected by their mutual relation. We cannot be conscious of a pure *ego*, or subject affected in

---

* A word in passing on the often used and often misused terms *subjective* and *objective*. All consciousness has a subject and an object; but sometimes the object determines the character of the subject, and sometimes the subject determines the character of the object. In the former case the product is objective, in the latter it is subjective. Thus, a nervous affection dependent on the constitution of my animated organism is subjective; a quality perceived or conceived as existing in the constitution of the object is objective: a code of morality which allows each man to fix his own standard of right and wrong, is subjective; one which requires the opinions of men to conform to a rule independent of themselves, is objective. This explanation, however, applies only to the modern signification of the terms.

no particular manner; nor yet of a pure *non ego*, or object out of relation to our own cognitive powers. Hence arises a distinction between *phenomena*, or things in consciousness, and *things in themselves*, or things out of consciousness. We know the object only as it stands in relation to our faculties, and is modified by them. We are not sure that, if our faculties were altered, the same things would appear to us in the same form as they do now : we are not sure that they do appear in the same form to all existing intelligent beings ; for we know not how far the faculties of other beings resemble our own. But, on the other hand, we have no right to dogmatise on the negative side, and to assume, with equal absence of ground, that things *are not* in themselves as they appear to us. This question, however, belongs to Ontology, and will be examined in its proper place. Psychology is concerned with *the phenomena of consciousness as such*. It has nothing to do with the ulterior realities, whose existence and nature consciousness perhaps indicates, but certainly does not ascertain.

Nevertheless, though consciousness exists, and can be conceived to exist, only in the psychological relation of a subject to an object, it is possible in some degree to distinguish between the elements apparently due to each. Not that these can be directly discerned apart from each other ; but that in their combination each exhibits certain features which appear to indicate a subjective or an objective origin. If there are in every act of consciousness certain invariable elements, which no change of consciousness can ever obliterate or alter, which no effort of thought can get rid of or conceive as absent, and without which consciousness itself cannot be imagined as possible,—these may be conjectured to owe their existence to the constitution of the subject, which remains one and unchanged in successive acts; while the changeable features which distinguish one mode of consciousness from another are probably due to the different constitutions of the several things of which the subject is successively conscious.* The

---

* An apparently opposite use of this criterion is made in some of the current theories of philosophy. Thus, in the distinction, which we shall shortly have to notice, between the primary and secondary qualities of body, those attributes of which the cognition is common to the several senses are usually regarded as existing in the bodies themselves; while those which are peculiar to this or that act of sensation are considered as affections of the sentient subject. But in truth the opposition is rather apparent than real. For the secondary qualities, as they are commonly distinguished, depend for their cognition, not on the constitution of the pure mind or subject proper of consciousness, but on that of the nervous organism as animated; and this latter, though in particular acts of sensation it is regarded as pertaining to the subject, yet, in reference to consciousness in general, and to the personal self properly so called, must be regarded as belonging to the object, and, as such, is present or absent in different acts of consciousness. Indeed, the above distinction between form and matter, though not thoroughly carried out in reference to the sensibility till the time of Kant, had, in relation to thought, been long previously an established canon in logic.

former may therefore be distinguished as constituting the *form* or subjective ingredient of consciousness; the latter as constituting the *matter* or objective ingredient.

OF THE FORM OF CONSCIOUSNESS IN GENERAL.

The analogy which gives rise to the terms *form* and *matter*, as used to denote the subjective and objective elements of consciousness, is obvious. In a work of art, the *form* is that which is given *by* the artist; the *matter* is that which is given *to* him. The sculptor, for instance, receives the unshaped block of marble, and imparts to it the form of the statue. The conscious mind, in like manner, receives its materials from without, and imparts to them a form by its own act, according to its own laws. The form of consciousness in general consists in *relation to a subject*. Whatever variety of materials, whether for intuition or thought, may exist within reach of my mind, I can become conscious of them only by recognising them as *mine*. By this the several materials are in each case set apart or united, and known as *an object*, of which *I am conscious*; and without such knowledge no act of consciousness is possible. Relation to the conscious self is thus the permanent and universal feature which every state of consciousness, as such, must exhibit; while in every other respect the several states may differ from each other, being distinguished as sensations, volitions, thoughts, etc.; or more particularly as states of sight or hearing, as virtuous or vicious acts, as conceptions or judgments; or more minutely still, as the sight of a tree or the hearing of music, as an act of benevolence or ingratitude, as the conception of a triangle or the judgment that the angles of a triangle are equal to two right angles. But in all alike there is a necessary relation to one and the same conscious self : the sight is *my* sight, the act is *my* act, the thought is *my* thought. If we further examine the manner in which this universal relation manifests itself in the particular case of presentative consciousness, we shall find two special forms or conditions common to all possible states of external or internal intuition respectively—namely, SPACE and TIME.

OF THE FORMS OF INTUITIVE CONSCIOUSNESS—SPACE AND TIME.

Space is the form or mental condition of our perception of external objects. The phenomena of the material world may vary in an infinite number of ways; but, under every variety, they retain the condition of existing in space, either as being themselves sensibly extended, or as having a local position in the sensitive organism. Without this condition, their existence at all as phenomena is inconceivable. We may suppose the phenomena changed as we will in other respects, but we cannot suppose them to exist out of space. We may suppose any given phenomenon to be non-existent, but the non-existence of space is beyond our power of supposition. Hence space is necessarily regarded as infinite (though not positively conceived as such), for to suppose it finite is to suppose a point at which it ceases to exist. It has thus the characteristics of universality and necessity, which appear to mark it out as an *à priori* law or condition of the conscious mind, not as the adventitious result of any special experience. And this conclusion is confirmed by other considerations. For the consciousness of space, though accompanying the perceptions of various senses, cannot be regarded as properly the object of any one of them. There is a visible extension given in the apprehension, of space as occupied by light and colour ; there is a tangible extension given in the consciousness of certain portions of the organism as occupied by tactual impressions ; and there is probably a certain consciousness of locality in the exercise of the other senses. But pure space is not identical with any of these ; for the blind man may form as positive a notion of it as the seeing man ; and one debarred from the sensation accompanying the act of touch would not thereby lose all consciousness of space ; and the same argument applies still more clearly to the other senses. Again, the exercise of the locomotive faculty implies a consciousness of space as containing our own body; but the idea of space cannot be said to be derived from locomotion, since the mere volition to move implies a prior consciousness of this relation. Space is thus not by itself an object of sensible intuition, but forms one element of all such objects, being presented in the form of a relation between parts out of each other, and hence being distinctly conceivable only in conjunction with the things related. Pure space has thus one character in common with concepts or general notions— namely, that it cannot by itself be depicted to sense or imagination; but in all other respects it is essentially different from them. A concept is logically as well as chronologically posterior to the individuals which it represents. It implies a prior perception of them, and it has no objective existence but in them. Space is logically, and in some degree chronologically, prior to the objects of sense. It is the condition of their existence as objects, and is itself necessarily conceived as existing independently of any *given* contents.* A concept is indifferently representative of many objects. Space is presented to consciousness as

---

* Space, though not positively conceived as devoid of all contents, is yet necessarily conceived as separable from any given contents, and thus as independent of each in succession.

one only (for the division of *spaces* is purely arbitrary), and thus is not conceived as predicable of individual objects under it, but as containing them in it. Space is thus an element of the sensitive consciousness presented in itself, not derived from or representative of anything else ; and, though always manifested on the occasion of some special experience, it cannot be regarded as the product of experience, nor can its notion be constructed from empirical data. It cannot properly be described as an *innate idea*, for no idea is wholly innate ; but it is the innate element of the ideas of sense which experience calls into actual consciousness. To describe experience as the cause of the idea of space, would be as inaccurate as to speak of the soil in which it is planted as the cause of the oak ; though the planting is the condition which brings into manifestation the latent powers of the acorn. To maintain that the mind contributes nothing to the formation of consciousness, because experience contributes something, is as unreasonable as to assert that the acorn may indifferently become an oak, or an ash, or an elm, according to the soil in which it is planted. Yet such reasoning has often been used to prove that the mind is but the passive recipient of impressions from without.

In the actual development of human consciousness, the condition of space accompanies every complete exercise of the bodily senses ; for in all there is a local

relation to a particular organ; and without this
relation no kind of sensation can be fully realised as
a mode of consciousness. And this is all that is
necessary to observe, so long as we are describing consciousness as it is, not constructing it as it might be.
Whether any single organ of sense—smell, for instance,
or hearing, supposing it to exist isolated from the rest—
would be competent to furnish the empirical conditions
under which the consciousness of space is realised, is a
question which can only be approximately and conjec-
turally answered by a special examination of each
sense. But such an examination would throw but little
light on human consciousness as it actually exists.
Consciousness is the result of a human intellect acting
in conjunction with a human organisation ; and if we
withdraw or mutilate either element, we produce, not
an actual man, but a hypothetical monster. A being
endowed, according to the hypothesis of Condillac, with
a sense of smell only, and identifying himself with his
successive sensations (it would be more correct to say
having no notion of self at all), would not, properly
speaking, be in any sense a *conscious being*. He would
be deficient in the essential conditions of consciousness,
the distinction of subject from object, and of objects
from each other. To be conscious of a particular
sensation we must know it as such ; and to know it as
such implies a concomitant knowledge of other sensa-

tions as different, and thus of the bodily organism as extended, or as *occupying space*.

Much of what has been said of Space is applicable to Time also. This is the condition, not merely of external perception, but of the entire consciousness, external and internal alike. Consciousness in every form implies a permanent and a variable element—a continuous self subject to successive modifications. It is thus necessarily manifested as a *change*, and that change as taking place in time. Pure time, like pure space, is not in itself an object of consciousness, but an element which, to be realised in consciousness, must be combined with the results of experience. We can form no notion of time *per se* with no events taking place in it. Time is thus manifested in the form of a relation of successive modes of consciousness to the one conscious self. It might be conjectured with some plausibility that a being not subject to any change of consciousness, or, on the other hand, one not cognisant of his personal identity in the midst of change, would have no idea of time. But then such a being would have no consciousness at all in the proper sense of the term. Time, like space, cannot be annihilated by any act of thought, and cannot be conceived as subject to any limitation, as having either beginning or end, or as absent from any mode of consciousness. Indeed, these conditions mutually imply each other; for to conceive a limit of time would be to conceive a consciousness in which time is present, preceded or followed by another from which time is absent. Time has thus, in common with space, the characteristics of universality and necessity, which appear to indicate a subjective condition, or law of consciousness itself. Like space, too, it is manifested in conjunction with and on the occasion of experience, being presented simultaneously with the empirical element of change, the apprehension of which constitutes the first step of positive consciousness.*

We are not at present concerned with the question whether space and time have any real existence apart from that of the mind which gives these forms to the objects of its consciousness. This question belongs to Ontology, not to Psychology. Space and time are known to us as formal conditions of consciousness; whether they are anything more than such conditions, is a question which at present we have no means of answering. The laws of consciousness must be primarily manifested as binding upon the conscious mind. As such, they necessarily accompany every manifestation of consciousness; and in their utmost objective reality

---

* The apparent paradox, on the one hand, that consciousness must have had a beginning in time, and on the other, that consciousness is only possible under the form of a change of state, will be further explained in the sequel.

they could do no more. But we do not deny the real existence of space and time, though at the present stage of our inquiry we are not able to affirm it. We shall hereafter have occasion to consider whether this question can be answered at all. It is sufficient for the present to say that it cannot be answered by Psychology.

OF THE MATTER OF INTUITIVE CONSCIOUSNESS.

The Matter of intuitive consciousness cannot be specified with the same exactness as the Form; for while in all cognate acts of consciousness the form is one and the same, and therefore admits of a distinct examination apart from the several modes of consciousness into which it enters, the matter is the variable element by which one act of consciousness differs from another, and which, therefore, can only be fully analysed by a separate examination of each individual case. The various phenomena of the matter of consciousness, however, admit of being classified and partially described under certain general heads; and such a classification has accordingly been attempted in the distinctions, which form the substance of most psychological treatises, between the various states, operations, and faculties of the human mind.

The *Matter* of intuitive consciousness, in its widest

sense, denotes all that distinguishes one object from another, as given in and by this or that special *experience*. Of experience there are two principal sources : 1. *Sensation,* or *external intuition,* by which we become cognisant of the phenomena connected with our material organisation ; and 2. *Internal intuition* (called by Locke *reflection*),* by which we become cognisant of the several successive states of our own minds. To the former we owe the materials of our knowledge of what takes place without us ; from the latter, in like manner, is derived our knowledge of what takes place within us. The subdivisions of these two constitute the several states and operations of the human mind.

OF SENSATION AND PERCEPTION.

Sensation, in its most general acceptation, is sometimes used to signify the whole of that portion of con-

* There is an ambiguity in Locke's use of the term *reflection,* which has given rise to considerable misunderstanding. Etymologically, the term should denote a *turning back* of the mind upon an object previously existing, so that the existence of a state of consciousness is distinct from the reflection on that state. In this sense, a sensation, like any other mode of consciousness, may be an object of reflection ; and those philosophers who understood Locke in this sense were only consistent in reducing his two sources of ideas to the single one of sensation alone. But, in the greater part of Locke's Essay, reflection is treated of in a different sense, namely, as the immediate consciousness of our internal states of mind — a consciousness identical with the existence of those states, and thus forming an original source of ideas.

sciousness which comes to us by means of the bodily organs of sense. *Perception,* too, has been used by various writers in a wider or a narrower sense—sometimes as synonymous with consciousness in general, sometimes as limited to the apprehensions of sense alone.* Under the latter limitation it has been found convenient to make a further restriction, and to distinguish between *sensation proper* and *perception proper.*

Sensation proper is the consciousness of certain affections of our body as an animated organism.

Perception proper is the consciousness of the existence of our body as a material organism, and therefore as extended.

The sensitive organism may be considered in two points of view:—1. As belonging to the *ego,* or conscious subject, which, in its actual concrete existence, is susceptible of consciousness only in and by its relation to a bodily organism. 2. As belonging to the *non ego,* or material object of consciousness, from which the mind, as an abstract immaterial being, is logically separable; though, in actual consciousness, the two are

---

* Thus Locke enumerates sensation and reflection as the two sources of our ideas, meaning by *sensation* what, in the language of Reid, would be sensation and perception together. In this he is followed by Condillac. The distinction between sensation proper and perception proper originated with Reid ; but its most accurate development is due to his editor, Sir William Hamilton. From the notes of the latter the greater part of the remarks in the text have been taken.

always united. The bodily organism is thus the debate-able land between self and not-self. In one sense, my eye is a part of my conscious self; for sight is an act of consciousness, and sight cannot exist except by means of the eye. In another sense, my eye is not a part of myself; for a man whose eyes are put out continues to be the same person as before. Hence the organism, as the vehicle of sensation, exhibits in the same act attributes of mind and attributes of body. In the former point of view, the act of sensitive consciousness is regarded as a *sensation*; in the latter, as a *perception*.

Perception is sometimes defined as "the knowledge we obtain, by means of our sensations, of the qualities of matter."* This definition may be admitted, if *matter* is understood as including our own bodily organism, as well as the extra-organic objects to which it is related. The former is the only kind of matter that is *immediately* cognisable by the senses. The existence of a material world, distinct from, though related to, our organism, is made known to us, not by the senses themselves, but, as will be noticed hereafter, by the *faculty of locomotion*. Sensation and perception, as above explained, are always correlative to each other; every sensation being accompanied by a consciousness of the extension of the sensitive organism, and this consciousness being a perception. But, though always coexistent,

* Stewart, *Outlines of Moral Philosophy*, § 15.

they are not proportionally coexistent. On the contrary, the sensation, when it rises above a certain low degree of intensity, interferes with the perception of its relations, by concentrating the consciousness on its absolute affection alone. Hence Sir William Hamilton, from whom the above remark is taken, has enunciated the important rule, *that, above a certain point, the stronger the sensation, the weaker the perception ; and the distincter the perception, the less obtrusive the sensation.* In other words, *though perception proper and sensation proper exist only as they coexist, in the degree or intensity of their existence they are always found in an inverse ratio to each other.*[*]

OF THE FIVE SENSES.

Sensation and perception, according to the above law, coexist, though in an inverse ratio to each other, in each of the five senses. But in addition to the relation which each bears to the other, when viewed with reference to the same sense, they are also found to be combined in different proportions when one sense is compared with another. In some the sensation so far predominates over the perception, that the sense manifests itself as a source of feeling rather than of knowledge, and has often, though erroneously, been

* Reid's *Works*, p. 880. The same rule had been in substance previously given by Kant, *Anthropologie*, § 20.

regarded as consisting of the former element only. In others the reverse is the case ; the perceptive element, or cognition of an object, predominating over the sensitive element, or consciousness of a personal affection. In this point of view, the senses of smell and taste may be distinguished as especially subjective or sensational ; those of hearing and sight as objective or perceptional. Touch, inasmuch as it has no special organ, but is diffused in various degrees over the various parts of the body, will require a separate consideration. In other words, smell and taste are chiefly known as vehicles of the mental emotions of pleasure and pain ; hearing and sight, as informing us of the nature of the bodily attributes of sound and colour. Touch may contribute to the one or the other end, according to the part of the body in which it resides, and the manner in which it is brought into exercise.*

Of Smell.

In Smell, as in the other senses, it is necessary to distinguish between the sensation itself and its object, which, in ordinary language, are not unfrequently con-

* This remark of course applies only to the senses as they exist in the human subject. A similar general rule, indeed, probably holds good with regard to the lower animals ; but it is differently manifested in the several senses. Of the senses of taste and smell it has been observed by Sir William Hamilton, that " precisely as in animals these latter senses gain in their objective character as means of knowledge, do they lose in

founded together. Thus we speak of the organ of *smell*, and of the *smell* of a rose, using the same term indifferently to signify the act of inhaling an odour and the odour inhaled. The act of smell, apart from the physiological inquiries connected with it, requires no description, being familiar to every one from his own experience. It will be sufficient for our present purpose to distinguish the sensation from the accompanying perception; and this will be best accomplished by an examination of the object.

The true object of smell is to be found in the odorous particles in contact with the organ. It is incorrect to say that we *smell a rose*, meaning by a *rose* the flower as seen or touched. We smell only the effluvia emanating from the rose and coming in contact with the nervous organism. What these effluvia or odorous emanations are in themselves, natural philosophy is unable to determine. "Although it may be surmised," says Dr. Carpenter, "that they consist of particles of extreme minuteness, dissolved as it were in the air, and although this idea seems to derive confirmation from the fact that most odorous substances are volatile, and *vice versa*, yet the most delicate experiments have

their subjective character as sources of pleasurable or painful sensations. To a dog, for instance, in whom the sense of smell is so acute, all odours seem in themselves to be indifferent" (Reid's *Works*, p. 863). Compare Kant, *Anthropologie*, § 15, whose distinction slightly varies from that given in the text.

failed to discover any diminution in weight, in certain substances (as musk) that have been impregnating with their effluvia a large quantity of air for several years; and there are some volatile fluids, such as water, which are entirely inodorous."* But whatever these odorous particles may be, it is important to remember that they, and not the bodies from which they proceed, are the proper objects of smell ; and, consequently, that this sensation (and the same may be said of all the others) is in fact a modification of touch. Hence it is incorrect to speak, as Aristotle and many subsequent writers have spoken, of the object of smell as perceived through a medium, such as the atmosphere. The atmosphere is not the medium of communication between the sensitive organ and its object, but only the vehicle by which the object is brought into contact with the organ.

Smell conveys to us no knowledge of the existence of extra-organic matter. The only matter of which we are directly conscious in this, as in other actions of sense, is our own organism as extended ; and this consciousness constitutes the *perception* of smell, as the consciousness of the same organism as affected constitutes the *sensation*. In the remarks upon the consciousness of space as the form of all sensitive intuition, enough has been said to explain in what sense the knowledge of locality and extension forms part of the

* *Principles of Human Physiology*, p. 905.

energy of smell as it actually exists, and to show that the lowest degree of intelligence that is sufficient for sensation proper is sufficient for perception also. But the object perceived is not a quality of body as such, but only the proper action, or rather passion, of our nervous organism; an action or passion of which the external cause is, so far as perception is concerned, wholly unknown, and which may even be excited in a similar manner by totally different causes. This is not so evident in the case of smell as in some others of the senses; yet it is a known fact in physiology that the sensation of smell may be produced in the olfactory nerve by electrical action without the presence of any odorous body. This fact is sufficient to show that the operation of a sense by itself does not afford any legitimate grounds for determining the qualities, or even the existence, of an extra-organic world. On this subject we shall have more to say when we come to treat of the distinction between the primary and secondary qualities of body.

Of Taste.

The principal characteristics of the sense of Smell are common to that of Taste also. The two senses resemble each other in being both powerful as instruments of feeling, and proportionally weak as sources of information. Tastes, like smells, admit of hardly any classification, except in respect of their relation to the sensitive organism, as pleasant or painful. Like smell, too, the sensation appears to be produced by means of sapid particles emitted from the body, and brought into contact with the nerves; and these particles, which constitute the object of the sense of taste, are in their own nature as little known as those of smell, and can as little be regarded as bearing any resemblance to the sensations which they excite. Taste, like smell, is thus a modification of touch; the object in contact with the organ being the sapid particles, and not, as might at first be supposed, the body from which those particles proceed. The body is in contact, not with the nerves, but only with their exterior covering; and in order to produce the distinctive sensation of taste, it appears to be necessary that the sapid particles should be dissolved in the saliva, and thus penetrate through the investments of the papillæ into their substance.* But, not to enter here on questions more properly belonging to physiology, it will be sufficient for our present purpose to observe, that taste, like smell, conveys no knowledge of the existence of extra-organic matter, and that the sensation, properly so called, consists in the consciousness of the organism as affected in a particular manner, agreeable or disagreeable; while the perception is to be found in the corresponding consciousness of the locality of the affection in the organism as extended. Though

* Carpenter's *Principles of Human Physiology*, p. 900.

these two are always to a certain extent coexistent, yet the former predominates so far over the latter as to form the principal characteristic of this class of sensations. For this reason, the organs of taste and smell are distinguished as being pre-eminently the sources of *sensation* in the strict sense of the term.*

Of Hearing.

In Hearing, the functions of sensation and perception are perhaps more nearly balanced than in any other of the senses. The subjective character of various sounds, as sources of pleasure or pain to the hearer, may be contrasted with their objective character, as resembling or differing from each other; and as in the latter relation this sense affords more accurate distinctions than those of taste and smell, so in the former the sensation is less capable of being carried to an extreme degree of pleasure or pain.† Hearing, therefore, though con-

* Kant, *Anthropologie*, § 15; Tissot, *Anthropologie*, vol. i. p. 37.

† A lover of music might perhaps demur to the conclusion that the pleasures of hearing are less intense than those of taste or smell. In explanation, it should be remembered that we are speaking only of the pleasure conveyed by the sensation itself. The pleasure derived from music is mainly intellectual, and is chiefly derived, not from the sound heard in any one sensation, but from the cognition of its relation to others, which are not heard, but remembered ; or from associations which may be suggested by, but are not actually contained in, the sound as heard. In short, the natural sensation, which is common to all mankind, must be distinguished from the acquired sensation, which is in a great degree the result of education.

tributing in different degrees both to enjoyment and to information, may be characterised as a source of the latter rather than of the former; and if, according to the rule already mentioned, the sensation and the perception are in an inverse ratio to each other, it will follow, that in proportion as our attention is more directed to the discrimination of various sounds from each other, we are less immediately conscious of the pleasure or pain which they are capable of communicating. In hearing, as in the senses previously described, we are directly cognisant, not of the sonorous body, but of the change in the condition of the auditory nerve produced by contact with a medium by which the vibrations are transmitted (the fluid inclosed in the labyrinth of the ear); and hence hearing, like the other senses, is a modification of touch, and does not directly inform us of the existence of any other material object than our own nervous organism. Hence it follows, that neither the *distance* nor the *direction* from which a sound proceeds is immediately perceived by the ear; and this conclusion is confirmed by the facts connected with the exercise of this sense in its uneducated condition, as by children, and occasionally also by adults. The child does not appear to be conscious at first of the direction or distance of voices that attract his attention; and a remarkable instance of the same kind in a grown person is mentioned by Dr. Reid. "I remember," he says, " that once lying a-bed, and having been put into a fright, I heard my own heart beat; but I took it to be one knocking at the door, and arose and opened the door more than once, before I discovered that the sound was in my own breast." . . . . " It is probable," he continues, " that, previous to all experience, we should as little know whether a sound came from the right or left, from above or below, from a great or a small distance, as we should know whether it was the sound of a drum, or a bell, or a cart?"* In this respect the sense of hearing presents a remarkable analogy to that of sight; and this property of both will be considered when we come to treat of acquired perceptions.

Of Sight.

Sight is of all the senses the most communicative as a vehicle of information, and consequently the one in which there is the least immediate consciousness of pleasure or pain in the exercise. Most of the knowledge, however, which this sense, in its matured state, conveys to us, belongs to its acquired, not to its original power, and is the result, not of a direct perception, but of an inference from a perception. In sight, as in the other senses, the direct perception is produced by contact; and the proper object of this sense is not the

* *Inquiry into the Human Mind*, chap. iv. sec. 1 (*Works*, ed. Hamilton, p. 117).

distant body from which the rays of light are emitted or reflected, but the affection of the organ of sight (the retina and the nervous system connected with it) produced by the rays impinging upon it. The essential characteristics of this affection are *brightness* and *colour*, which, however, are necessarily accompanied by a consciousness of *extension;* for a luminous point, however small, must itself occupy some portion of space, and can be perceived only as in contrast to a surrounding expanse of obscure or differently-coloured surface.* The immediate object of sight being in contact with the extremities of the optic nerve of the person seeing, it is as impossible for two persons simultaneously to see the same object with their eyes as to touch the same spot with their fingers ; and every movement of the eye which brings a different portion of rays into contact with the organ, produces a different object of vision.† The object of vision being thus neither the rays alone nor the organ alone, but the organ as affected by the rays ; and the sensation of colour being a purely organic affection ; it follows that sight, like the other senses, gives us no immediate knowledge of an extra-organic world ; though it is immediately cognisant of extension, and therefore of matter, as presented in the organism itself. Hence we have no immediate perception by sight of the *figure,* the *size,* or the *distance*

* See Sir W. Hamilton, Reid's *Works*, p. 860.   † *Ibid.* p. 304.

of bodies ; and we cannot, in strict accuracy, be said to *see* a distant body, such as the sun, at all ; though in practice the direct perception becomes so intimately united with the indirect inference, that it is difficult to imagine that either can exist apart from the other. Admitting this view of the true object of sight, which may be regarded as established by physiological as well as psychological testimony,* we may notice some remarkable contrasts between the *presented object*, or that which we actually see, and the *represented object*, or that which we appear to see. The presented object is on the surface of the retina : the represented object appears without, and at a greater or less distance from the eye. The presented object is of such a size as can be contained within the spectator's visual organism : the represented object may be many times larger than his whole body. The presented object is a flat surface : the represented object is a solid body. The presented object is inverted : the represented object is erect. The presented object is double, there being a distinct image on the retina of each eye : the represented object is generally single, the two images being in normal vision united into one body.   These and other apparent anomalies in the exercise of the senses will be discussed under the head of " Acquired Perceptions."

* See Sir W. Hamilton, Reid's *Works*, pp. 160, 301, 304, 814 ; and Dr. Carpenter, *Principles of Human Physiology*, pp. 925, 928 (4th edit.)

Of Touch and Feeling.

Touch is regarded by many writers as the most objective and the most trustworthy of all our faculties. It has been described as the source of our knowledge of the existence of an external world, and of the real magnitudes, figures, and distances of objects; as the instructor of the other senses, and the corrector of their aberrations. It appears certain, however, that the sense of touch in itself is equally limited in its sphere with the rest of the senses, and that it can convey no other proper perception than that of the existence of its own organism as extended. The sensations of touch, considered by themselves, present no characteristics which can distinguish them from those of the other senses, as regards an immediate cognisance of the external world. Like smell, or sound, or light, they are affections of the nervous system, which may be produced by internal as well as external causes, and which directly indicate no other existence than that of the organised sentient being.* The fact is, that in the examination of this faculty, philosophers have often made a two-fold confusion between things in themselves distinct. In the first place, the sense of touch proper, in which the

---

* See Destutt Tracy, *Elémens d'Idéologie*, p. i. chap. 7 ; or his follower, Brown, Lecture xxii. Both these authors, however, are wrong in denying an immediate tactual perception of our own organism, though right as regards an extra-organic world.

G

sentient subject is as passive as in any other state of sensation, is confounded with the faculty of locomotion, which originates in a voluntary act of the same subject. In the second place, the sense of touch having no special organ, but being common to all parts of the surface of the body, it has sometimes happened. that perceptions have been assumed to be invariable and absolute, which, in truth, are relative to one part only of the organism, and assume a different character in relation to other parts.   To mention only one eminent instance out of many, both these confusions occur in Bishop Berkeley's *Essay towards a New Theory of Vision.*   That illustrious philosopher distinguishes between two kinds of magnitude,—the one tangible, which is perceived and measured by touch ; the other visible, by the mediation of which the former is brought into view.   The tangible magnitude he considers to be fixed and invariable, while the visible magnitude changes as we approach to or recede from the object.   Hence he concludes that tangible and not visible figures are the objects of geometrical reasoning ; the latter having no other use than words have, being merely signs to suggest the former.   Now, in the first place, it is obvious that mere touch, without the power of locomotion, can inform us of no other magnitude than that which corresponds to the touching organ.   In point of fact, it informs us only of the extension of the organ itself ;

but under no possible hypothesis could it inform us of more than the magnitude of that part of a body with which we are actually in contact. In the second place, it has been proved by experiment that the same object will appear of a different magnitude when in contact with different parts of the human body, and cousequently that the sense of touch, regarded by itself, is not only variable, but even self-contradictory in its testimony. Hence it follows that the sense of touch alone has no pre-eminence over the other senses as a criterion of truth in relation to a material world beyond our own organism : in fact, like the other senses, it is silent as to the existence of such a world. Touch, however, differs in some remarkable particulars from the other senses. There is no distinct organ appropriated to the tactual sensations alone ; and the various parts of the body by which these may be communicated may also be the instruments of other classes of sensations, all of which have been confounded under the general name of "touch" or "feeling." The object of touch proper has no special name, like *sound, colour*, or *smell ;* but in itself it is familiar to every one who has experienced the state of consciousness which results from the contact of his own body with another, when not sufficiently violent to rise into a positive sense of pleasure or pain. In this state there is a two-fold consciousness ; that part of the bodily organism being known at the same time as *affected* and as *extended..* The former constitutes the *sensation*, the latter the *perception;* and in proportion as the former rises to a higher consciousness of pleasure or pain, the latter grows feebler, though never becoming wholly extinct. This double state, which has no appropriate name, may perhaps be distinguished in its twofold character by the name of *Tactual Impression.* In addition to this may be mentioned other modes of feeling communicated, partly at least, through the same organs, such as those of heat and cold, which have sometimes been regarded as the proper objects of the sense of touch, and the various kinds of pain and pleasure produced by external applications. It will be sufficient for our present purpose to notice, that all of them belong to the class commonly known as *secondary qualities of body;* that is to say, affections of the different parts of the nervous organism, which, as apprehended, have no resemblance to any property of inorganic matter, though generally caused by some unknown power by which that matter is capable of affecting our organs.

GENERAL REMARKS ON THE FIVE SENSES.

The psychological characteristics of the five senses in general, omitting those which properly belong to physiological inquiries, may be summed up as follows:—

The proper function of each and all of them is a *sensation*, or affection of the nervous organism as *animated;* which affection, however, does not, and in all probability cannot, exist in consciousness without an accompanying intellectual cognition of the same organism as *extended* or *occupying space.* This cognition (the *perception* proper) is referred to the intellect rather than to the sense, chiefly for two reasons : Firstly, because it is not, like the sensation proper, limited in each case to a single form of sensibility, but appears as the common condition of consciousness in all. Secondly, because it is not in any case the consciousness of a single object as such, but of a relation, either between the parts of the sensible object, viewed as out of each other, or between that object as a whole, and the concomitant conditions under which it is presented to the sense. Thus, for example, the rays of light in contact with the retina may be perceived either as forming a visible surface, whose parts are related to each other, or as a luminous spot related to the surrounding obscurity : and even a smell or a sound, whether themselves perceived as extended or not, are at all events discerned in and by their relation to different parts of an extended organism.* The sensation and the perception are thus each

---

* Notwithstanding the general opinion of philosophers to the contrary, I am inclined to think that some consciousness of extension is simultaneous with the earliest exercise of sensation. Of course I do not

the necessary condition of the other; and the union of the two is requisite to constitute a state of consciousness. But consciousness is not complete, even when these two elements are united. The consciousness of any mental state (whether of sensation or otherwise) never does, and probably never can take place, without the accompanying consciousness that something else preceded it. This *something* need not be distinctly known as a former state of consciousness (which would make a beginning of consciousness impossible), just as the space to which the object of perception is related

mean that this consciousness is distinct, and can be at that time separated by analysis from its concomitants; but this is equally the case with all the characteristics of sensation. I only mean that the element of locality is there from the beginning, at least as distinctly as anything else, and that it could be detected if the sensation in its original state could be reproduced in a mind sufficiently developed to be capable of analysing it. In this respect it differs from the acquired perceptions properly so called, such as externality, distance, magnitude, etc., which may be chronologically as well as logically separated from the original sensation. So long as sensations are spoken of as affections of mind only, there is plausible ground for the opposite opinion; not so, however, when they are viewed in their true character, as affections, neither of mind alone nor of matter alone, but of an animated organism—*i.e.* of mind and matter together. Professor Müller allows that there is a perception of the extension of the organism in sight, touch, taste, and even smell, though slightly, if at all in hearing. It may be conjectured, however, that the compound action of the two ears in hearing will naturally give rise to some perception of extension, though this may become obliterated in acquired perception, from the attention being withdrawn from it to other sources of information. (See Baly's translation of Müller's *Elements of Physiology*, pp. 1073, 1075, 1086.)

need not be distinctly discerned as containing other objects; but every act of consciousness as such is accompanied by the conviction, indefinite it may be, of something having gone before, just as a coloured spot in sight is perceived as having something surrounding it.* In other words, every act of consciousness, as such, is presented as a *change in the state of our existence*, not as the beginning of that existence, and thus implies the continuous existence of a permanent self, presented in and through the several modes of consciousness, but not identified with any. We can have no knowledge of an abstract self apart from its successive states of consciousness, nor yet of any one of those states, save as a mode of the existence of one and the same indivisible self. The sensitive consciousness is thus revealed

---

* "Puisque réveillé de l'étourdissement on s'appercoit de ses perceptions, il faut bien qu'on en ait eu immédiatement auparavant, quoiqu'on ne s'en soit point apperçu ; car une perception ne sauroit venir naturellement, que d'une autre perception, comme un mouvement ne peut venir naturellement que d'un mouvement" (Leibnitz, *Monadologie*, sec. 23). This position, which Leibnitz maintained on metaphysical and psychological grounds, is confirmed by the researches of physiology, which tend to show that consciousness has a physical as well as an intellectual growth ; that impressions may be made on the organism which may leave perceptible traces in the subsequent development of consciousness, without having been themselves present to consciousness at all. (See Carpenter's *Human Physiology*, p. 818.) This may, perhaps, help to explain the apparent paradox, on the one hand, that consciousness must have had a beginning in time, and, on the other, that an absolutely first act of consciousness is inconceivable. Thus time is the universal form of consciousness as such.

to us as composed of three elements; a permanent self, having a sensitive organism extended in space, and with successive affections of that organism taking place in time. None of these elements, apart from the rest, can be presented or represented in consciousness; and the distinction between sense and intelligence is thus verbal only, not real, constituting, like the concave and convex circumference of a circle, different sides of the same consciousness, but incapable in any act of thought of being considered apart from each other. In the words of Sir William Hamilton—"It is manifestly impossible to discriminate with any rigour sense from intelligence. Sensitive apprehension is in truth only the recognition by intelligence of the phenomena presented in or through its organs.*

The *proper sensibles*—smell, taste, sound, colour, and tactual sensation—all belong to the class commonly called *secondary qualities of body;* which are in reality affections of the nervous organism, which have no resemblance to any attribute of inorganic bodies. It is true that, in their normal state, they are excited by the presence of such bodies; but that in themselves, as apprehended, they are states of the nervous organism, and not qualities of other bodies, is evident from the fact that they may be abnormally called into existence by any circumstance which produces the appropriate ner-

* Reid's *Works*, p. 878.

vous action, even when the ordinary bodily correlative is not present. In fact, as Professor Müller has observed, *"external agencies can give rise to no kind of sensation which cannot also be produced by internal causes, exciting changes in the condition of our nerves."** Such is the case in the well-known phenomena of dreams, of spectral illusions, of ringing in the ears, of bitterness in the mouth, etc; to which may be added the several artificial means by which various sensations may be produced—light and colours by pressure on the optic nerves, ringing by a blow on the ear, and the sensations of all the senses by electricity.† Similar though less striking evidence to the same point is furnished by the familiar instances of the sensation remaining in the organism when the body is withdrawn, or the communication intercepted. Thus a luminous body, passing rapidly backwards and forwards before the eye, appears as a continuous line of light; a rapid succession of sounds will produce a continuous tone; the spectrum of a bright object may be distinctly seen after the eyes are shut, etc. It is manifest, therefore, that the senses cannot in any case furnish direct evidence of the existence or properties of an extra-organic world; for, even if we are compelled by a law of our constitution to suppose the existence of an

* *Elements of Physiology*, translated by Baly, p. 1059.

† See Müller's *Elements of Physiology*, p. 1064; Carpenter's *Principles of Human Physiology*, p. 888; Abercrombie's *Intellectual Powers*, p. 61.

external cause of our internal states, such a supposition is representative, not presentative,—suggested by, not contained in the sensation ; it gives us no knowledge of the nature of the cause which it suggests, and in some instances, as has been shown, is deceptive even in suggesting its existence.

What, then, it may be asked, is the nature of our sensations as thus described? Are they affections of mind, or of body, or of both? On the one hand, consciousness, in all its modes, seems manifestly to be a state of mind. On the other hand, sensitive consciousness appears with the concomitant condition of extension, which is an attribute of body. The general voice of modern philosophers has pronounced that sensations, as such, belong to mind, and not to body. This is asserted both by those who admit and by those who deny the existence of perceptible primary qualities of body in addition to the mental sensation.* And rightly, so long as by *body* is meant something distinct from our own

---

* See Descartes, *Principia*, iv. 197 ; Malebranche, *Recherche*, l. i. ch. x. *sqq. ;* Locke, *Essay*, b. ii. ch. 8 ; Condillac, *Traité des Sensations*, p. iv. ch. 5 ; Berkeley, *Principles of Human Knowledge*, i. 3 ; Reid, *Inquiry*, ch. vi. sec. 4, 5, 6 ; Stewart, *Essays*, ii. chap. ii. sec. 2 ; Brown, *Lectures*, xxii. Leibnitz speaks more guardedly on this question,—" Il est vrai que la douleur ne ressemble pas aux mouvemens d'une épingle, mais elle peut ressembler fort bien aux mouvemens que cette épingle cause dans notre corps, et representer ces mouvemens dans l'ame, comme je ne doute nullement qu'elle ne fasse " (*Nouveaux Essais*, l. ii. ch. 8).

organism ; but wrongly, or at least inaccurately in language, so long as no distinction is made between body
as brute matter and body as part of a sentient being.
A dead body, though its eyes are open, has no sensation
of colour ; so far, sight is an affection of mind rather
than of body.   But a living man, if his eyes are put out,
is equally deprived of the sensation : so far it appears
to belong to body rather than to mind ; for mind in its
purest sense,—the abstract, immaterial, personal *ego*,—
cannot be conceived as destroyed, or even as in any way
diminished by the deprivation of a bodily organ.   But
the above inaccuracy of language assumes more than a
verbal importance, when it is made, as is sometimes the
case, the foundation of theories of perception, as though
the distinction which it indicates were strictly, not
merely approximately, true.   Thus it is argued that
we can have no immediate perception of extension in
space, " because it is not explained how the mind, which
alone can have sensation or knowledge, and which certainly is not square itself, is to be made acquainted
with the squareness of its own corporeal organ, or of the
foreign body."*   The whole force of the reasoning, and,
at the same time, its whole fallacy, lies in the word *alone*.
Mind is not *alone* capable of sensation : for it is sentient
only in so far as it animates a bodily organism.   That
a disembodied spirit has consciousness we must indeed

* Brown, *Lectures*, xxii.

believe ;—at least it is impossible to conceive how
spiritual existence can be otherwise manifested ;—but,
at the same time, it is impossible to conceive such consciousness as at all resembling our own, at any rate in the
particular phenomena which are conveyed by means of
the senses.   Sensation, then, is not an affection of mind
alone, nor of matter alone, but of an animated organism
—i.e. of mind and matter united.*   How this union is
effected ; whether the soul as a substance is one or
many : whether it has or has not a local habitation ;
whether, in short, we have any knowledge at all of a pure
immaterial being, apart from its modes of consciousness
when embodied ;—these and similar questions belong
to the Ontological branch of Metaphysics.   At present
we are concerned only with the phenomena of sensation,
and with the soul as the subject of those phenomena in
and through its connection with the body.   In this respect the soul cannot be assigned to any peculiar bodily
organ as its seat, but, as manifesting its existence in sensation, must be regarded as present in all the sensitive
organs alike.†

* In this respect the language of Aristotle is more accurate than that
of the majority of modern philosophers,—'Επεὶ δ' οὔτε τῆς ψυχῆς ἴδιον τὸ
αἰσθάνεσθαι οὔτε τοῦ σώματος (οὗ γὰρ ἡ δύναμις, τούτου καὶ ἡ ἐνέργεια · ἡ δὲ
λεγομένη αἴσθησις, ὡς ἐνέργεια, κίνησίς τις διὰ τοῦ σώματος τῆς ψυχῆς ἐστί)
φανερὸν ὡς οὔτε τῆς ψυχῆς τὸ πάθος ἴδιον, οὔτ' ἄψυχον σῶμα δυνατὸν αἰσθάνεσθαι (De Somno, chap. 1, sec. 5).

† See Müller's Elements of Physiology, p. 1335. In the above remarks,
and throughout this treatise, no notice has been taken of the different

To the above account of sensation and perception an obvious objection presents itself, which it is necessary to consider before proceeding further. " The perception as it ought to be," it may be urged, " is very different from the perception as it is. We are told that we only perceive our own organism; we are conscious of actually perceiving things external to our organism. We do not see the image on the retina; we see the object at a distance from the eye. Even in hearing and smell, the object of which we are actually conscious is not presented as an affection of the nerves, but as situated in and proceeding from a distant body." The answer to this objection is to be found in the fact, that in the actual exercise of our senses, in their matured state, we never perform a pure act of perception, but one of per-

functions of the nerves and the sensorium in sensation. This question is confessedly one of the most difficult in physiology, and, in its proper place in that science, one of the most important. But in reference to the present remarks its decision is of little consequence. The visible image, or other sensible impression, is not itself transmitted to the sensorium; and the irritation of the interior nervous system can only serve to arouse the attention to the affection localised at the surface. The notion of a *seat of the soul*, in the literal sense of the term, is utterly meaningless to any but a materialist; and all that the minutest anatomy can hope to discover is the material *occasion* which acts as the immediate stimulant to consciousness. But the consciousness, once aroused, is as capable of acting in one part of the system as in another, and is, in fact, *present* wherever it acts. This is expressed with philosophical accuracy in the words of St. Augustine :—" Ideo simplicior est corpore, quia non mole diffunditur per spatium loci, sed in unoquoque corpore, et in toto tota est, et in qualibet ejus parte tota est." (*De Trinitate*, vi. 6).

ception united with something else. It is as certain as
any fact of science can be, that the perception of distance is not originally conveyed by the eye, but is an
inference of the understanding derived from certain
concomitant visible phenomena, principally from the
degree of distinctness of the colour and outline of the
object. Yet of this inference we are never conscious in
the exercise of our matured senses, but appear to see the
distance of objects as immediately as their colour. The
most ordinary judgments apparently derived from sense
are instances of the same kind. When I say, " I see a
horse," in reality I see nothing of the kind. Even
granting for the moment that the external object is seen,
it can be seen only as a coloured body of a certain
figure. That the coloured body before me is a horse is
not a perception of the sight, but a judgment of the
understanding; a judgment which implies acts of
memory, of comparison, of conception, etc. Yet we are
not conscious of the data from which we make the
inference, but refer the entire result to the act of sight
alone. These instances sufficiently show the necessity
of distinguishing between *original* and *acquired* perceptions; for which purpose we must first consider the
operations of that faculty to which our intuitions of
external objects as such properly belong.

The Locomotive Faculty, which we have next to consider, differs from the Senses, both in other respects, and
especially in the circumstance, that in its exercise, and
partly also in its results, it is dependent upon the will
of the person exercising it.   By this it is not meant
that the will is in all cases consciously exercised ; that
all motion is the result of a knowledge of two alternatives, and a deliberate preference of one of them.   This
is not always the case in the most undeniably voluntary
acts performed in the maturity of our faculties.   A man
in the midst of a walk, when engaged in conversation or
thought, is not distinctly conscious of each successive
movement of his limbs ; yet there can be no doubt that
the acts are his own, as much as when he is attending to
and conscious of the exertion, and that, in either case, it
depends on himself to continue or discontinue the
motion.   How far the will itself is free or determined
by antecedent causes, is a question which cannot be
considered here ; but, whatever theory we may adopt
upon this point, as regards the actions of men or of
brutes, there is an obvious difference between saying,
" You may bring a horse to the water, but you cannot
make him drink ;" and saying, " You may fire a cannon
in his ear, but you cannot make him hear ;" or, " You

may lay on the whip, but you cannot make him feel." This difference, whatever amount of liberty it may imply, is all that is insisted upon in distinguishing between the exercise of the locomotive faculty and that of the senses.

It is the locomotive faculty which first informs us immediately of the existence and properties of a material world exterior to our organism. This exterior world manifests itself in the form of *something resisting our volition*; and to this general head of *resistance* may be reduced the whole of those attributes which exterior bodies immediately exhibit in their relation to our organism ; namely, gravity, cohesion, repulsion, and inertia. This consciousness of our locomotive energy being resisted by something external, though in practice accompanied by the sensation of touch, is so far distinct from that sensation that either may be conceived as taking place without the other. The sensation of touch is a consciousness of an irritation of the nerves spread over the surface of the skin ; a consciousness which experience may teach us to connect with a pressure from without, but which may be, and sometimes is, also communicated from within, and which has no immediate relation to the will of the sentient person. The consciousness of resistance, on the other hand, implies a volition to move the limb ; and this volition may be conceived as impeded externally without any accompanying organic feeling. The various qualities of the body, moreover, are manifested in proportion to the amount of volition exercised. A slight effort makes known to us the existence of a resisting body : a stronger or more continued effort is followed by a consciousness of a more vigorous resistance, or of a yielding on the part of the opposing body, either wholly or in a certain direction. Hence we obtain a knowledge of the attributes of hardness or softness, of mobility or immobility. All these are different manifestations of a relation between self and not-self ; between an organised body acted upon by the will, and a foreign body in antagonism to it. This consciousness of resistance to our voluntary motion is something very different from that of a mere inability to move, such as may take place when a stroke of paralysis destroys the power of the will over the bodily motions. We have in it, not the mere negative consciousness of will not followed by motion, but the positive consciousness of will followed by motion, and that motion resisted from without. In this relation both elements are equally *presented*, and one of them is the external body.

The manner in which the locomotive energy may be supposed originally to exert itself, and the foundation which by such exertion would be laid for the education of the sensitive consciousness, even before the latter is called into actual existence, has been graphically described by Professor Müller, in language which I will not attempt to weaken by alteration ; though I may remark, in quoting it, that that eminent physiologist has hardly marked with sufficient accuracy the distinction between the sense of resistance and that of touch properly so called ; and consequently has made some confusion between the objective and the subjective, the presentative and the representative consciousness. " If we imagine a human being in which—as in the fœtus in utero, for example—the sense of vision has never received any impressions, and in which sensations of touch merely have been excited by impressions made upon its body from without, it is evident that the first obscure idea excited would be no other than that of a sentient passive *self*, in contradistinction to something acting upon it.* The uterus, which compels the child to assume a determined position, and gives rise to sensations in it, is also the means of exciting in the sensorium of the child the consciousness of something thus distinct from itself and external to it. But how is the idea of two *exteriors*—of that which

* Perhaps it would be more correct to say only, " a sentient passive self, modified in a certain manner." So far as touch alone, without motion, is concerned, it may be doubted whether there can be any consciousness of a something exterior to *self*. It may perhaps be possible to distinguish the one conscious self from its successive modifications ; but the relation thus manifested can hardly be described as one of interior and exterior. The sentient self is on each occasion of sensation present in the organism, and has no conscious relation to anything beyond.

the limbs of the child's body form in relation to its
internal self and of the true exterior world—developed ?
In a twofold manner: In the first place, the child
governs the movement of its limbs, and thus perceives that they are instruments subject to the use
and government of its internal *self;* while the resistance
which it meets with around is not subject to its will, and
therefore gives it the idea of an absolute exterior.
Secondly, The child will perceive a difference in the
sensations produced according as the parts of its own
body touch each other, or as one part of the body only
meets with resistance from without. In the first instance, where one arm, for example, touches the other,
the resistance is afforded by a part of the child's own
body, and the limb thus giving the resistance becomes
the subject of sensation as well as the other. The two
limbs are in this case external objects of perception and
percipient at the same time. In the second instance,
the resisting body will be represented to the mind as
something external and foreign to the living body, and
not subject to the internal *self.* Thus will arise in the

There may, indeed, be a consciousness of a local relation between different parts of the body successively affected ; but these, though exterior
to each other, will not thus be recognised as exterior to the conscious
self. The relation of interior to exterior can only exist between two
bodies occupying space ; and, in this case, can only arise when we become
conscious of the double *non ego*, of the bodily organism in relation to
some other body. This will be the consequent, not the antecedent,

mind of the child the idea of a resistance which one part of its own body can offer to another part of its own body, and at the same time the idea of a resistance offered to its body by an absolute *exterior*. In this way is gained the idea of an external world as the cause of sensations.* Though the sensations of the being actually inform him only of the states of himself, of his nerves and of his skin, acted upon by external impressions,† yet henceforth the idea of the external cause becomes inseparably associated with the sensation of touch ;‡ and such is the condition of sensation in the adult. If we lay our hand upon the table, we become conscious, on a little reflection, that we do not feel the table, but merely that part of the skin which the table touches ;§ but, without this reflection, we confound the sensation of the part of the skin which has received the impression with the idea of the resistance, and we maintain boldly that we feel the table itself, which

* Rather "as existing and resisting our volitions." To describe the external world merely as the *cause of sensations* is to make it no more than a hypothetical object, invented to account for certain states of the subject.

† True of the sensations proper, but not of the locomotive volition ; and, in the case of the former, the impressions need not be *external*.

‡ How can it be *associated*, unless it has been first *given* without association ; *i.e.* in itself, and not merely in its effect ? Otherwise there is a relation with only one related term.

§ True of the mere feeling, but not of the consciousness that arises when we try to penetrate into the substance of the table and find ourselves unable to do so.

is not the case. If the hand be now moved over a greater extent of the table's surface, the idea of a larger object than the hand can cover is obtained. If, to encompass the resisting object, the hand require to be moved in different directions and planes, the idea of surfaces applied to each other in different directions is conceived, and thus the notion of an external solid body occupying space is obtained."[*]

From the consideration of the locomotive faculty, we should pass, by a natural transition, to that of the acquired perceptions, in which the information originally furnished by this faculty is transferred to other modes of consciousness. Before taking this step, however, it will be necessary to say a few words on another organ of sensation, which, in the opinion of some eminent authorities, is entitled to contest with the locomotive faculty the claim of giving rise to our knowledge of the properties of external matter.

OF THE MUSCULAR SENSE.

The motion of a limb, whether free or resisted, being accompanied by certain sensations arising from the contraction or relaxation of the muscles, it has been some-

* Müller's *Elements of Physiology*, p. 1080, Baly's translation. The notion of a solid body occupying space, may, however, arise from simpler data than those supposed in the last sentence. This will be considered hereafter, when we treat of the primary qualities of body.

times thought that to these sensations, and not to the motion which they accompany, is owing our earliest apprehension of the fact of external extension and resistance.* A few words on this question will be necessary to complete this portion of our inquiry.

In the first place, it is unquestionable that these muscular sensations exist, and that they are distinct from the proper impressions due to the five commonly acknowledged senses. The feeling of *fatigue*, for example, belongs, partly at least, to this class; but this feeling is only an increased degree of one which accompanies every muscular exertion, and which, in its more moderate forms, is pleasant instead of painful. When we move a limb after a sufficient rest, the motion is accompanied by a sensation similar to, though less intense than, that which ensues when it is moved after long previous exercise. To the same class belongs the sensation which accompanies the act of stretching, which is only another degree of the feeling of muscular tension.† In the second place, these sensations may in some cases be the means of indicating to us the fact of the motion; and such is probably the office which they

* See Brown, Lecture xxii. In giving a prominent place to the muscular sensation, and taking but slight notice of the volition by which it is accompanied, Brown departs from the teaching of his master Destutt Tracy, and in the same degree vitiates the theory.

† See Brown, Lecture xxii.; and Mill, *Analysis of the Human Mind*, chap. i. sec. 7.

perform in the earliest exercises of the locomotive faculty. As at that stage of our existence our other senses have not yet come into operation, or, at least, have not been developed to that degree which suffices for the perception of foreign bodies, it is clear that the fact of our limb being in motion must be made known to us by some feeling connected with the act itself, not by observation of it from any other centre. We cannot as yet *see* that our limb moves : we must therefore, in some manner, *feel* that it does so ; and this, in point of fact, is effected by means of the muscular sensations of the limb itself.*

But this is not sufficient to convey a knowledge of external bodies. The muscular sensations, viewed by themselves, are, like all other sensations, merely the consciousness of a particular state of our organism, and do not, any more than other sensations, give us a direct perception of the cause from which they proceed. The

---

* It does not, however, follow that the muscular sensation is in this case the only possible evidence of the motion.   On this point Sir William Hamilton observes :—"Supposing all muscular feeling abolished (the power of moving the muscles at will remaining, however, entire), I hold that the consciousness of the mental motive energy, and of the greater or less degree of such energy requisite, in different circumstances, to ac-complish our intention, would of itself enable us always to perceive the fact, and in some degree to measure the amount, of any resistance to our voluntary movements, howbeit the concomitance of certain feelings with the different states of muscular tension renders this cognition not only easier, but, in fact, obtrudes it upon our attention" (Reid's *Works*, p. 864).

muscular sensation that arises when our motion is resisted is not a consciousness of resistance, but of a state of our organism caused by resistance; and it is the state, and not the causation, that we immediately feel; the latter, as in the case of the other senses, being not *presented* in the sensitive act, but *represented* as a consequence of association. Hence, while we grant the existence and the importance of the muscular sensations, we are as far as ever from the knowledge of an extra-organic world. This knowledge depends, not on the relation in which that world stands to our *sensations*, but on that in which it stands to our *volitions*. We will in the first instance to move a limb: the sensation may inform us that the limb obeys our volition; but it is the motion, and not the sensation, which is resisted by the external body. The two are unlike in all their most important features. The sensation is chiefly, if not entirely, a passive state; the motion is an active energy. The sensation is in the organism; the motion is derived from the will. The sensation conveys an immediate knowledge of the *ego;* the motion, when resisted, conveys an immediate knowledge of the *non ego.* I am conscious at one time of a voluntary effort to move; I am conscious also (whether through the muscular sensation or otherwise) that I have overcome the inertia of the limb, and put it in motion; and I am conscious of the amount of effort necessary to effect this purpose. This consciousness contains, as its condition, a concomitant intellectual apprehension of *space*, without which the effort to move could not be made or willed; and this apprehension appears to be original and inexplicable, as it is implied in the first consciousness of a power of locomotion, prior to its actual exercise. I next become conscious that the motion is resisted from without, and that an additional effort is needed to overcome the resistance and continue the motion. This is an immediate perception of a relation between *self* and *not-self*, between the resisted effort and the resisting object. In this the voluntary energy is the primary source of knowledge; the muscular sensation, the secondary, and possibly the contingent accompaniment. The language of Destutt Tracy—"Il reste donc constant que le mouvement volontaire nous donne seul un vrai sentiment de resistance"*—can hardly be called exaggerated.

OF THE PRIMARY AND SECONDARY QUALITIES OF BODY.

The theory of the action of our senses, and of their relation to the material world, would be incomplete without some notice of a famous distinction which has played an important part in various systems of philosophy,—the distinction between Primary and Secondary

* *Elémens d'Idéologie*, p. 162.

Qualities of Body.   The history of this distinction, under various names, in ancient and modern times, has been given at considerable length in a learned note appended to Sir William Hamilton's edition of Reid's *Works*, to which we must content ourselves with referring.   Our limits will only allow a few remarks on the nature of the distinction itself, and its relation to the theory of perception which has been adopted in the preceding pages.

By modern philosophers, the distinction between these two classes of qualities has been based, sometimes on a psychological, sometimes on a physical principle. In the former point of view, the primary qualities have been distinguished as those which cannot by any act of thought be separated from the conception of body, being essential to that conception itself, in whatever relation it may be viewed ; while the secondary qualities are mere modifications of the primary, by which the bodies are enabled to produce certain sensations in us.   In the latter point of view, the primary qualities are considered to be such as really exist, in the bodies themselves, in the same manner in which they are perceived by us ; whereas the secondary qualities are but the occult causes of certain sensations, which, as experienced, bear no resemblance to the powers by which they are produced. Under the former class are comprehended extension and solidity, to which have sometimes been added figure, number, motion and rest,[*] hardness and softness, roughness and smoothness.[†]

Against the first of the above principles of distinction it has been objected that some secondary qualities, as well as the primary, are inseparable from the conception of body. Thus colour, of some kind or other, accompanies every perception, and even every imagination of extended substance ; and of two contradictory qualities, one or other must be attributed to every object.[‡] Against the second principle it may be objected that, even if we admit that in perception we are immediately conscious of the existence of a body as presented, still we know not what any of its qualities may be in themselves, out of relation to our faculties. Both mind and matter may be immediately present in an act of perception, yet the object perceived may be, like a chemical compound, the result of a relation between the two, and may resemble neither of the elements from which it is produced. We can never be certain how much of the perceived phenomena of a body depends on the constitution of our own faculties, and how much belongs to the absolute nature of the body irrespectively of its relation to us. To determine this point, it would be necessary that we should perceive it without our faculties.

[*] As by Locke, *Essay*, b. ii. chap. viii. sec. 9.

[†] As by Reid, *Inquiry*, chap. v. sec. 4 ; and by Stewart, *Essays*, i. chap. ii. sec. 2.

[‡] Sir W. Hamilton, Reid's *Works*, p. 839.

Yet both the above principles of distinction are fundamentally sound, though, to free them from misapprehension, they require a somewhat different explanation and application from that which is usually given. The *body* which is directly perceived by the senses is not inanimate matter, but our own organism ; and of this, as extended, we have an immediate consciousness in every act of perception. Hence the distinction between primary and secondary qualities as perceived by the senses, if it is tenable at all, must be tenable only in relation to certain qualities existing in our own organism. We can therefore no longer distinguish between attributes existing in bodies, and powers of affecting our sensitive organism ; for the *body* in relation to which the distinction has to be made is not that which affects, but that which is affected. In this point of view, it is obvious that colour, for example, is a quality of body, as well as extension. Our visual organism is presented in the act of sight as *extended* and as *coloured*. We cannot say that the extension belongs to the inanimate, the colour to the animated body ; for of the inanimate body the senses tell us nothing. Nor yet can we describe the one as an attribute of body *per se*, the other of body in relation to our senses ; for the whole nervous organism, as such, exists for us only as it is perceived, and is perceived only as it is affected. Destroy or alter the faculty of sense ; and the whole organism of sight, as it is perceived in sensation, exists no more, or exists in a different manner.

The true ground of distinction between primary and secondary qualities of body is, we think, to be found in the fact, that some attributes of body are presented in the exercise of all the senses alike, while others are peculiar to one sense only. In every act of sensation we are conscious of our own organism as extended or occupying space. In the act of sight we are conscious of it as coloured. The two impressions, when once acquired, may be inseparable from each other ; but the first may be acquired without the second, as in the case of a man totally blind, who would have a knowledge of extension but not of colour.* Hence the former class of attributes are essential to our conception of body, and indeed form that conception : the latter are accidental in so far as the conception of body may exist without them ; though, when the association between the two has once been formed, it may not be possible to separate them by any subsequent act of thought.

We are thus brought back to the old Aristotelian distinction between *common* and *proper sensibles*, which

* Sir W. Hamilton asserts that "light and darkness, white and black, are, in this relation, all equally colours ;" and this is true, when the sensation of both has been once given. But if objects are only discerned by difference, a man totally blind could not be said to have a consciousness of darkness as such, or to associate its idea with the positive impressions derived from the other senses. Ordinary blindness, how-

has been pointed out by Sir William Hamilton, as in substance identical with the modern distinction between primary and secondary qualities. In this point of view, the secondary qualities of body may be easily indicated. To this class belong all the affections peculiar to certain parts of our sensitive organism, whether as the proper objects of the respective senses, or as the accidental accompaniments of certain sensations. "Such are the idiopathic affections of our several organs of sense, as colour, sound, flavour, savour, and tactual sensation; such are the feelings from heat, electricity, galvanism, etc.; nor need it be added, such are the muscular and cutaneous sensations which accompany the exercise of the locomotive faculty. Such, though less directly the result of foreign causes, are titillation, sneezing, horripilation, shuddering, the feeling of what is called setting the teeth on edge, etc. etc. Such, in fine, are all the various sensations of bodily pleasure and pain determined by the action of external stimuli."[*]

The primary qualities require somewhat more consideration to determine them. They are the universal attributes of body, common to every mode of its existence as an object of consciousness. Hence they are not, properly speaking, known by sense, but by intellect, having no special organ adapted to their perception, but being equally present in every exercise of the bodily

[*] Sir W. Hamilton, Reid's *Works*, p. 854 (slightly altered from the original).

senses. Hence, too, they cannot, in their pure form, be depicted to the sense or the imagination, but require, in every instance, to be united with one or other of the secondary qualities which are the proper objects of the several senses. Pure extension, for example, is not an object of sight or touch, but only visible or tangible extension ; *i. e.* extension combined with colour or tactual sensation. The perception of the primary qualities, in its original manifestation, is in fact an intellectual cognition of the relations between the several parts of our sensitive organism ; and, as such, both implies a present consciousness of that organism as affected, and is implied by it. For on the one hand, the consciousness of a relation implies the simultaneous consciousness of the objects related ; and, on the other hand, the consciousness of an object as such implies so much of relation to other objects as is necessary to its distinct cognition. A coloured surface, for instance, can only be perceived as composed of several coloured points exterior to each other; and a coloured point can only be discerned as forming a portion of a coloured surface. The primary and secondary qualities are thus necessarily perceived in conjunction with each other ; though the primary constitute the permanent element, implied in the cognition of body in general ; the second-ary constitute the variable element implied in the cog-nition of body by this or that sense.

The primary qualities of body may be all included under the one general head of *relation to space*. This implies the twofold condition of—1. *Solidity*, or occupation of space in the three dimensions of length, breadth, and thickness ; 2. *Being contained in space*, or surrounded by space on every side.* Though the sensible affection, as confined to the surface of the organism, may appear at first sight to indicate two dimensions only, yet it is obvious, on a moment's reflection, that the intelligible relation of parts to parts which necessarily accompanies the affection, is only possible under the condition of a simultaneous immediate consciousness of solidity. Space, in all its dimensions, is the form of all our perceptions of sense : a surface, or even a visible point, can only be perceived as occupying a portion of space, and as surrounded by space on all sides of it. It is impossible to conceive a surface as having no space behind or before it, or as not breaking the continuity of that space, and thus occupying a part of it. The geometrical line which has length without breadth, and the geometrical surface which has length and breadth without thickness, are, as objects of perception, equally inconceivable with the geometrical point which has no magnitude ;† though it is possible logically to distin-

* Sir W. Hamilton, Reid's *Works*, p. 847.

† This is perfectly consistent with the fact, to be noticed hereafter, that the *actual perception* of solidity by sight is not original, but acquired.

guish between these various elements of body, and to ascertain the special properties of each. We have in this circumstance a further confirmation of the character which has throughout these pages been assigned to space, as an *à priori* condition of consciousness, manifested on the occasion of experience, but in no way to be evolved from it.

From the general attribute of solidity or occupation of space, in its two constituent features of *geometrical solidity* or trinal extension, and *physical solidity* or ultimate incompressibility, Sir W. Hamilton has deduced the three necessary relations of *number* or *divisibility*, *size* or *magnitude*, and *shape* or *figure;* and from the correlative attribute of being contained in space, those of *mobility* and *situation.* These may be all regarded as primary qualities of body, involved in, and deducible by analysis from, the conception of body in general as presented in every act of sensitive perception.

Those attributes which are immediately perceived as existing in extra-organic bodies are distinguished by Sir W. Hamilton under the name of *secundo-primary qualities.* These are not essential constituents of the conception of body in general, but attributes contingently observed to exist in bodies in relation to our organism. They are all contained under the general head of *resistance* or *pressure,* and are immediately discerned only by means of the locomotive faculty. To this general head belong the attributes of *weight, cohesion,·inertia,* and *repulsion,* all of which are made known to us as different modes of resistance to our locomotive energy. It is by the apprehension of the secundo-primary, not by that of the primary qualities, that we immediately learn the existence and nature of an extra-organic world.   We are conscious, to use the words of Sir W. Hamilton, " that our locomotive energy is resisted, and not resisted by aught in our organism itself.   In the consciousness of being thus resisted is involved, as a correlative, the consciousness of a resisting something external to our organism.   Both are therefore conjunctly apprehended."* For a more detailed exposition of this important subject, which our limits do not permit us to treat at greater length, the reader is referred to the dissertations of Sir William Hamilton.† It only remains for us to sum up briefly the substance of the above remarks.

By *primary qualities of body* must not be understood qualities of body *per se,* as it exists *out of relation to our faculties;* for of body in this sense we have not, and cannot have, any knowledge.   The nearest approximation which we can make to a conception of body *per se* is that of body as it appears *in relation to all our faculties;* and, consequently, the primary qualities can only be directly given as existing in our own organism, which is the only body of which we are immediately cognisant

---

* Reid's *Works,* p. 882.   † Reid's *Works,* notes D and D*.

in every act of external perception. The secundo-primary and the secondary qualities are not in this sense qualities of body *per se*, being given only in certain special modes of cognition; the former as attributes of an extra-organic substance resisting our locomotive energy, the latter as affections of our organism in this or that particular state of sensation. The primary qualities are thus the essential constituents of our empirical notion of body, from whatever form of experience it may be derived; while the others are attributes superadded to that notion, as manifested by body in certain special relations only.

But though the primary qualities of body as such are immediately given only as existing in our own organism, it is obvious that they are apprehended as forming the essential attributes of all matter alike, organic or otherwise; for the body which resists our locomotive energy can only do so as occupying a portion of space into which we attempt to penetrate, and thus as possessing the same primary qualities with the organism to which it is related. The secondary qualities, too, though immediately apprehended only as affections of our organism, are, in the later development of consciousness, necessarily associated with exterior objects. The nature of this association next claims our attention, as that which gives rise to the important phenomena of *acquired perception*.

OF THE ACQUIRED PERCEPTIONS.

The examination of the Acquired Perceptions should, in strict accuracy, be undertaken in connection with the representative, not with the presentative consciousness. They are not, properly speaking, *given* in the sensitive act to which they are supposed to belong, but *inferred* by the understanding, according to a law of association, from the presence of something else. But inasmuch as the inference is one which is never consciously performed; as it takes place by a necessary law of our mental constitution at a period too early to leave any trace in the memory; as, consequently, in the complex acts of our matured consciousness the inferred elements are not directly distinguishable from the data which suggest them; and as the explanation of the former is intimately connected with the preceding remarks on the latter, it will be better to sacrifice the strictly logical arrangement, in order to present in a more connected view the entire series of phenomena usually referred to the evidence of the senses.

It has been already observed that, in the exercise of our faculties in their mature state, no perception occurs pure and isolated, but is, in all cases, united with an act of judgment or inference. To ascertain by actual experience the relative proportions of these ingredients, so as to separate the independent acts of the senses from the results of their education, it would be necessary to have an exact recollection of our first impressions as they existed before the formation of habits. Nay, even this, were it possible, would be hardly sufficient; as it may be questioned whether the education of the senses does not in some respects precede even the first occasions of their exercise. From what has been said in treating of the locomotive faculty, it appears that the sense of sight, for example, can never be said to have existed in a wholly uneducated state ; inasmuch as certain obscure notions of an external world already exist, and have made their influence felt, before the eyes of the child have come in contact with the light, or its acts been exposed to the observation of others. When, in the absence of experience of the simple, we attempt to supply its place by analysis of the compound, it must be borne in mind that the results at which we arrive will represent a theoretical rather than an actual process, and that some of the conclusions elicited by the theory will be only approximately true in practice. It must not be supposed, for instance, that the several stages through which the sense of sight is represented as passing, actually occur as distinct phenomena of vision during the unremembered days of infancy. When theory declares that the object which we really see is in the organ of sight, it does not follow that the infant has ever actually seen it there. The approximate truth, that the perception of distance is of gradual acquisition, may be ascertained by positive observation; but no observation can tell us whether the actual exercise of sight began with the first or with a later member of the series. The remark which we have before had occasion to make, that the distinctions of Psychology represent the elements of consciousness rather than separate acts, is equally applicable here.

Of the acquired perceptions, those of vision are by far the most important; so much so that it will be sufficient to notice a few of the principal of these, leaving the reader to apply our observations, *mutatis mutandis*, to the other senses. The principle which must guide him in making the application is that which we have more than once had occasion to repeat; namely, *that no sense, in its original state, informs us of anything more than certain states of our own organism.* In addition to this, it will be necessary to bear in mind another principle of no less importance; namely, *that all representation must be founded on a presentation; in* other words, *that nothing can be inferred in connection with one phenomenon of consciousness which has not been given in connection with another.* The examination of this principle belongs to a later stage of our inquiry. For the present we must content ourselves with taking it for granted.

Among the acquired perceptions of the sense of sight, the most important are the following :—1. The perception of an *external field of vision* distinct from the retina, and the consequent judgments concerning the *distance* and *magnitude* of objects in that field. 2. The perception of the *unity* of a visible object, which presents a separate image to each retina. 3. The perception of the object as *solid* or extended in three dimensions of space, and of its *figure* or boundary in each direction. 4. The perception of its *position*, which is the reverse of that of its image on the retina. A few remarks on each of these will, it is hoped, furnish sufficient information for the explanation of acquired perceptions in general.

I. *Field of vision.*—The true or perceived field of vision is the surface of the retina itself ; and this may, in certain cases, be actually discerned as such. Thus, the sensation of darkness is the consciousness of the condition of the retina in a state of repose ; and in this there is no perception of any field of vision exterior to the retina itself. The apparent or inferred field of vision is a space of greater or less extent, exterior to the eye, on which the images of the retina are projected by an act of the mind. In the majority of cases, we appear to perceive this field immediately ; but many observations have been adduced to show that this apparent perception is not part of the original faculty of sight. An infant appears at first to have no perception

by sight of the distance of objects, but stretches out its
hands towards distant and near bodies alike.   The youth
who was couched by Cheselden saw at first all objects
in one plane, and apparently touching the eye.   It is true
that the patient in this instance saw the objects as *on*
not *in* the eye; and this may, perhaps, be the case with
the infant also; but it must be remembered that the
ideas of externality and distance are already partially
acquired by the locomotive faculty before the sense of
sight comes into exercise.   From these approximate
facts, joined to what we know of the theory of vision, we
may conclude, with some probability, that a being destitute of the power of motion would, on first opening his
eyes, discern nothing but the images existing on the
surface of the retina.

But, when the knowledge of an external world has
been once given by the locomotive faculty, the education
of the sense of vision follows rapidly and imperceptibly.
A certain image on the retina accompanies the perception of an object in contact with the hand.   The object
is pushed further off, and the size and outline of the
image undergo a corresponding change.   The hand is
placed over the object, and its image takes the place of
the other.   It is placed over the eye, and the images
vanish altogether.   Certain sensations of sight are thus
at first associated with certain perceptions of distance;
then suggest those perceptions when the latter are not

immediately present; and finally, as the process becomes more familiar, are substituted for them. Something similar to this takes place more perceptibly in
some of the associations of ideas which are formed at a
later period. In many cases, where the association is
frequent, the antecedent is gradually forgotten, and the
attention wholly fixed on the consequent. There is no
original connection between the meaning of a word and
its sound, or between the sound and the written charac-
ters by which it is represented to the eye; yet the sight
of certain black figures on a white ground suggests to
the child, first the sound, and through the sound the
meaning. At a later stage the intermediate links of
the chain are forgotten; the sound vanishes entirely;
the form of the letter is scarcely, if at all, noticed; and
the sight of the printed page plunges us at once into
communion with the thoughts of the writer. Yet the
mere visual perception remains as it was, one and the
same to the man who can read and to the man who
cannot. All beyond this is acquired by habit; and the
process, when most familiar and most imperceptible, is
in its successive steps precisely the same as in those
early days when we painfully combined distinct letters
into syllables, and distinct syllables into words, and
distinct words into sentences. The principal difference
which distinguishes this and similar operations from
the acquired perceptions of sight is, that the associa-

tions are formed in the one case consciously, after the mind has acquired a power of reflecting on its own operations, and of acting in consequence of reflection; in the other, unconsciously, by an instinctive law of our constitution. Hence the latter may be described as a natural association common to all men; the former, as an artificial association peculiar to the educated. Yet our natural powers are not, as natural, necessarily born with us. It is natural for man to see distant objects; in the same way as it is natural for him to walk upright and to use his hands. Yet there was a time when he could not discern distances by the eye; just as there was a time when he crawled on all fours, and employed his hand for no other purpose than that of sucking its extremities.

The following remarks of Professor Müller are important, in illustration of the phenomenon in question :—"Several physiologists—as Tourtal, Volkmann, and Bartels—suppose the interpretation of the sensations of the retina, as objects forming part of the exterior world, to be a faculty of the sense of vision itself. But what, in the first place, constitutes the external world? Since, in the first acts of vision, the image of the individual's own body cannot be distinguished from those of other bodies, the referring of the sensations of vision to something external can be nothing else than the discrimination between the sensations of vision and the subject of them—between the sensations and the sentient *self*. It is by the operations of the judgment that the objects of vision are recognised as exterior to the body of the individual. . . . It is said that the new-born infant perceives from the first that the objects of vision are external to its body and to its eye; but the infant perceives neither its own eye nor its body in the form of sensations of vision, and only learns by experience which of the images which it sees is its own body. We can therefore only say, that the new-born infant distinguishes the sensations from the sentient *self;* and in this sense only does it perceive the sensation as something external. In brutes, the co-operation of instinct renders this reaction of the sensorium under the impression of external objects much less indefinite; for the young animal soon applies itself to the nipple of the mother; so that its sensorium must be the seat of an innate impulse to attain to the image, which it sees, and which is an object, or something external to the sentient self, by appropriate movements. Though the new-born infant be at first unable to distinguish between the image of its own body and those of external objects, it will soon remark that certain images in the field of vision are constantly reappearing, and that these images move when its body is voluntarily moved. These are images of parts of its own body. All the other images in the field of vision

either change quite independently of the body of the
infant, or the changes which they undergo do not correspond with its voluntary movements. These are
images of objects appertaining to the external world,
which, now recognised as existing in a space external
to the body of the individual, are henceforth continually presenting themselves in this space, which, according to the conception of the mind, is subject to the
operations of vision. Of the eye, as the organ of vision,
the new-born infant knows nothing."*

The field of vision being thus by association perceived as external to the eye, our judgment of the relative *distance* and *magnitude* of objects within that field
is determined by similar associations. That of distance
is an inference chiefly drawn, in the first instance, from
the degrees of distinctness in the colour and outline of
the objects, aided, perhaps, in the case of near objects,
by the muscular sensations accompanying the conver-
gence of the optic axes.† That of magnitude may be
considered as partly original, partly acquired. Original,
in so far as there is a difference in the size of the object actually perceived (*i. e.* the image on the retina),
dependent upon the visual angle made by the central
rays of two pencils of light from the extreme points of
a luminous body, intersecting after refraction within

---

* *Elements of Physiology*, p. 1168.
† Carpenter, *Principles of Human Physiology*, p. 922.

the eye; acquired, inasmuch as the inferred magnitude of the external object is the result of a combination of the size of its image with other phenomena, chiefly with those which give rise to our estimate of its distance. This is, in substance, the theory of distance and magnitude first proposed by Bishop Berkeley,—a theory which, while it has been amended and completed in some of its minor details by the discoveries of modern science, remains in its essential features unshaken.

II. *Single vision with two eyes.*—The above remarks are also applicable in a great degree to the phenomenon of single vision with two eyes; a phenomenon which many eminent physiologists have referred to a special provision in the structure of the visual apparatus,* but which is sufficiently proved by the observations and experiments of Professor Wheatstone to be an inference from the mental combination of the two images actually seen. To this combination it is necessary that the two images should fall on portions of the two retinæ which have been accustomed to act in concert; and the principle on which it mainly depends is doubtless the association of a single perception of resistance with the double image of the corresponding visible phenomena.†

* See Müller's *Elements of Physiology*, p. 1197.

† See Dr. Baly's remarks in his translation of Müller's *Elements of Physiology*, p. 1205; and Carpenter's *Principles of Human Physiology*, p. 917.

III. *Solidity and Figure.*—The perceptions of solidity and figure are results of the same law of association. The former, as Professor Wheatstone's experiments show, is like the unity of the object, the effect of the combination of the two visible images, and depends, as far as sight is concerned, upon the different perspective exhibited by the projection of each. The phenomena of the stereoscope present a now familiar illustration of this ; two plane projections being, by means of this instrument, made to act upon the eye in the same manner that solid figures do in ordinary vision ; and the two being, by an act of the mind, combined into the appearance of one external solid body.* The perception of resistance, however, has also some share in the origin of this association. Figure, like magnitude, is partly an original, partly an acquired perception. Plane figures, such as a square or a circle, can be depicted on the surface of the retina, and can thus be distinguished from each other by the original power of the sense of sight. Solid figures, such as a sphere or a cube, are discerned in a great measure by the simultaneous use of both eyes, though the accuracy of the discrimination

---

* This explanation is of course inapplicable to the case of persons who have the sight of one eye only. Here, however, the same perception of solidity will be produced, partly by the associations suggested by resistance, and partly by the different perspective of the projection, conequent on changes in the position of the single eye.

is, no doubt, assisted by associations derived from touch assisted by motion.*

IV. *Erect vision.*—The explanation of the erect position of external objects has been attempted in various ways, none of which, however, can be considered as quite satisfactory.† It seems to be a law of the mind, in projecting images beyond the retina, to follow in some degree the course of the rays, and thus to produce an inverted impression when the image is projected beyond the point where the rays intersect. But to investigate

* Molyneux proposed to Locke the question whether a person born blind, who was able by touch to distinguish a cube from a sphere, would, on suddenly obtaining his sight, be able to distinguish them by the latter sense (see Locke, *Essay*, b. ii. chap. 9). Professor Müller finds it "difficult to conceive wherefore these two philosophers answered the problem in the negative." That figures, solid as well as plane, can be distinguished by sight alone, when the perception of an external field of vision has once been acquired, seems unquestionable; but the real problem is to determine whether each perception of sight can be at once identified with the corresponding perception of touch. That this cannot be done has been recently shown experimentally in a case reported by Mr. Nunneley of Leeds. The patient in this case was actually in the circumstances supposed by Molyneux, capable of distinguishing a cube from a sphere by touch. On first exercising his sight he could perceive a difference in the shapes, but could not say which was the cube and which the sphere. This interesting case confirms, in many respects, the experiment of Cheselden. See Nunneley *On the Organs of Vision*, p. 32.

† Sir David Brewster's theory of the line of visible direction is objected to on physiological grounds by Dr. Carpenter, *Human Physiology*, p. 916. That proposed by Professor Müller, and adopted by Dr. Carpenter, may be briefly stated thus. Up and down, right and left, are relative terms; therefore the inversion of everything is equivalent to

this and similar points fully, it would be necessary to know the exact relations of mind and body to each other in the act of sensation. This is impossible, as we cannot trace the action of the mind apart from that of the organism. The explanation of many of the phenomena of sensation probably depend on some inscrutable condition of consciousness, which no examination of the mere nervous organism is able to reveal to us. " There is," says Mr. Morell, " a perilous distance for the materialist to travel between the retina and the living soul. The eye does not see of itself, neither, if the optic nerve be severed, can any visual perception reach the mind. How, then, we may ask, can the image on the retina travel along the nerve, and impress the brain with its own form and hue? The moment we get beyond the mere *mechanism* of the case, our power of tracing the image is lost, and we can only detect at the other, or spiritual end of the process, a mental phenomenon, differing as widely as possible from the mere material substance without." *

The acquired perceptions of the other senses may be the inversion of nothing. This explanation, however, does not tell us why the inversion takes place, but only accounts for the fact of our not noticing it. The fact still remains unexplained, that the external object and the image on the retina are, *to the eye of a stranger*, in a position the reverse of each other. *Query*—Are they likewise so *in different stages of the vision of the person himself?* This we have as yet no means of determining.

* *Elements of Psychology*, p. 131.

explained on the same principles.   Such, for instance,
are the judgments which we form of the direction and
distance of an object by the hearing or the smell ; these
two senses having, like that of sight, both an original
and an acquired field for their exercise.   Cognate to
the subject of acquired Perceptions is that of acquired
Sensations.   The feelings of pleasure and pain, which
an object imparts through the senses, may be as much
the result of practice and association as the information
which we gain by the same means concerning its nature.
Instances of this may be found in the artificial tastes
which we gain by the constant use of objects which at
first were considered as indifferent or disagreeable ; and,
again, in the strong feelings of dislike with which we
often regard various sensations, solely in consequence of
some early association.   And hence it will often be the
case that the different degrees of pleasure which the
several senses are capable of affording to an educated
man, will by no means correspond to those which they
materially impart as vehicles of mere animal enjoyment.
Thus the senses of sight and hearing, which are less
intense than the other senses in the merely nervous
affections which they are calculated to excite, are, notwithstanding, the vehicles of a mixed enjoyment (partly
sensitive, partly intellectual) of a far higher order.   But
the pleasure which we enjoy from the sight of beautiful
scenery, or from the hearing of music, is something

K

very different from the natural sensation, or affection of
the nervous organism.   The natural sensation is limited
to that amount of enjoyment of which the sense is susceptible at the moment of its exercise.   When our eyes
are gratified by a variety of visible objects, or our ears
by a succession of sounds, the memory, and not the
sensation, plays the principal part.   We see the various
objects, we hear the various sounds, *in succession ;*
though by an act of thought we necessarily combine
them into a single whole.   But the *discernment of relations* is in no case a work of sense ; and beauty and
deformity, harmony and discord, are almost entirely
the result of *relations.*   To estimate the merely sensual
pleasure imparted by sight and hearing, we must suppose the eye to be limited to a succession of detached
colours, and the ear to a succession of isolated sounds,
with no consciousness of any relation between them,
and no power of comparing the past with the present.
This distinction between original and acquired sensations has been perhaps too much neglected in the various attempts that have been made to construct an exact
philosophy of taste.

OF ATTENTION.

That sensation, as before observed, is neither a purely
bodily nor a purely mental affection—that it belongs

neither to the nervous organism alone, nor yet exclusively to the active self by which that organism is animated, but to that mysterious union of both, whose elements and laws philosophy has ever failed, and probably ever will fail, to penetrate—appears conspicuously when we come to examine two states of consciousness which appear to form the connecting links between the external and the internal affections, between the passive and the active elements of our nature, partaking of both, and identical with neither. These two are *Attention* and *Imagination*. Attention, in particular, partakes of this twofold character in a remarkable degree. To a hasty inspection it appears as if the operation of this faculty were at once the antecedent and the consequent of the sensible impression, as if the mind were at the same time active and passive in its production. It appears certain, on the one hand, that, in order to arouse the attention to any sensible phenomenon, that phenomenon must first be presented to consciousness ; while, on the other hand, it has been argued, with some plausibility, that unless the attention be previously aroused, consciousness has no intimation of the existence of the phenomenon at all. All the physical conditions of sensation may exist in full perfection, without any corresponding impression being produced upon the mind. "When two persons," says Reid, " are engaged in interesting discourse, the clock strikes within their hearing, to which they give no attention. What is the consequence? The next minute they know not whether the clock struck or not. Yet their ears were not shut. The usual impression was made upon the organ of hearing, and upon the auditory nerve and brain; but, from inattention, the sound either was not perceived, or passed in the twinkling of an eye, without leaving the least vestige in the memory."* Of the two alternatives here offered to our choice, the latter is adopted by Dr. Reid's successor as the more accurate explanation of the phenomenon. That attention is not necessary to the existence of a sensation in the consciousness seems at first sight manifest, both *à priori*, because a phenomenon must exist before the attention can be aroused to observe it, and *à posteriori*, from the very narrow limits within which experience testifies that our power over our own sensations is confined. When the mind is unoccupied, the slightest and most familiar sounds will make themselves heard as a matter of course. It is not necessary that the attention should be previously directed towards the object from which the sound proceeds; it is sufficient that it be not engaged with any other object. A louder or more unusual sound forces itself on the consciousness, however much the attention may be engaged elsewhere. The striking of a clock may be unheard during an interesting discourse; but

* *Active Powers*, Essay ii. chap. 3.

the report of a gun, or any unwonted noise, will be heard in spite of it. These and other considerations may be urged in favour of the hypothesis so ably maintained by Dugald Stewart,—namely, that we are in all cases conscious of the sensation, but are not always able to recollect that we have been conscious. "The true state of the fact," says that distinguished philosopher, "I apprehend, is, that the mind may think and will, without attending to its thoughts and volitions, so as to be able afterwards to recollect them. Nor is this merely verbal criticism; for there is an important difference between consciousness and attention, which it is very necessary to keep in view, in order to think upon this subject with any degree of precision. The one is an involuntary state of mind; the other is a voluntary act: the one has no immediate connection with the memory; but the other is so essentially subservient to it, that without some degree of it, the ideas and perceptions which pass through the mind seem to leave no trace behind them. When two persons are speaking to us at once, we can attend to either of them at pleasure without being much disturbed by the other. If we attempt to listen to both we can understand neither. The fact seems to be, that when we attend constantly to one of the speakers, the words spoken by the other make no impression on the memory, in consequence of our not attending to them, and affect us as little as if they had not been uttered. This power, however, of the mind to attend to either speaker at pleasure, supposes that it is at one and the same time conscious of the sensations which both produce. Another well-known fact may be of use in illustrating the same distinction. A person who accidentally loses his sight never fails to improve gradually in the sensibility of his touch. Now there are only two ways of explaining this. The one is, that in consequence of the loss of the one sense, some change takes place in the physical constitution of the body, so as to improve a different organ of perception. The other, that the mind gradually acquires a power of attending to and remembering those slighter sensations of which it was formerly conscious, but which, from our habits of inattention, made no impression whatever on the memory. No one, surely, can hesitate for a moment in pronouncing which of these two suppositions is the more philosophical."*

But this ingenious reasoning is not quite so conclusive as at first sight it appears to be. It proves clearly that the attention cannot be directed to an object in contact with an organ of sense unless something intervenes to arouse it; but it assumes without proof that this something must itself be a phenomenon of consciousness. The question remains, Is the phenomenon of which we become fully conscious by attention

---

* *Elements of the Philosophy of the Human Mind*, part ii. chap. 2.

the *same phenomenon* that it was before we attended to
it? or has attention itself added an element which
brings it within the sphere of consciousness? It seems
at first sight a paradox to maintain that our consciousness can be stimulated by anything of which we are not
conscious. Yet this apparent paradox is a fact which
in some degree takes place at every moment of our
lives. When we look at the smallest visible point of
light, this is obviously compounded of parts so small as
to be invisible; yet each of these contributes its share
to the sum total of consciousness. When we see a distant forest, the indistinct impression of green is made
up of the greenness of every individual leaf, not one of
which could be singly discerned. The theory of *latent
modifications of mind*, or, as they are called by Leibnitz, *obscure representations*, which is well calculated to
explain many of the most curious phenomena of consciousness, has been almost entirely neglected by the
philosophers of this country; yet it is one which,
though in most of its details belonging to physiology
rather than to psychology, must be assumed by the
latter science as the basis of many of its researches. In
the recently-published *Lectures on Metaphysics* of Sir
W. Hamilton, this deficiency has been in a great degree
supplied; and the English student of philosophy has
now the means of seeing this question treated with
the fulness and ability which its importance deserves.

But whether, in the widest sense of the term *consciousness*, it can or cannot be correctly described as prior to and independent of the act of attention, yet in the narrower and more accurate sense, in which alone it can be the object of scientific analysis, attention becomes a necessary condition of its existence, or rather is identical with consciousness itself. Every phenomenon of consciousness proper, as before observed, must possess in some degree the attributes of *clearness* and *distinctness*, without which it can leave no trace in the memory, and cannot be compared with other phenomena of the same class. But to a clear or distinct consciousness it is necessary that an act of reflection should accompany the intuition ; and to the act of reflection it is necessary that the phenomenon in question should have been observed with some degree of attention. The act of attention is therefore a necessary condition, possibly of the existence of a sensation in consciousness, but certainly of its recognition as such ; and, in strict language, it would not be inaccurate to define Attention as Consciousness in operation relatively to a definite object. This intimate union of the active with the passive functions of the human mind; this presence in every complete act of consciousness of a voluntary and personal factor—a permanent *self* in the midst of transitory modes,—exhibits man as in some degree the master of his own consciousness, and the author of the phenomena which it reveals to him. It is the exaggeration or exclusive consideration of this element which is the source of most of the extravagances of idealist metaphysics, as its neglect or suppression has given rise to most of the opposite extravagances of sensationalism.

OF IMAGINATION, MEMORY, AND HOPE.

In the art of attention the mind selects certain prominent features of an object of intuition, which thus become fixed in the memory, and capable of reproduction when the object is no longer present. The reproductive Imagination is thus the sequel of attention, forming the second link in the chain of connection between the intuitive and the reflective consciousness.[*] Hence, in a strictly methodical arrangement, the treatment of attention and imagination should be postponed till after the complete examination of the phenomena of intuition. But the prominence which, in the majority of treatises on the subject, has been given to the sensible relations of these two cognate acts, may furnish both an excuse for the consideration of them in the present place, and an opportunity of pointing out some of the chief defects which may be noticed in the ordinary treatment of them. "Imagination," says Dr. Reid, "when it is distinguished from conception, seems to me

* See Morell, *Elements of Psychology*, p. 169.

to signify one species of conception—to wit, the conception of visible objects."*   In this he follows the language of Descartes,—"Imaginari nihil aliud est quam rei corporeæ figuram seu imaginem contemplari."†   Mr. Stewart, though differing in his language, virtually limits the office of the same faculty to the reproduction of sensible impressions, though he does not, like the two authors last cited, confine it to the impressions of sight. Under the name of *conception*, he defines it as "that power of the mind which enables it to form a notion of an absent object of perception, or of a sensation which it has formerly felt."‡   Of the proper sense of the term *conception* we shall have occasion to speak hereafter. For the present, it will be sufficient to observe that Imagination, in the proper psychological sense of the term, should not be confined to the reproduction of the phenomena connected with the bodily senses.   It should rather be defined as the consciousness of an image in the mind, resembling and representing an object of possible intuition.   Not the objects of sense alone, but the presentations of intuition, external or internal,—desires,

---

* *Intellectual Powers*, Essay iv. chap. 1.

† *Meditatio Secunda.*   The office of imagination in relation to two other senses is accurately described in the lines of Shelley—

> "Music, when soft voices die,
> Vibrates in the memory ;
> Odours, when sweet violets sicken,
> Live within the sense they quicken."

‡ *Elements of the Philosophy of the Human Mind*, part i. chap. 3.

affections, volitions, thoughts, as well as sounds, or
colours, or figures,—everything, in short, that can be
experienced in consciousness as an individual thing, act,
or state of mind, may remain as an image in the
memory, or be reproduced in the mind at a future
period. Or the detached portions of objects once perceived may be combined by the imagination in a manner
in which they have never been presented in any actual
experience. Thus, when the upper parts of a man and
the lower parts of a horse have been perceived by the
sense in separate objects, the image of a centaur may be
formed as readily as that of a horse or a man. It is to
this last "power of modifying our conceptions, by combining the parts of different ones together, so as to form
new wholes of our own creation," that Mr. Stewart
would confine the term *imagination*. The distinction
really lies not so much in the image obtained as in the
manner of obtaining it; and, though worthy of notice
on many accounts, should, I think, be expressed in different language.

Imagination is of two kinds, which, following the
plan of classifying the phenomena of mind by the
leading characteristics of each, may be distinguished as
belonging to the intuitive and the reflective consciousness respectively. The first, in which the mind is
comparatively passive, consists in the continuance, in a
weaker form, of a sensible or otherwise intuitive impres-

sion, when the object which gave rise to it is no longer present.* This is the imagination which is described by Aristotle as a *kind of weak sensation,*† and as *sensitive imagination.*‡ When coupled with a consciousness of the past existence of the impression which it represents, it forms the *memory,* as distinguished from the *reminiscence* of Aristotle.§ The other kind of imagination is more properly an act of thought,|| and consists in constructing in the mind an individual image (whether actually resembling a former impression or not) in accordance with the attributes contained in a given general notion. In this instance, imagination coincides with a faculty to be hereafter described,—*conception.* It is, in fact, individualising the contents of a

* Arist. *Anal. Post.* ii. 19. Ἐνούσης δ' αἰσθήσεως τοῖς μὲν τῶν ζῴων ἐγγίνεται μονὴ αἰσθήματος, τοῖς δ' οὐκ ἐγγίνεται. Ὅσοις μὲν οὖν μὴ ἐγγίνεται, ἢ ὅλως ἢ περὶ ἃ μὴ ἐγγίνεται, οὐκ ἔστι τούτοις γνῶσις ἔξω τοῦ αἰσθάνεσθαι· ἐν οἷς δ', ἔνεστι [μὴ] αἰσθανομένοις ἔχειν ἔτι ἐν τῇ ψυχῇ. The negative inserted by Trendelenburg appears indispensable to the sense.

† *Rhet.* 1. 11.

‡ *De Anima,* iii. 11. Ἡ μὲν οὖν αἰσθητικὴ φαντασία καὶ ἐν τοῖς ἄλλοις ζῴοις ὑπάρχει, ἡ δὲ βουλευτικὴ ἐν τοῖς λογιστικοῖς.

§ Aristotle, *De Memoria,* c. i. Τίνος μὲν οὖν τῶν τῆς ψυχῆς ἐστὶν ἡ μνήμη; φανερόν, ὅτι καὶ οὗπερ ἡ φαντασία· καὶ ἔστι μνημονευτὰ καθ' αὑτὰ μὲν ὅσα ἐστὶ φανταστά.

|| *De Memoria,* c. ii. 25. Διαφέρει δὲ τοῦ μνημονεύειν τὸ ἀναμιμνήσκεσθαι, οὐ μόνον κατὰ τὸν χρόνον, ἀλλ' ὅτι τοῦ μὲν μνημονεύειν καὶ τῶν ἄλλων ζῴων μετέχει πολλά, τοῦ δ' ἀναμιμνήσκεσθαι οὐδέν, ὡς εἰπεῖν, τῶν γνωριζομένων ζῴων πλὴν ἄνθρωπος. Αἴτιον δ' ὅτι τὸ ἀναμιμνήσκεσθαί ἐστιν οἷον συλλογισμός τις.

concept or general notion, so as to depict them (which in their general form is impossible) to the intuitive consciousness. This kind of imagination may be simpler or more complex, according as the image is constructed immediately, from the data furnished by the given notion, or mediately, from a train of associations which that notion suggests. It includes under it as a species the *deliberative imagination* of Aristotle ; and, when coupled with the conscious effort to recall a past impression, corresponds in some degree to the *reminiscence* of the same philosopher.*

Imagination, Memory, and Hope are psychologically one and the same faculty.† In Imagination, the presence of the image is necessarily accompanied by a conviction of the *possible* existence of the corresponding object in an intuition. Memory is the presence of the same image, accompanied by a conviction of the fact, that the object represented has actually existed in

* By reminiscence, Aristotle means the process of endeavouring to reproduce something formerly on the memory, indirectly, by means of associated ideas. Memory proper comes in at the conclusion of the process, though it may also exist without it. (See *De Memoria*, ii. 4.) In this point of view, it is obvious that memory is the result of a process of thought, and therefore should not have been identified with that retention or remembrance which in the same chapter is described as common to men and brutes. It would be more accurate to distinguish between *intuitive* and *reflective* remembrance, according as it is performed without or with the intervention of a concept ; and of the latter the Aristotelian ἀνάμνησις is a special form.

† See Sir W. Hamilton, *Discussions*, p. 52.

a *past* intuition. Hope, in like manner, is the presence of the same image, together with an anticipation, more or less vivid, of the actual existence of the object in a *future* intuition. Imagination, memory, and hope are thus (whether formed by a reflective process or not) in their actual results partly *presentative*, partly *representative*. They are presentative of the image, which has its own distinct existence in consciousness, irrespectively of its relation to the object which it is supposed to represent. They are representative of the object, which that image resembles, and which, either in its present form or in its several elements, must have been presented in a past act of intuition. Thus there is combined an immediate consciousness of the present with a mediate consciousness of the past. An immediate or presentative consciousness of the past or the future, as such, is impossible.

Imagination, being representative of an intuition, is, like intuition, only possible on the condition that its immediate object should be an *individual*. If we try to form in our minds the image of a triangle, it must be of some individual figure,—equilateral, isosceles, or scalene. It is impossible that it should, at the same time, be all of these, or none. It may bear more or less resemblance to the object which it represents; but it can attain to resemblance at all only by being, like the object itself, individual. I may recall to mind, with more or less vividness, the features of an absent friend, as I may paint his portrait with more or less accuracy ; but the likeness in neither case ceases to be the individual representation of an indivdiual man. On the other hand, my *notion of a man in general* can attain to universality only by surrendering resemblance ; it becomes the indifferent representative of all mankind, only because it has no special likeness to any one in particular. This distinction must be carefully borne in mind in comparing imagination with the cognate process of conception.

OF INTERNAL INTUITION IN GENERAL.

Locke, as is well known, referred the origin of our ideas to two sources—*sensation,* by which we acquire our knowledge of external objects ; and *reflection,* by which we become acquainted with the internal operations of our own minds. The latter term is unfortunately chosen, as it naturally suggests the notion of a *turning back* of the mind upon an object previously existing ; and thus represents the phenomena of consciousness as distinct from the act of reflecting upon them. Understood in this sense, reflection can have no other objects than the phenomena of sensation in some one of its modes ; for sensation and reflection are the only recognised sources of knowledge ; and if reflection implies a previously existing operation of mind, that operation can be none other than sensation. Interpreting Locke in this sense, Condillac and his followers were only carrying out the doctrine to its legitimate consequences when they maintained that sensation was the only original source of ideas, and furnished the whole material of our knowledge. But though the language of Locke is both unfortunate in its choice of terms and vacillating in the use of them, the general tenor of his philosophy demands a different interpretation of the term *reflection*, as synonymous with *internal consciousness*; that is to say, as a knowledge of the presence of certain inward phenomena of mind, which exist only as they are known, and are known only as they exist. Reflection is thus an original and independent source of ideas not distinct from, but identical with, the acts that are its objects. It is, in fact, the consciousness of those states of the mind by which it is placed in relation to itself, as Sensation is the consciousness of those states of the mind by which it is placed in relation to the material world. Both sensation and reflection thus denote original states of consciousness, which exist only in so far as we are conscious of them. For example, *I see, and I am conscious that I see.* These two assertions, logically distinct, are really one and inseparable. Sight is a state of consciousness; and I see only in so far as I am conscious of seeing. Here, then, is one source of ideas,—the consciousness of certain affections of our bodily senses in relation to external objects. Whatever comes from this source is classed by Locke under the general head of *ideas of sensation*. But again ; I am angry, and I am conscious that I am angry ; I fear, and I am conscious that I fear ; I will, and I am conscious that I will. Here, too, are acts which exist only in so far as we are conscious of them, and which point to another and a distinct source of ideas,—the consciousness, that is to say, of internal phenomena taking place in the mind itself. Whatever comes from this source is classed by Locke under the general head of *ideas of reflection*. It is in this sense that he describes reflection as a source of ideas which every man has wholly in himself, and which, "though it be not sense, as having nothing to do with external objects, yet it is very like it, and might properly enough be called *internal sense*."* And thus, also, in another passage, he says, "I cannot but confess that *external and internal sensation* are the only passages that I can find of knowledge to the understanding."† We may thus, retaining the substance of Locke's teaching, though slightly altering his language, divide the presentative consciousness into two kinds :—1. External Intuition, which embraces the various phenomena of sensation and perception, together with that knowledge of the

* *Essay*, b. ii. chap. i. sec. 4.   † *Essay*, b. ii. chap. xi. sec. 17.

L

attributes of matter which is obtained through the locomotive faculty; and 2. Internal Intuition, which
includes all those modes of consciousness in which we
become immediately cognisant of the various states of
our own mind, as well as the concomitant consciousness
of our own personality as the one permanent subject of
these successive states. The phenomena of external
intuition have been described in the preceding pages.
We have next to consider those of internal intuition;
and here it will be most convenient to begin with the
variable element, as exhibited in the several mental
states of which we are successively conscious. The
Form of this consciousness, as has been already observed,
is *time*. The phenomena which we are about to describe
constitute the Matter.

OF THE CLASSIFICATION OF INTERNAL INTUITIONS.

Internal Intuition, in the widest sense of the term,
includes among its modes the whole of the phenomena
of consciousness; for consciousness in general denotes
a state of the mind; and all states of the mind are
objects of internal intuition. In this extended signification, the phenomena of sensation and those of thought
are both included under this head; for sensation,
though in respect of its object it is external to the
conscious mind, is in itself an affection of which that
mind is intuitively conscious; and thought, in like

manner, though in respect of its object it is mediate and representative, is in itself an individual act of which we are immediately and presentatively conscious. Thus, for example, *colour*, the object of sight, is an affection of the nervous organism, and therefore external to the immaterial self, the subject of consciousness; but *sight*, as a species of sensation, is a state of the personal consciousness, and, as such, internal. So, again, when I think of any material object, such as a tree or a stone, the object of which I think is external to the mind, and represented by the notion which I form of it; but the act of thinking about it is an individual affection of the conscious self, having its own definite position in time, and thereby numerically distinguished from every other affection, however similar. I may think of the same tree on twenty successive occasions; but my several thoughts, however identical in their objects, are nevertheless twenty successive, distinct, and individual states of my own mind, and, as such, belong to the class of internal intuitions. But in the practical treatment of the subject it is not necessary to take into consideration either of the above classes of mental phenomena; for the distinction between an act of consciousness and its object, though logically valid, has psychologically no existence. In no actual operation of consciousness can the act be separated from the object, or the object from the act. By no mental abstraction can either of these correlatives be conceived apart from the other,—though they are conceived together, not as identical, but as related and logically distinguishable. A perception cannot be conceived except as the perception of some object; an object of perception cannot be conceived except as in relation to a perceiving mind. In treating, therefore, of the phenomena of sensitive perception in relation to their external objects, we have at the same time sufficiently exhibited their internal character as acts of mind. A similar remark may be made with respect to the operations of thought. These will be examined hereafter in relation to the objects which they represent, and to their manner of representing them; and this examination will, at the same time, necessarily include their presentative aspect as individual phenomena of consciousness. The perceptive and discursive faculties, which are thus excluded from our present consideration, embrace all those operations of consciousness which are usually referred to the head of *cognitive* or *intellectual powers.* There will still remain for consideration the various phenomena which in the same division are classified, not very accurately, as belonging to the *appetitive* or *active powers;* * and which may, perhaps, be more

Of this classification Sir W. Hamilton observes :—" The division of the powers into those of the *understanding* and those of the *will* is very objectionable. It is taken from the peripatetic distinction of these into *gnostic* or *cognitive,* and *orectic* or *appetent;* but the original

exactly comprised under the three appellations of—1. *Emotions or Passions; 2. Moral Judgments; 3. Volitions.* *

division is far preferable to the borrowed ; for, in the first place, the term *understanding* usually and properly denotes only a part—the higher part—of the cognitive faculties, and is thus exclusive of sense, imagination, memory, etc., which it is now intended to include. In the second place, the term *will* is also usually and properly limited to our higher appetencies, or rational determinations, as opposed to our lower appetencies, or irrational desires, which last, however, it is here employed to comprehend. In the third place, both the original and borrowed divisions are improper, inasmuch as they either exclude or improperly include a third great class of mental phenomena—the phenomena of *feeling.*" The distribution of our powers into *speculative* and *active* is also very objectionable. Independently of the objection common to it with that into the powers of the understanding and the powers of the will—that the feelings are excluded or improperly included —it is liable to objections peculiar to itself. In the first place, *speculation* or theory is a certain kind or certain application of knowledge ; therefore *speculation* is not a proper term by which to denote the cognitive operations in general. In the second place, *speculation* and *knowledge* are not opposed to *action*, but to *practice* or *doing*, or, as it is best expressed in German, *das Handeln. Speculative* powers ought not, therefore, to have been opposed to *active*. In the third place, the distinction of *active* powers is in itself vicious, because it does not distinguish or distinguishes wrongly. *Active* is opposed to *inactive ;* but it is not here intended to be said that the cognitive powers are inactive, but merely that the action of the powers of appetency is different in kind from the action of the powers of knowledge. The term *active* does not, therefore, express what was meant, or rather does express what was not meant. It is to be observed, however, that the English language is very deficient in terms requisite to denote the distinction in question " (Reid's *Works*, p. 511). A somewhat similar criticism has been made by Brown, Lecture xvi., who uses the term *emotions* to denote the internal intuitions in general. For the classification approved by Sir W. Hamilton himself, see the next note.

* Sir W. Hamilton, in the advertisement to the second volume of

It is difficult to fix upon any positive mark which shall express the distinctive characteristic of this group of mental phenomena, viewed as constituting a single class; though they may, perhaps, be sufficiently distinguished from other states of mind by the negative criterion of attributes which they do not possess. The internal intuitions, as a class, may, in this way, be described as comprehending all those affections of mind which are neither directly caused by conditions of the nervous organism, nor representative of an object distinct from themselves. The first criterion will distinguish them from the sensitive affections; the second, from the intellectual powers properly so called. An instance will perhaps explain the distinction more clearly than a definition. A man may be affected with fear at the sight of a lion. The emotion of fear may in

Stewart's *Works*, observes that, "if we take the mental to the exclusion of material phenomena, that is, the phenomena manifested through the medium of self-consciousness or reflection, they naturally divide themselves into three categories or primary genera :—the phenomena of knowledge or cognition,—the phenomena of feeling, or of pleasure and pain,—and the phenomena of conation, or of will and desire." This division, which had previously been given by Kant in his *Kritik der Urtheilskraft*, though made on a somewhat different principle, coincides to a great extent with that given in the text. The phenomena of knowledge will include the external intuitions already treated of, together with the moral judgments and the operations of thought proper. The phenomena of feeling answer to the class of emotions, and those of conation in some degree to that of volitions. But in the present treatise the desires are classed with the feelings, and not, as in the above-mentioned arrangement, with the will.

one sense be said to be caused by an affection of the optic nerve—the sight, and to have an object distinct from itself—the lion ; but it is neither the immediate and necessary consequence of the one, nor is it representative of the other. It is quite possible for the man to see the lion without fearing him ; and it is quite possible that he should fear him if he suspected that he was concealed near him, without any sensible intimation of his presence. And though the lion is the ultimate object of the mental affection, both when we think of him and when we are afraid of him, yet he is not represented in the mind by our fear as he is by our thought. An emotion, or other internal intuition, may accompany an act either of perception or of thought, though it is perfectly distinguishable from the one and the other. The pleasure which we experience at the sight of a beautiful prospect, and the desire which we have to see it, are both distinct from the sight itself,— just as the liking for mathematical studies, and the gratification arising from the solution of a problem, are distinct from the demonstrative process itself.

OF THE PASSIONS OR EMOTIONS.

Perhaps the nearest approach to a positive definition of the Passions or Emotions may be found in the language of Aristotle, who describes them as *those states of*

mind which are accompanied by pleasure or pain; *
but the definition requires some explanation before it
can be accepted as satisfactory. A toothache is accompanied by pain ; but a toothache is not an emotion.
The pursuit and acquisition of knowledge is a source
of pleasure ; but neither the pursuit nor the acquisition
can be classed among the emotions. But it is necessary to distinguish between the bodily sensation or the
mental energy, considered in itself, and the feeling of
liking or disliking by which it is accompanied. The
bodily sensation is not pleasant or painful *per se,* but
may be the one or the other, according to the degree
in which it exists. The sensation of heat, for example,
up to a certain point, is the pleasant feeling of warmth ;
beyond that point it is the painful feeling of burning.
The sensation of touch may be pleasant or painful or
indifferent, according to the nature of the body with
which we are in contact, or the degree of resistance
which it offers. Light, within certain limits, is pleasant to the eye ; increased beyond those limits, it is
dazzling and painful. The sensation itself is in no case
an emotion : the feeling of liking or disliking, which
accompanies it is so. The essence of the bodily sensation consists in its being a nervous affection of a
particular kind. The accident, or emotion, which in

* *Eth. Nic.* ii. 5. Λέγω δὲ πάθη μὲν ἐπιθυμίαν, ὀργήν, φόβον, θράσος,
φθόνον, χαράν, φιλίαν, μῖσος, πόθον, ζῆλον, ἔλεον, ὅλως οἷς ἕπεται ἡδονὴ ἢ
λύπη.

certain cases accompanies it, is, that that particular affection is agreeable or disagreeable. The same may be said of the mental energies likewise. The *desire* of knowledge, and the *pleasure* which it imparts, are emotions: the act of pursuit and the state of possession are not so. It is perfectly conceivable that men might be so constituted as to seek after knowledge, from a rational conviction that it is their duty to do so, without deriving the slightest gratification from the pursuit or the acquisition; just as they might take food, from a conviction of the duty of preserving life, without being actuated either directly by the appetite of hunger, or indirectly by the love of life. Under this explanation, we may, with tolerable accuracy, define the emotions or passions as *those states of mind which consist in the consciousness of being affected agreeably or disagreeably;* and consistently with this point of view, an eminent modern philosopher has observed that there are, strictly speaking, but two passions,—the one arising from the consciousness of pleasure, manifesting itself in the successive stages of *joy, love,* and *desire,* the other arising from the consciousness of pain, and exhibiting the successive forms of *grief, hate,* and *aversion.** The various subdivisions of these two classes are, properly, not so much distinctions in the nature of

* Jouffroy, *Mélanges Philosophiques,* p. 269. Cf. Damiron, *Psychologie,* vol. i. p. 247.

the emotion itself, as in that of the objects upon which it is exercised.

Hitherto we have used the words *passion* and *emotion* as synonymous. The above remarks will suggest, in stricter language, a distinction between them, which, though by no means accurately observed either in philosophical writings or in popular use, is yet in many cases perfectly intimated by both. To distinguish, indeed, between these terms, in strict accordance either with philosophical or general usage, is out of the question ; for scarcely any two writers or speakers are in all respects consistent with each other. Sometimes emotion is a species of passion ; sometimes passion is a species of emotion ; sometimes the two terms are used as exactly synonymous ; and at others the word *passion* is used to designate a violent degree of emotion. A more serviceable, and therefore a better, distinction than any of these may, we think, be furnished by the characteristics of the phenomena themselves,—a distinction which, though not warranted by the etymology of the two words, yet appears to express with tolerable accuracy the difference imperfectly intimated in their popular use. Our internal as well as our external intuitions have both a subjective and an objective phase, inseparable from each other, but logically distinguishable. This distinction, which in the case of our external intuitions is expressed by the terms *sensa-*

tion and *perception,* may be marked in its internal aspect by the corresponding usage of *emotion* and *passion.* The mental phenomena of this class are composed of two principal ingredients,—a consciousness of being affected agreeably or disagreeably by a certain object, and a desire to obtain or avoid, to advance or impede, the object thus affecting us. This is equally the case, whether the object affecting us be a physical good, as in the feeling of hunger ; a mental enjoyment, as in the desire of honour or knowledge ; or the welfare of another, as in the benevolent affections. In all alike we may trace the fundamental distinction of consciousness, the distinction between myself affected and the object affecting me, whether that object be regarded as a reality separate from myself or not. The subjective feeling of pleasure or pain may, we think, be appropriately expressed by the term *emotion ;* while the objective tendency to the thing by which that emotion is caused may be indicated, not improperly, by the term *passion,* which, in its ordinary signification, appears to denote those particular propensities of our nature which, in the language of Bishop Butler, have for their objects "external things themselves, distinct from the pleasure arising from them."* The passions, as thus described, may be excited by an object either perceived as present, or imagined as absent ; the object being in

* Sermon xi.—"On the love of our neighbour."

the one case presented, in the other represented. When this representation is accompanied by a conviction of the possibility or impossibility of obtaining the object, the passion assumes the form of *hope* or *despair*—terms which, in their widest sense, do not denote special passions, but general relations in which any particular passion may stand towards its own object. But the passion, as actually existing, whether directed towards a present or an absent object, is in every case an individual state of mind, intuitively discerned as now present in consciousness.*

The further subdivisions of the passions may be made on various principles, and from various points of view. The general features which have been above described as characteristic of this class of mental phenomena will, in their special manifestations, be subject to various modifications, according to the nature of the object upon which they are exercised, or the constitution and training of the subject in whom they exist. To attempt a complete enumeration of the complex modes of consciousness thus arising would be impossible : we must content ourselves with selecting some one principle of division, and pointing out a few of the

---

* Aristotle, *Rhet.* i. 11. Ἀνάγκη πάντα τὰ ἡδέα ἢ ἐν τῷ αἰσθάνεσθαι εἶναι παρόντα, ἢ ἐν τῷ μεμνῆσθαι γεγενημένα, ἢ ἐν τῷ ἐλπίζειν μέλλοντα· αἰσθάνονται γὰρ τὰ παρόντα, μέμνηνται δὲ τὰ γεγενημένα, ἐλπίζουσι δὲ τὰ μέλλοντα.

most important and universal of the feelings comprehended under it. Perhaps, on the whole, the least
objectionable principle of classification is that derived
from the various classes of objects in relation to which
the emotions of pleasure and pain, and the corresponding feelings of attraction or repulsion which constitute
passion, may take place. In this point of view the
passions may be divided, generally, into the two classes
of *desires* and *affections,* according as the object to which
they are related is a *thing* or a *person,*—regarded as a
possession to be sought for or avoided, or as a moral
agent, capable of mutual relations of sympathy or
antipathy. Under the general head of Desires may be
specified the *appetites,* which take their rise from bodily
conditions, and are common to men and brutes,—com-
prising the feelings of hunger, thirst, and sexual instinct ;
and the *desires,* as they are sometimes called in a special
sense, such as the desire of knowledge, of society, of
esteem, of power, and of superiority, together with the
counter-feelings of repugnance to the opposite class of
objects.* The Affections embrace our social, domestic,
and religious feelings in general ; the love of friends, of
kindred, of God ; and the special modifications of feeling
arising from our particular relations with individuals
among our fellow-men ; such as respect, gratitude, com-

* For the details of this classification, see Stewart's *Philosophy of
the Active and Moral Powers.*

passion, anger, contempt, and so forth. The principles of Self-love and Benevolence, which are sometimes included in this enumeration, should be considered, not as original intuitions, but rather as derived conceptions, in which the several personal or social passions and their respective objects, together with their moral relations and observed consequences, are generalised into the comprehensive notions of a *regard for the welfare* of ourselves or of others.

The complete treatment of the emotions and passions belongs to the province of moral philosophy. To the metaphysician they are important, chiefly in two points of view, *psychologically*, as individual phenomena of consciousness, perceived intuitively, and therefore capable of being conceived reflectively; and *ontologically*, as regards the light which they may be able to throw on the problem of the real existence of the subject or object to which they are related. In this latter point of view they will come again under our notice hereafter.

OF THE MORAL FACULTY.

Every passion, as we have seen, is ultimately related to an object regarded as the cause of agreeable or disagreeable emotions. But between the passion and its object there is always an intervening medium of communication,—the *action* by which the object is to be obtained or avoided. Pleasure and pain, so far as they are the objects of desire and aversion, do not properly lie in the things by which they are caused, but in the actions by which those things are brought into contact with the person affected. But the actions, and in some degree also the feelings which prompt them, may be exhibited in another point of view, not merely as pleasant or painful, but as *right* or *wrong*. The existence of these terms, or their equivalents, in every language, indicates a corresponding phenomenon in the universal consciousness of mankind, which no effort of ingenuity can explain away. Indeed, the very ingenuity of the various attempts that have been made to identify the conception of *right* with that of *expedient*, or *agreeable*, or any other quality, is itself a witness against them; for no such elaborate reasoning would be required, were it not necessary to silence or pervert the instinctive testimony of a too stubborn consciousness.* That the terms *right* and *wrong* indicate a special class of mental phenomena, discernible in the contemplation of actions in themselves, and not merely inferred from observation of their consequences, is a truth guaranteed by the universal language of mankind, by the testimony of every man's own consciousness, and by the inconsistencies and

* For some valuable remarks on the moral faculty as an original intuitive principle, See M'Cosh, *Method of the Divine Government*, pp. 294, 301.

mutual contradictions of its several antagonists. But what are these phenomena, and by what means are they discerned? Are they qualities of actions in themselves, or states of the mind which contemplates actions? Are they simple qualities, or complex; perceived intuitively, or conceived reflectively? Are they the objects of a special mental faculty, or are they discerned by the same faculty which perceives truth and falsehood in other cases? These doubts may be summed up, in the language of Stewart, in the two following questions, which, as he says, seem to exhaust the whole theory of morals:—"First, by what principle of our constitution are we led to form the notion of moral distinctions,— whether by that faculty which perceives the distinction between truth and falsehood in the other branches of human knowledge, or by a peculiar power of perception (called by some the moral sense) which is *pleased* with one set of qualities and *displeased* with another? Secondly, what is the proper object of moral approbation; or, in other words, what is the common quality or qualities belonging to all the different modes of virtue? Is it benevolence, or a rational self-love, or a disposition (resulting from the ascendant of reason over passion) to act suitably to the different relations in which we are placed?"*

The two alternatives proposed in the first of the

* *Philosophy of the Active and Moral Powers*, b. ii. chap. 5.

above questions represent the antagonist views of the two schools of philosophy which made common cause with each other in protesting against the denial of all natural right and wrong, which characterised the philosophy of Hobbes. The first represents the opinion of Cudworth and his followers, who refer our knowledge of right and wrong to a decision of the *reason or understanding*. The second is the opinion of Hutcheson and those who with him maintain the existence of a faculty of *moral perception* or *sense*. The language in which the two theories are worded, though historically accurate, as representing the views of their respective authors, is in some degree defective in philosophical precision. On the one hand, there is no single faculty of mind which distinguishes between truth and falsehood in the various branches of knowledge. The understanding or reason, taken in its widest sense to denote the reflective faculty in general, contributes only one element to the decision. Truth and falsehood depend upon the agreement or disagreement between the representations which we make of an object in thought, and the qualities presented by that object in intuition; and this agreement or disagreement can only be ascertained by the co-operation of the two faculties. How, for instance, do we know that it is true to conceive snow as white, and false to conceive it as black? The understanding furnishes the conception; but has the

M

sight, therefore, nothing to do with the decision? Could we answer the question by the mere act of thought, without reference to the perception of a present, or the recollection of a past fact of intuition? If there were no moral intuition, truth and falsehood could have no place in moral thought; for the conception of right or wrong, even supposing that it could exist, would be related to no facts with which it could agree or disagree. Moral truth and falsehood, like all other truth and falsehood, must consist in the agreement or disagreement of thoughts with facts; and this may take place in two different ways, as regards the mental phenomenon or the extra-mental reality. For example : I may, owing to an inaptitude for mental analysis, have an inaccurate conception of the characteristics of a moral judgment which I have myself exercised. Hence will result a false representation of the phenomenon of moral approbation. Or I may have conceptions of right and wrong, perfectly in accordance with the facts of my own consciousness, but at variance with some higher standard of right and wrong *per se.* The latter is an ontological falsehood, the criterion of which we are not yet in a position to determine. The former is a psychological falsehood, which can only be corrected by comparing the thought with the intuition to which it is related. But in neither case can the act of thought guarantee its own accuracy; else would every conception be equally true, for the sole reason that it is conceived. On the other hand, Hutcheson and his followers, as Stewart has observed, while rightly admitting the existence of a moral intuitive faculty (whether it be called *sense* or not is unimportant), unfortunately, in their description of its operation, were too much misled by a false analogy derived from the perception by the bodily senses of the secondary qualities of matter. It is no necessary part of the theory of a moral sense that it should be represented as perceiving qualities only in so far as they are *pleasing* or *displeasing*. It is true that the exercise of our bodily senses produces pleasure as well as information ; but the perception of a fact is logically distinguishable from the sensation of an affection ; and, however much in practice they may be united, either may be conceived to exist independently of the other. If, in like manner, we distinguish between the *moral perception* of an act as right or wrong, and the accompanying *moral sensation* of the pleasing or displeasing manner in which we are affected by those qualities, the hypothesis of a moral sense may be freed from most of the excrescences which have hitherto disfigured it in the systems of its advocates, and have afforded the chief handle to the criticisms of its antagonists.

An illustrious critic of this hypothesis* has remarked

* M. Cousin. See his review of Hutcheson's system. *Cours de* 1819, Leçon 14.

with truth, that in our perception of the moral character of an act, whether done by ourselves or by others, we may trace the united action of a *moral judgment* and a *moral sentiment*. Our *feeling of indignation* at an act of treachery may be more or less vivid, according to our proximity to the time and place at which the act was committed, or to our relation to the doer or the sufferer. Our *condemnatory judgment* is independent of the accidents of time, place, or circumstance ; we pronounce the action to be evil with the same assurance, whether it was done yesterday, or ten years, or a thousand years ago; whether the victim was our dearest friend or a complete stranger. Of these two elements of moral consciousness, the judgment is the superior, the permanent, the essential factor ; the sentiment is the inferior, the fluctuating, the accidental one. The sentiment, he adds, may be due to a moral sense; but the judgment, which is derived from the universal and necessary ideas of good and evil, can belong to no other faculty than the reason.

The above analysis, though true so far as it goes, is, like that which it criticises, incomplete. The moral judgment itself may be further divided into two constituent parts ; the one, an individual fact, present now and here ; the other, a general law, valid always and everywhere. That this particular act of my own, at the moment of being committed, is wrong, is a fact presented immediately by the judgment of conscience. That all acts of the same kind, whensoever or by whomsoever committed, are necessarily wrong, is a judgment formed by the reason through the medium of the general notions of acts of a certain class, and of right and wrong. The latter, as an universal and necessary truth, may be referred to the same faculty, and formed under the same conditions, as other truths of the same kind. The former, as the *presentative condition of moral thought*, must be allowed to possess that chronological priority which in other cases is admitted to exist in individual facts, as compared with universal notions.

A more accurate theory of the nature and origin of moral judgment than is contained either in the moral reason of Cudworth, or in the moral sense of Hutcheson, or even in M. Cousin's union of the two, may, we think, be proposed in accordance with what has been said in the preceding pages of the complex nature of consciousness in general. It has been before observed, that every mode of consciousness, to be known as such, must possess a certain degree of clearness and distinctness, and that this is the product of the combined action of the presentative and representative faculties. The distinctions of language are doing their work ; the task of education is going on ; the phenomena of consciousness are assuming shape and consistency, before we are capable of discerning the various transitory conditions of our minds, or of distinguishing them one from another. A conscious act of pure moral sense, like a conscious act of pure physical sense, if it ever takes place at all, takes place at a period of which we have no remembrance, and of which we can give no account. To have a clear notion of moral obligation as such, we must have reflected upon it ; and to reflect upon it, we must have obscurely experienced various acts in unison with it, and others distinct from it. At what time the notions of *good*, *bad*, and *indifferent*, first clearly presented themselves to the mind, it is as impossible to say, as it is to determine when we first distinctly recognised as such, and severed from each other, the visible phenomena of *white, black*, and *grey*. All that we can hope to do is, by subsequent analysis of the compound phenomenon, to detect in its composition an intuitive and a reflective element, growing side by side from the first dawn of intelligence, and contributing their respective shares to the gradual development of their mutual product. Our mental, no less than our bodily constitution, testifies that we are the work of One whose judgments are unsearchable and his ways past finding out. The results alone we know ; the creative process we can but darkly conjecture. "As thou knowest not what is the way of the spirit, nor how the bones do grow in the womb of her that is with child ; even so, thou knowest not the works of God who maketh all."

The preceding remarks have in some degree furnished by anticipation the answer to an objection which a distinguished author has recently urged against the theory of a moral sense as usually understood. " The judgment of man," it has been said, " concerning actions as good or bad, cannot be expressed or formed without reference to language, to social relations, to acknowledged rights ; and the apprehension of these implies the agency of the understanding in a manner quite different from the perceptions of the bodily senses."* If there is any truth in the view which has been taken in the preceding pages of the operations of the bodily senses, it appears that the perceptions of these also are not so independent of the agency of the understanding as is usually supposed ; and that there is at least sufficient analogy between our physical and moral intuitions to justify the metaphorical use of the term *sense*, to denote the mode of action of the latter. But there still remains a point in which the ordinary theory needs correction. It is commonly said, that by the operation of the moral sense we perceive immediately the character of acts, whether done by ourselves or by others. The assertion, that we are immediately conscious of the morality of another person's actions, appears to be an error of the same kind in relation to our moral perceptions, as the assertion that we are immediately conscious

* Whewell, Preface to Butler's Three Sermons.

of the past in memory is in relation to our bodily senses. To be directly conscious that this act, now being committed, or about to be committed, is right or wrong, I must be directly conscious of two things : of a law of obligation, commanding a certain person to act in a certain way, and of the course now before that person, as agreeing or disagreeing with such law. But I cannot be directly conscious of a law of obligation as it exists in another person's mind : I can only infer its existence by *representing* his mind as similarly constituted to my own. If man were not a free agent, his acts, whether beneficial or hurtful in their physical results, could have no moral character as right or wrong. But I cannot be immediately conscious of the free agency of any other person than myself; and, were it not for the direct testimony of my own consciousness to my own freedom, I could regard human actions only as necessary links in the endless chain of phenomenal cause and effect. It is obvious, therefore, that the intuitive perception of moral qualities cannot extend beyond our own actions, in which alone we are directly conscious of a law of obligation and of a voluntary obedience or disobedience to it. The actions of other men may be known presentatively in their material aspect as beneficial or hurtful; for this is a relation external to the mind of the agent. They cannot be presentatively known in their moral aspect as good or evil; for this is an internal relation, existing in the hidden depths of another's consciousness.

The substance of the above remarks may be briefly summed up as follows :—Moral consciousness, in the only form in which it can be distinctly recognised in the mind, consists, like all other consciousness, of a presentative and a representative element ; the one being necessary to its first formation, the other to its completeness and recognition as what it is. Neither reason alone nor sense alone can account for the existence of the moral judgment as a fact of consciousness, whether we regard it in its subjective aspect, as an emotion, pleasant or painful, analogous to sensation proper, or in its objective aspect, analogous to perception proper, as exhibiting a voluntary act in relation to a law. The presentative element must be referred to a special faculty of moral intuition or sense,—in one word, to avoid more objectionable phrases, to *conscience,* —whose object, like that of all intuitions, is an individual phenomenon now present :—a special faculty, we say, in the only point of view in which the mind can be said to have distinct faculties at all, namely, on the ground of a difference of which we are conscious in the corresponding objects. The representative element, on the other hand, in common with all other general notions, may be referred to the single faculty of the *understandin .*

Up to this point, the moral problem is properly psychological; its purpose being only to determine what are the characteristic features and origin of the moral judgment, regarded as a fact of consciousness. The second question which Stewart proposes as completing the theory of morals,—" What is the proper object of moral approbation? or what is the common quality or qualities belonging to the different modes of virtue?"—is one which belongs not to Psychology, but to Moral Philosophy, which, in this point of view, may be considered as a branch of. Ontology; its office being to inquire into the nature of virtue, regarded, not as a mental perception, but an extra-mental reality. The moral decisions of conscience cannot by themselves be the ultimate criterion of right and wrong; for if so, whose conscience is to be taken as the standard? If the individual conscience is ever mistaken in its judgments; if crimes can ever be committed which seem no crimes to the perpetrator; there must be a standard of right and wrong *per se*, by which our moral intuitions and our moral conceptions must both, in ultimate appeal, be tested. To ask what this standard is, though the most important of all questions in speculative morals, would be out of place here; the only legitimate office of the psychological inquirer being to analyse and exhibit the characteristic features of the mental phenomenon of moral approbation.

The correlative terms, *will* and *volition*, are usually distinguished, in the language of philosophy, as applying, the one to the general faculty, the other to the special acts in which it manifests itself. A volition is an act of the will; and our several volitions are classified as proceeding from one and the same faculty. *Will*, then, like *sense* and *reason*, does not indicate a special phenomenon of consciousness, but is a general name for the power from which special phenomena prooecd, and which itself exists in consciousness only as it is manifested in operation. The examination, therefore, of this portion of our consciousness must be attempted in relation to the internal acts, which, in the usual language of philosophy, are denominated *volitions*.

That Volition is not identical with Desire, and cannot properly be classed with the phenomena of emotion, was one of the earliest results of psychological analysis, and is, indeed, obvious to the consciousness of every man who has experienced the two, however much they may have been confounded together by the perversity of a few unscrupulous system-makers. A man may be thirsty, and yet refuse to drink; his desire drawing him one way, and his will determining him in the

other.* Desires are not under our own control; they
arise naturally and necessarily on the occasion of the
presence of objects which affect us agreeably or disagreeably. We cannot help being so constituted as to
derive pleasure from certain objects; we cannot help
feeling attracted to pleasant objects; for the pleasure
constitutes the attraction. But we can help yielding to
the attraction of desire when felt; and we can help
putting ourselves in the way of feeling it. Desire may
be vicious as well as action; but only in so far as
either is combined with volition. I may place myself
in the way of desirable objects, and, in so doing, my
act is voluntary. I may give my attention to thoughts
calculated to excite desire, and the attention is a voluntary act; but in the mere fact that an object, when
present, no matter how its presence is procured, raises a
corresponding emotion in the mind, there is no volition,
and consequently no moral character. Hence it has
long been established as a canon in morals by the
soundest writers on the question, that virtue and vice
depend, not on the existence of desires, but on their
relation to the will.†

---

* Plato, *Republic*, b. iv. p. 439. Cf. Aristotle, *Eth. Nic.* B. iii.
c. 2. Προαιρέσει μὲν ἐπιθυμία ἐναντιοῦται, ἐπιθυμίᾳ δ' ἐπιθυμία οὔ. The
distinction between will and appetite or desire is well stated by Hooker,
E. P. B. 1, ch. vii. sec. 3.

† See especially Bishop Butler, *Sermons* i. ii. v. xi.; *Analogy*,
chaps. iv. v.

But volition must be further distinguished, both from the judgment which precedes, and from the external act which follows it.* For example, a man determines to take a walk for the benefit of his health. The feeling that health is desirable is not voluntary; the conviction that walking is beneficial to health is not voluntary. The one is an emotion, which by his constitution he cannot help having: the other is a relation between natural cause and effect, which he cannot make other than it is, and cannot judge to be other than he knows it to be. But, while conscious that health is desirable, and while conscious that walking promotes health, he is also (and this forms a distinct phenomenon) conscious that it is in his own power to take or not to take the means necessary to the end. We cannot at present inquire how far this consciousness of power answers to any corresponding reality in the nature of things. We are not yet in a condition to examine the paradox maintained by some philosophers, that consciousness deludes us with a fallacious appearance of liberty. We are concerned only with the mental phenomenon that a man does, in certain states of consciousness, feel possessed of a power of choosing between two alternatives, which in certain other states he does not feel. But again : Suppose that the man determines

* Cousin, *Cours de* 1819, Leçon xxiii. *Cours de* 1829, Leçon xxv.

to walk, but finds himself, by a sudden stroke of paralysis, deprived of the use of his limbs; here again we
must distinguish between the fact of determination,
which is always in our own power, and the fact of
bodily motion, which may or may not be in our own
power, according to circumstances. The power of locomotion (I do not now speak of that of muscular effort)
is not, properly speaking, a fact of consciousness at all ;
that is to say, it is not a fact whose existence is identical with our knowledge of its existence. We may
suppose the case of a man whose limbs have become
paralysed without his being aware of it. The conscious
portion of the effort to move is the same as before, but
the physical sequence is interrupted. Or we may suppose the act of motion to take place as a consequence
of volition, without the person being conscious of the
relation between the volition and the act. The latter
supposition, indeed, is actually true in all cases ; for
motion is the remote, not the immediate, consequence of
volition; and between the one and the other there is
an intervening nervous and muscular action, of which
we not only are not conscious in the act of moving,
but which we may pass a whole lifetime without dis-
covering.

Some philosophers of no small eminence, especially
in this country, have maintained that we are not directly
conscious of mind or self, but only of its several modifi-

c̄ations.* It is in relation to the phenomena of volition
that the error of this theory is most manifest. If, in the
mental state which corresponds to the ;judgment, *I will*,
there is no consciousness of *I*, but only of *will*, it is impossible to place the essential feature of volition, as has
been done above, in *the consciousness of myself having
power over my own determinations.* *Will*, and not *I*,
being the primary fact of consciousness, the causative
power of volition must be sought in the relation between
will and some subsequent phenomenon ; and so sought,
it will assuredly never be found.† It cannot be found
where Locke sought it,—in the relation between the
determination of the will and the consequent motion of
the limb ; for the determination is not the immediate
antecedent of the motion, but only of the intervening
nervous and muscular action. I cannot, therefore, be
immediately conscious of my power to move a limb,
when I am not immediately conscious of my power to
produce the antecedent phenomena. Nor yet can the
causative power be found where Maine de Biran sought
it,—in the relation of the will to the action of the nerves
and muscles ; for this relation may at any time be interrupted by purely physical causes, such as a stroke of

* Locke, *Essay*, b. ii. chap. xxii. sec. 3, 5. Hume, *Treatise of
Human Nature*, p. iv. sec. 5, 6. Reid, *Intellectual Powers*, Essay v.
chap. ii. Stewart, *Elements*, Introduction, part i. See the next section
on the "Consciousness of Personality."

† Cousin, *Fragments Philosophiques*, Preface de la première edition.

paralysis; and in that case no exertion of the will can produce the desired effect. We can escape from this difficulty—the stronghold of scepticism and necessitarianism—by one path only, and that is by a more accurate analysis of the purely mental state, which will discover an immediate consciousness of power in *myself determining my own volitions.*

The essential characteristic of Volition, as presented to the mind, consists in *the consciousness of a power of choosing between two alternative determinations.* But, by a natural association, as in the case of the acquired perceptions, we are led to connect the volition with its most striking, not with its most immediate consequence, and thus to believe that we have an immediate consciousness of our power to move the limbs of the body. The latter act is indeed voluntary, as being the foreseen, though remote, consequence of a volition; the remoteness of the consequence not affecting the moral responsibility; just as a man who shoots another is guilty of murder, though his immediate act is not to inflict the wound, but to pull the trigger. But the connection between volition and its remote consequences is not *presented* in consciousness, but *inferred.* The importance of the will as an element of consciousness, and its influence upon the other phenomena, may be in some degree estimated by comparing the characteristics of consciousness in its ordinary state with those which it presents during a *dream.* In the latter state the functions of volition, properly so called, are altogether suspended.* We may seem to ourselves to act as well as to suffer; but the action is not accompanied by a consciousness, at the moment of its performance, of a power to act otherwise. In other words, our actions during a dream are *spontaneous,* but not *voluntary,* being never presented to the consciousness in the form of a choice between two alternatives. Hence our inability during sleep to break off or change the direction of the train of ideas which is passing through the mind. Hence, too, the absence of all power of reflecting upon those ideas ; and the natural consequence, that fancies the most absurd, and events the most improbable, are never at the time discerned as being so.

---

* Stewart, in one of the most interesting chapters of his *Elements of the Philosophy of the Human Mind,* argues that the power of volition itself is not suspended during sleep, but only the influence of the will over the thoughts and actions. But he has not sufficiently distinguished between merely *spontaneous* acts and those which may properly be called *voluntary.* We are conscious in a dream of making an effort ; but we are not conscious at the moment that it is in our power not to make it. Thus, though the active function of the mind is retained, the essential feature of volition has disappeared. This remark, however, applies only to the conscious exercise of volition in determining our own mental states. It is probable that spontaneity itself, at least in rational beings, is but a lower form of volition ; and attention, in which some amount of volition is always implied, seems to be a necessary condition of all consciousness, sleeping or waking. At any rate, it is necessary to recollection ; and thus the phenomena of dreaming would, without some co-operation of the voluntary energy, either not take place at all, or be to the waking man as though they had never been.

It is impossible to compare the events of a dream with the natural course of things ; for to do so we must make a voluntary effort to recall the latter to mind ;—we must will to withdraw our attention from the phenomenon before us, and to fix it upon the remembrance of our past experience. It may be conjectured, with all the probability of which conjectures on such points are susceptible, that if man were, as so many philosophers have maintained, a necessary agent, determined even in his volitions by antecedent phenomena, his waking state would resemble that of a dream : he would be astonished at nothing.   Astonishment, as Plato and Aristotle have said, is the commencement of philosophy.* When we examine, compare, judge, and pronounce sentence upon the phenomena of our own consciousness, we assert our right to a place distinct from, and superior to, that of a mere link in the chain of phenomena ; we exercise the privilege of our conscious existence as beings above phenomena ; though the being and the phenomenon are manifested together as parts of one and the same complex act of consciousness.

We may notice, in conclusion, the light that is thrown, by the phenomena of dreaming, on some of those remarkable cases of passive subjection to another person, which, under the names of Mesmerism, Hypnotism, or

---

* *Theatetus,* p. 155.   *Metaph.* i. 2, 9.

Electro-Biology, have of late years excited so much public attention, and given rise to such strange and unfounded theories of physical or hyperphysical agency. These states exhibit, in their ordinary features, little more than the mental phenomena of sleep without the accompanying bodily conditions. The mental phenomena of sleep exhibit two principal characteristics:—1. They show the power of the mind to produce, by its internal agency, sensible phenomena, having all the vividness and apparent reality of those communicated by impressions from without. 2. They show that the mind, under certain circumstances, may be so completely under the influence of a leading idea as to follow passively the train of associations suggested, without the slightest power of judging of their truth or falsehood, probability or absurdity. The principal difference between these phenomena and those of the above-mentioned states consists in the circumstance that the leading suggestion is, in the latter case, conveyed from without, by the operator, instead of from within, by the patient's own mind. Is there any necessary law of connection between the mental state of suspended volition and the bodily state of suspended susceptibility to external impressions? If, by any artificial means, the former of these states can be produced without the latter (and this is partially the case, even without artifice, in reverie and absence of mind), we have a link to connect these psychological

marvels with the most familiar facts of our everyday
experience.*

OF THE CONSCIOUSNESS OF PERSONALITY.

The universal language of mankind has established
a distinction between the capacities of mind and matter,
which philosophy has often, but in vain, attempted to
explain away. We speak of the *properties* of material
agents, of the *faculties* of the human mind.† It is a
property of fire to burn, of metals to conduct electricity,
of a tree to bear fruit after its kind. Sensibility, memory,
reason, are *faculties* of the mind. Yet the attributes of
mind, as well as those of body, are known only by their
effects. I know that I have a power of thinking, only
because I actually think,—as I know that fire is capable of burning, only because it actually burns. What,
then, is the distinction between the nature of intelligent
and unintelligent beings, to the existence of which our
language instinctively bears witness? The foundation
of the distinction is to be found in the *consciousness of
self.* Whatever variety of phenomena may succeed one
another within the field of consciousness, in all alike I
am directly conscious of the existence of one and the

* See Sir Henry Holland's *Chapters on Mental Physiology*, chap. ii.
v. ; Carpenter's *Principles of Human Physiology*, p. 859 ; *Quarterly
Review*, No. 186.

† Jouffroy, *Mélanges Philosophiques*, p. 312.

same indivisible Self, the centre and the possessor of each and all. Let system-makers say what they will, the unsophisticated sense of mankind refuses to acknowledge that mind is but a bundle of states of consciousness, as matter is (possibly) a bundle of sensible qualities. There may be no material substratum distinct from the attributes of extension, figure, colour, hardness, etc. Matter may be merely a name for the aggregate of these, for we have no immediate consciousness of anything beyond them ; but, unless our whole consciousness is a delusion and a lie, *self* is something more than the aggregate of sensations, thoughts, volitions, etc. Our whole consciousness is manifested as a relation between a permanent and a changeable element,—a conscious self, affected in various manners. The notion of a state of consciousness, with no one to be conscious of it, is as absurd as the opposite fiction of a conscious self with nothing to be conscious of. If the latter has given rise to the extravagances of rational pyschology, the former is the basis of a not less extravagant reaction, which in its logical consequences leads to the consistent denial of personality, of freedom, of responsibility ; nay, of the very conceptions of substance and cause, the foundations of all philosophy.

Consciousness is given to us as a relation ; and no effort of analysis can separate the two correlatives ; for analysis is itself an act of consciousness, and contains the same relation. We cannot conceive either factor of consciousness apart from the other; but, on the other hand, we cannot annihilate either in conceiving their product. We cannot analyse the judgment *I will*, and set an abstract *I* on the one side, and an abstract *will* on the other; but neither can we conceive the entire judgment, save as the product of two constituent elements. Whatever may be the variety of phenomena of consciousness,—sensations, volitions, thoughts, imaginations,—of all we are immediately conscious as affections of one and the same self. It is not by any subsequent effort of reflection that I combine together sight and hearing, thought and volition, into a factitious unity or compounded whole: in each case I am immediately conscious of *myself* seeing and hearing, thinking and willing. This Personality, like all other simple and immediate presentations, is indefinable; but it is so because it is superior to definition. It can be analysed into no simpler elements; for it is itself one element of a product which defies analysis. It can be made no clearer by description or comparison; for it is revealed to us in all the clearness of an original intuition, of which description and comparison can furnish only faint and partial resemblances.

Relation is the law of consciousness, and relation is the end of philosophy: for philosophy is only the articulate expression of consciousness. *Cogito, ergo sum,* may indicate a legitimate passage from Thought to Being, from Psychology to Ontology; but the thought and the being alike are manifested only in the form of relation. Whether that dualism, which in another country has become a byword for unphilosophical thinking, may be made the basis of a sounder philosophy than the mutilated and shapeless fragment which aspires to the name of unity, is a question which is probably reserved for a future generation to answer. This much, however, appears to be proved by experience as well as testified by reason, that it is hopeless to attempt to found philosophy on the annihilation of consciousness.

We have now described the principal phenomena of the Intuitive Consciousness, in which are presented to us individual states of the mind in relation either to itself or to the material world. We have next to describe the phenomena of the Reflective Consciousness, in which the several intuitions, external or internal, are represented under general notions, and thus become objects of thought.

OF REPRESENTATIVE OR REFLECTIVE CONSCIOUSNESS.

The term *representation* has been used by philosophers in various senses. In the Leibnitzian and subsequent philosophies of Germany, this word, or its German equivalent *Vorstellung*,* is employed to denote any

* Etymologically, the term *Vorstellung* means presentation rather than representation ; but in its actual use in philosophy it is generally equivalent to the latter.

cognitive act, including even those obscure cognitions,
as they are termed by Leibnitz, which do not amount to
a conscious apprehension of an object as such. Thus
Kant includes under the common genus of *representation* the successive sub-classes of representation with
consciousness, or *perception ;* which is divided into subjective perception or *sensation,* and objective perception
or *cognition ;* the latter containing under it immediate
cognition or *intuition,* and mediate cognition or *conception.** On the other hand, Sir William Hamilton,
distinguishing between *presentative* and *representative
knowledge,* and rightly referring the perceptions of the
senses to the former class, uses the term *representation*
to denote exclusively the cognition of individual objects
by means of images resembling them.† Representation,
thus distinguished, is synonymous with imagination, and
does not include the operations of thought properly so
called, which have for their immediate object general
notions or concepts. In the present work it has been
found convenient to adopt an intermediate course.
Kant's extension of the term *representation,* to include
the intuitions of sense, involves, even on his own theory
of sensitive perception, at least an unnecessary ambiguity of language.   The intuition, on that theory, is representative of nothing that can possibly come within

* *Kritik der reinen Vernunft,* Transc. Dial. B. i. Abschn. 1.
† Reid's *Works,* pp. 805, 809. *Discussions,* p. 13.

the sphere of consciousness, but of an unknown and unknowable *thing in itself*, or absolute reality out of all
relation to human faculties. Concepts, on the contrary,
are representative of intuitions, from which they are
originally derived, and whose place they occupy in the
processes of thought. But it is obvious that, in the analysis of consciousness, the thing in itself, being *ex hypothesis* unknown and unknowable, may be dropped out of
our reckoning altogether. The intuition, or consciousness of an individual object, being the commencement
of our knowledge and the point beyond which it cannot
penetrate, may be more accurately described as a state
of *presentative consciousness*, of which thought, or *representative consciousness*, is the reflective sequel. On the
other hand, Sir W. Hamilton, by confining the term
representation to those modes of consciousness in which
there is an actual and adequate imagination of an object,
has perhaps narrowed the term too much from its original meaning, and restricted it to a sense which, however
convenient in the controversy concerning perception, is,
out of that controversy, unnecessary and likely to mislead. The general notion of *man* is representative of
many individuals in their common qualities, and of any
one individual, so far as those qualities are concerned, as
much as the image which the mind forms of James or
John is representative of the proper characteristics of
that person. The notion is generalised from the indivi-

duals, and must be ultimately verified by reference to them ; and, though not resembling the individuals, and therefore incapable by itself of being depicted in the imagination, it becomes their substitute in the act of thought, just as the written word, which likewise bears no resemblance to the sound of speech, becomes the substitute and representative of the word spoken.   In one respect, indeed, the thought proper may be called *representative* in a stricter sense than the imagination ; for the imaginative consciousness, though representative, is presentative also, and, so far, has more affinity to sense than to thought.   It is presentative of the image, which is itself an intuition, as well as representative of the object of sense.   But the concept, so far as its object is concerned, is purely representative.   It presents nothing on which the mind can rest as an adequate object of consciousness,—nothing which is not in its nature obviously incomplete and relative,—nothing, in short, but the fact of thinking at a particular time, and the sign in which the thought is exhibited.

Representative Consciousness, like presentative, cannot be considered as forming a complete act by itself. The phenomena of intuition by themselves present nothing but a confused impression of diversity, until they are classified and distinguished from each other under separate general notions ; and the notion, on the other hand, though in the ordinary exercise of thought it may be employed apart from the consciousness of the object which it represents, can only be so separated by being associated with a further representation of itself, such as is furnished by the symbols of language. Pure thought, if by that expression is meant the consciousness of general notions and of nothing else, is an operation which may perhaps be possible to higher intelligences, but which never takes place in the human mind. Our only choice lies between notions as exemplified in individual objects, and notions as represented in signs spoken or unspoken; for the sign, the clothing of our thought, accompanies our silent meditations as well as our audible utterances : εὐφήμου στόμα φροντίδος* is not a mere poetical metaphor, but the literal statement of a philosophical fact. Thinking, as Plato has observed,† is but the conversation of the soul with herself; and the instrument employed is the echo of that which forms the medium of communication with others. To this it may be added, that the notion, as represented in language, is but the substitute for the notion embodied in intuition, and derives all the conditions of its validity from the possibility of the latter; for language, though indispensable as an instrument of thought, lends itself with equal facility to every combination, and thus

---

* Sophocles, *Œd. Col.* 132.

† *Theatetus*, p. 190. Ἔγωγε τὸ δοξάζειν λέγειν καλῶ · καὶ τὴν δόξαν λόγον εἰρημένον, οὐ μέντοι πρὸς ἄλλον οὐδὲ φωνῇ, ἀλλὰ σιγῇ πρὸς αὐτόν.

furnishes no criterion by which we can judge between sense and nonsense—between the conceivable and the inconceivable. *A round square* or *a bilinear figure,* is, as a form of speech, quite as possible as *a straight line* or *an equilateral triangle.* The mere juxtaposition of the words does not indicate the possibility or impossibility of the corresponding conception, until we attempt to construct, by intuition, an individual object in accordance with it. Language, like algebra, furnishes a system of signs, which we are able to employ in various relations without at the moment being conscious of the original signification assigned to each. But what our thoughts thus gain in flexibility they lose in distinctness, and the logical and algebraical perfections are thus in an inverse ratio to each other. It therefore becomes necessary, at the end of the process, and even occasionally during the intermediate stages, to submit the result to the test to which each step has been tacitly assumed to conform ; namely, the possible coexistence of the several groups of attributes in corresponding objects of intuition.*

* " Plerumque, præsertim in analysi longiore, non totam simul naturam rei intuemur, sed rerum loco signis utimur, quorum explicationem in præsenti aliqua cogitatione compendii causa solemus prætermittere, scientes aut credentes nos eam habere in potestate : ita cum chiliogo. num, sec polygonum mille æqualium laterum cogito, non semper naturam lateris, et æqualitatis, et millenarii (seu cubi a denario) considero, sed vocabulis istis (quorum sensus obscure saltem atque imperfecte menti obversatur) in animo utor loco idearum, quas de iis habeo, quoniam

From this use of language in thought arises the distinction, originally pointed out by Leibnitz, between *intuitive* and *symbolical* cognition. In the former we deal with the notions themselves, as exemplified in an individual object of intuition, real or imaginary. In the latter we deal with the same notions as represented by their symbols in language. The latter, however, is rather a substitute for consciousness than an act of consciousness itself. It implies a consciousness, indeed, of the act of thinking, but not immediately of the object about which we think.* Like the bank-note, it is the

memini me significationem istorum vocabulorum habere, explicationem autem nunc judico necessariam non esse ; qualem cogitationem *cœcam*, vel etiam symbolicam appellare soleo, qua et in algebra, et in arithmetica utimur, imo fere ubique " (Leibnitz, *Meditationes de Cognitione Veritate et Ideis*).

* Cognitio quæ ipso idearum intuitu absolvitur, dicitur *intuitiva*, seu, rem intuitive cognoscere dicimur, quatenus ideæ ejus, quam habemus, nobis sumus conscii. E. gr. Dum arborem præsentem intueor, mihique conscius sum corum quæ in eadem obtutu comprehendo, intuitivam arboris habeo cognitionem. Si triangulum mihi vi imaginationis tanquam in tabula delineatum, vel asserem triangularem representem, atque hujus figuræ mihi conscius sim ; triangulum intuitive cognosco. Quodsi cognitio nostra terminatur actu quo verbis tantum enunciamus quæ in ideas continentur, vel aliis signis eadem repræsentamus, ideas vero ipsas verbis aut signis indigitatas non intuemur, *cognitio symbolica* est. Ita cognitionem symbolicam habeo trianguli, si cogito ipsum esse figuram tribus lineis terminatam, trianguli vero ideam nullam, multo minus linearum quibus terminatur, ac numeri ternarii earundem, ideas intueor. Similiter cognitionem chiliogoni symbolicam habeo, si verbis tacite quasi loquens mihi ipsi indigito, chiliogonum esse figuram mille lateribus terminatam, laterum vero singulorum, ac numeri millenarii,

representative of value without having an intrinsic value of its own; and, like the bank-note, its real worth depends on the possibility of its being at any time changed for the current coin of the realm. But, as in practice the note is treated as if it were the money which it represents, so it will be convenient, in the following remarks, to treat symbolical knowledge as if it were itself the complete consciousness to which, if valid, it may be at any time reduced. We shall, therefore, treat both of intuitive and symbolical reflection under the general name of Representative Consciousness or Thought.

OF THE FORM AND MATTER OF THOUGHT.

The Form of consciousness in general has been explained as consisting in *relation to a conscious subject.* The Form of representative consciousness in particular must be ascertained by observing in what manner the subject, as a thinker, moulds into thought the raw materials furnished by intuition. The conditions under which this is done constitute the *laws of thought;* and

ipsiusque chiliogoni ideam nullam intueor.   Quod etiam signis aliis uti possimus ad res nobis repræsentandas, præter verba, vel sola arithmetica loquitur, ubi singularibus utimur notis numericis ad numeros quoscumque repræsentandos.   Habes igitur hic signa numerorum quæ sunt a verbis, quibus enunciantur, diversa.   Luculentiora exempla analysis recentiorum quam algebram vulgo dicimus suppeditat, ubi formulis ex literis atque signis aliis compositis notiones rerum exhibemus" (Wolf, *Psychologia Empirica*, sec. 286, 289).

the feature by which these laws are manifested in the product will be the *form of thought.* The former of these terms is strictly used with reference to an act of thought ; the latter, with reference to its product. Conceiving, judging, and reasoning are carried on under certain *laws.* Concepts, judgments, and reasonings exhibit certain *forms.* To ascertain what these are, we must endeavour to analyse the complex act of consciousness, and to separate those elements which appear to be contributed by the reflective act of the conscious subject.

The office of Thought consists in arranging the confused materials presented to it in such a manner as to constitute *an object.* This is done by *limitation* and *difference.* The object, as such, must contain a definite portion of the materials, and a portion only. Without the first of these conditions, there would be no contents out of which the object could be constructed : without the second, there would be no distinct representation of an actual object, but a confused and imperfect consciousness of the universe of all possible objects. An oak, for example, to be discerned as an oak, and as nothing else, must have certain constitutive features of its own ; and these must in thought be separated from those of the surrounding objects. These two conditions of all thought, expressed in the most general terms, are the well-known logical laws of Identity and Contradiction, *A is A*, and *A is not not-A ;* that is to say, every object, to be conceived as such, must be conceived as having a character of its own, and as distinct from all others. But these two conditions necessarily involve a third. The object which I distinguish and that from which I distinguish it must constitute between them the uni-verse of all that is conceivable; for the distinction is not between two definite objects of thought, but between the object of which I think and all those of which I do not think. *Not-A* implies the exclusion of A only, and of nothing else, and thus denotes the universe of all conceivable objects with that one exception. This re-lation, in its most general expression, constitutes a third law of thought,—that of Excluded Middle : *every possible object is either A or not-A.* (*Principium exclusi medii inter duo contradictoria.*) These three principles of identity, contradiction, and excluded middle, constitute the laws of *thought as thought,* and are the foundation of pure or formal Logic.

Every complete act of consciousness is a compound of intuition and thought ; and the portion which is due to the act of thought as such, conducted under the above laws, will be the *form of the representative con-sciousness.* Now, by the act of thought, the confused materials presented to the intuitive faculties are contem-plated in three points of view : as a single object, as distinguished from other objects, and as forming, in conjunction with those others, a complete class or universe of all that is conceivable. We have thus the three *forms* (or as they are called by Kant, *categories**) of *unity*, *plurality*, and *totality*; conditions essential to the possibility of thought in general, and which may therefore be regarded as *à priori* elements of reflective consciousness, derived from the constitution of the understanding itself, and manifested in relation to all its products. They are thus distinguished from the *matter*, or empirical contents, by which one object of thought is distinguished from another. The Matter of thought is derived from the intuitive faculties, and consists in the several *presented phenomena* which form the special characteristics of each object—as a man, a house, a tree,

---

* Besides these three, which are classified as categories of quantity, Kant enumerates nine others—viz. three of quality,—reality, negation, and limation ; three of relation,—inherence and subsistence, causality and dependence, and community or reciprocal action ; and three of modality,—possibility or impossibility, existence or non-existence, and necessity or contingence. But the Kantian categories are not deduced from an analysis of the act of thought, but generalised from the forms of the proposition, which latter are assumed without examination, as they are given in the ordinary logic. A psychological deduction, or a preliminary criticism of the logical forms themselves, might have considerably reduced the number. Thus the categories of quality are fundamentally identical with those of quantity ;—reality, or rather affirmation and negation, being implied in identity and diversity, and limitation in their mutual exclusion. The remaining categories are, to say the least, founded on a very questionable theory in logic ; and the two most important—those of substance and cause—present features which distinguish them from mere forms of thought. But these will have to be examined hereafter.

etc. In order to exhibit this distinction more completely, it will be necessary to notice in detail the different operations into which thought is ordinarily divided.

OF THE SEVERAL OPERATIONS OF THOUGHT.

The ordinary division of the representative faculties into Conception, or Simple Apprehension, Judgment, and Reasoning, is properly a logical rather than a psychological division, and relates to the products of thought rather than to the powers or operations by which those products are generated. Viewed as products of thought, projected, as it were, out of the thinking mind, and embodied in language, the Concept, the Judgment, and the Syllogism are expressed in different forms of speech, are susceptible of different relations one with another, and are subject to different logical rules and tests of validity. For logical purposes, therefore, they may properly be regarded as distinct objects, though susceptible of treatment upon common principles ; just as the different works of the same artist, though the result of the same productive power, may be arranged in different classes and criticised from different points of view. But the logical division of products does not necessarily imply a corresponding psychological division of faculties. The same faculty, operating by the same laws, may produce different results according to the nature of the objects submitted to it; just as the same artist may produce different works out of different materials. It is necessary, therefore, before we transplant our logical divisions into the field of psychology, to inquire upon what principles the latter science is justified in distinguishing at all between various powers of the human mind.

The only natural and necessary principle of distinction between objects is the numerical diversity of individuals. All other divisions are, to a certain extent, arbitrary and artificial, and subservient to the special purposes of this or that branch of study. The naturalist may class the man and the ape together, on account of certain points of similarity in their physical structure; the moralist will place them as widely as the poles asunder, as rational and irrational, responsible and irresponsible agents. But no possible system of arrangement can make Socrates the same individual as Plato, or regard an act performed to-day as numerically one with a similar act performed three days ago. Numerically, not only intellectual operations of various kinds, but every single act of each kind, is distinct from every other. An act of reasoning which I perform to-day is *numerically* distinct from any similar act performed yesterday; though both may be governed by the same laws, and applied to the same objects. But in the classification of acts as *specifically* the same or different, much must depend on the purpose which we have in view, and on the utility of certain relations for certain ends. A distinction which is useful for the purposes of logic may be worthless or injurious as regards psychology.

The distinction between various faculties of the internal consciousness, if made at all, must be made on a principle exactly the reverse of that by which a similar distinction is made with respect to the external senses. The bodily organs of sensation are given as locally and numerically distinct from each other, and thus furnish a pre-existing basis for the classification of their several operations. Seeing and hearing are not only distinct phenomena of consciousness, but are performed by means of distinct organs; and the faculty of seeing is at any rate so far distinct from that of hearing, that a man may be blind without being deaf, and deaf without being blind. But as regards the internal consciousness, we have no other ground for discriminating between different faculties than that which is furnished by the mental characteristics of the corresponding acts. We do not classify the acts from an acknowledged diversity of the faculties; but we attempt to classify the faculties from some admitted or supposed diversity in the acts. The acts, therefore, must, on independent grounds, be determined to be identical or distinct in species, before we can unite or separate them as related to the same or different mental powers.

The distinction between the various reflective faculties is therefore not so much to be considered with
regard to its truth or falsehood as with regard to its
convenience or inconvenience. The theory of distinct
mental organs corresponding to distinct acts of thought
is untenable on any hypothesis but that of the crudest
materalism. No sober-minded psychologist ever intends
to represent the mental faculties as substantially and
numerically distinct portions of the mind ; but, as *entia
rationis*, they may furnish more or less convenient heads
of classification, to connect or distinguish the similar
or dissimilar mental acts or states of which we are
successively conscious. In this point of view, the phenomena of conception, judgment, and reasoning, viewed
merely as acts of thought, without reference to the
diversity of the data from which the act commences and
with which it deals, appear to furnish far more prominent features of similarity than of difference. They are
effected by the same means ; they are governed by the
same laws ; they are confined within the same limits ;
they admit of the same distinctions of material and
formal validity. The pscyhological analysis of any one
may be applied, almost in the same words, to the others ;
and, so far as thought alone is concerned, the same
mental qualities are manifested in the right performance
of each. In a psychological point of view, to enumerate separate mental faculties and operations, as giving

rise to the various products of thought, is, to say the least, to encumber the science with unnecessary and perplexing distinctions. It will be sufficient to refer them to the single faculty of *thought* or *reflection*, the operation of which is, in all cases, *comparison*. The unit of thought is always a judgment, based on a comparison of objects ; and the several operations of thought are, in ultimate analysis, nothing more than judgments derived from different data. In order to exhibit this in special instances, it will be convenient to adopt provisionally the logical classification, and to examine the phenomena of thought under the several heads of Conception, Judgment, and Reasoning.

OF CONCEPTION.

The ultimate object of all complete consciousness, intuitive or reflective, is, as has been already stated, an *individual ;* that is to say, an object occupying a definite position in time or space, or both. It is not, however, necessary that the individual so presented to consciousness should be discerned as such by any distinctive features. We must distinguish between an individual act of consciousness and an individual object viewed out of relation to that act. The conditions of time and space are sufficient to distinguish *the act* from every other act, and the object *at the moment of perception* from every other object ; but they are not parts of *the object itself ;* and they furnish no marks by which that object may be *permanently* distinguished from others. The same object may occupy different places at different times ; or different objects may successively occupy the same place. Hence, in addition to these conditions, which serve only for the intuitive cognition of a single individual at a particular moment, it is necessary to select others, which may serve as marks for the reflective cognition of an individual, as such, when different objects are compared together. In any given intuition we may or may not be conscious of marks sufficient for this purpose. I may see, for example, at a distance, three men standing together. They are unquestionably three individual men, each occupying his own position in space ; and this at the moment is sufficient to distinguish them from each other. But I may be unable, on account of the distance, to discern any distinctive features belonging to the objects themselves. I discern them as three men, and that is all. I cannot say whether they are fair or dark, tall or short, acquaintances or strangers. I can distinguish them by nothing but their relative positions ; and these may at any moment be changed without my being able to discover it. In other words, I perceive in the individuals only such qualities as are characteristic of a class.

The above example may serve to illustrate the

process of *imperfect or intuitive generalisation,* which consists in directing the attention, voluntarily or involuntarily, to the common features of several objects presented to us, neglecting or not perceiving those qualities which are peculiar to each.* It is not a distinct cognition of the class as a class, nor of the individuals as individuals ; but a confused perception of both together. To form a complete cognition of the individual, I must, by the aid of imagination, supply those distinctive features which I am unable clearly to perceive. To form a complete cognition of the class, I must separate the common attributes from their connection with a definite time and place. But how are

* " *Si in cognitione intuitiva acquiescimus, prima intellectus operatio absolvitur, dum in ideis duorum vel plurium individuorum simul nobis occurrentibus ad ea successive attentionem dirigimus quæ in iisdem eadem sunt.* Dum enim attentionem nostram successive dirigimus ad ea quæ in ideis duorum vel plurium individuorum simul nobis occurrentibus eadem sunt ; magis nobis conscii sumus quod jam in pluribus eadem percipiamus, quam quod percipiamus alia, atque adeo operatione intellectus ea a subjectis, quibus insunt, quasi separamus. Distincte igitur percipimus quæ ad genus vel speciem illarum rerum pertinent, consequenter genera et species nobis distincte repræsentamus. Quare cum generum et specierum repræsentatio sit notio, distincta autem notio intellectus operatio sit eaque prima ; si in cognitione intuitiva acquiescimus, prima mentis operatio absolvitur, dum in ideis duorum vel plurium individuorum simul nobis occurrentibus ad ea successive attentionem dirigimus, quæ in iisdem eadem sunt. Hoc modo patet, quomodo nobis genera et species rerum in universali repræsentare debeamus. Quod alius non detur modus in cognitione intuitiva genera et species rerum repræsentandi, ex eo intelligitur, quod universalia, seu genera et species non existant nisi in singularibus, et ad notionem entis in universali non

attributes, apart from their juxtaposition in space, to be so connected together as to constitute a single object? The head and trunk and limbs of an individual man are connected together by continuity in space, and by that continuity constitute a whole of intuition, whether distinctly recognised in that relation or not. How are the attributes of mankind in general to be separated from their position in space, and yet so united together as to constitute a whole of thought? To effect this, we must call in the aid of language. The word is to thought what space is to perception. It constitutes the connecting-link between various attributes,—the frame, as it were, in which they are set,—and thus furnishes the

pertineant nisi determinationes intrinsicæ pluribus singularibus seu individuis communes. Ponamus e. gr. duas arbores, cerasum atque prunum, ooulis nostris una objici, ita ut utramque uno intuitu comprehendere valeamus. Quodsi jam attentionem nostram ad folia utriusque arboris simul dirigimus, nobis conscii sumus nos in utraque percipere folia, et magis quidem conscii sumus, quam quod alia vel in iisdem arboribus vel extra eas una percipiamus. Quodsi jam porro attentionem nostram promovemus ad surculos in utraque arbore simul, eorundem eodem prorsus modo conscii nobis sumus. Et idem tenendum est de ramis atque truncis. Hac ratione absque omni vocabulorum vel aliorum signorum usu, ea nobis distincte repræsentamus, quæ arboribus communia sunt, atque adeo notionem hujus gereris ingrediuntur, quod arboris nomine indigitamus. Atque ita simul intelligimus, quid sit mente separare ea, quæ individuis communia sunt. Neque vero utilitate sua caret nosse, quomodo in cognitione intuitiva prima intellectus operatio sese exerat, quoniam notionibus generum atque specierum claritas affunditur, si cognitio intuitiva cum symbolica conjungatur" (Wolf, *Psychologia Empirica*, sec. 326).

means by which the features characteristic of a class
may be viewed apart from the individuals in which
they are intuitively perceived, and combined into a
complex notion or concept. Conception is thus, in the
operations of thought, the counterpart of perception in
those of sense. In the latter we are conscious of objects
as extended; *i.e.* as possessing parts related to each
other by juxtaposition in space. In the former we are
conscious of notions as embodied in words, and as composed of subordinate notions, which are themselves also
expressed by similar symbols.

Conception, apart from intuition, is only possible
under the form of symbolical cognition, in which the
notions are contemplated in their signs. In this form it
consists in the enumeration, by means of verbal or other
symbols, of the different parts constituting a given
notion.* Conception, intuitive as well as symbolical,

---

* "*In cognitione symbolica prima mentis operatio absolvitur recensione
vocabulorum, vel aliorum signorum, quibis ea indigitantur, quæ notionem rei distinctam ingrediuntur.* Etenim in cognitione symbolica
tantummodo verbis enunciamus quæ in ideis continentur, vel aliis signis
eadem repræsentamus, ideas vero ipsas verbis aut signis aliis indigitatas
non intuemur. Quare cum in cognitione intuitiva prima mentis operatio absolvatur, si attentionem successive in idea rei ad ea dirigimus
quæ notionem distinctam generis vel speciei ingrediuntur, singula autem
hæc enunciabilia sint, adeoque vocabulis vel signis aliis indigitari pos-
sint; in cognitione symbolica prima mentis operatio absolvi debet
recensione vocabulorum, vel repræsentatione aliorum signorum, quibus
ea denotantur quæ notionem rei distinctam ingrediuntur. Ita prima
mentis operatio in cognitione symbolica arboris absolvitur, si dicimus

is thus in all cases a judgment. In intuitive conception we judge that an object now present to the mind
exemplifies a given notion : we pronounce, for example,
that this is a man. In symbolical conception we pronounce that the notion comprehends such and such
subordinate notions as its constituent parts. But symbolical cognition supposes intuitive cognition, actual or
possible, as its condition. The existence of a class is
possible if the existence of individual members is possible ; for the universal has no existence apart from the
individual. A class really exists, if individuals exist
possessing the attributes of that class : a class may
imaginably exist, if we can imagine the existence of individuals possessing the corresponding attributes. But
where neither perception nor imagination is possible—
where the attributes are such that we cannot, either by
observation or by construction, manual or mental, combine them into an individual unity of representation—

vegetabile, quod ex trunco, ramis, surculis et foliis constat : etenim sigillatim recensemus verba quibus ea indigitantur quæ in arboribus tanquam communia distinguimus, consequenter quæ notionem arboris in
genere, quatenus distincta est, ingrediuntur. Non autem jam nobis
quæstio est, utrum notio distincta sit completa atque determinata, atque
oratione ista talis notio significetur, ut hæc definitionis loco inservire
possit. Sufficit enim hic ea sigillatim enunciari quæ mente ab idea rei
separantur, dum distincte nobis genus vel speciem repræsentare cona-
mur. Pendet enim cognitio symbolica ab intuitiva, quam supponit et
ad quam refertur. Quicquid igitur huic deest, idem etiam illi deesse
debet " (Wolf, *Psychologia Empirica*, sec. 328).

the class is inconceivable, and the words by which it is represented, however separately intelligible, are, in their combination, utterly unmeaning.

Hence, as a general rule : *Conception is only possible within the limits of possible intuition,*—that is to say, those notions only are conceivable whose objects as individuals can be presented to intuition in themselves or represented in their images. It is not necessary that the intuition should in all cases actually take place : it is sufficient if, from our intuitive knowledge of the several attributes, we know that there is no incompatibility between them which renders their union in one representation impossible. I conceive a chiliagon when I define it as a regular figure of a thousand sides ; but I cannot distinctly represent in the imagination a thousand sides at once; nor do I think it necessary to draw the figure in order to convince myself by actual experience of the possibility of the intuition. But I know that the property of inclosing space contains nothing incompatible with the number of a thousand sides ; and that therefore the corresponding figure could be constructed, if necessary. Under this conviction, the symbolical takes the place of the intuitive cognition ; and we are enabled, by the aid of language, to think of the figure in certain relations without actually constructing it.* In

* " Quoniam vocabula sunt signa nostrarum perceptionum, vel rerum per eas repræsentatarum, dum verba recensemus quibus ea indigitantur

speaking of *possible intuition* as the test of conceivability, we do not mean merely the intuition of the bodily senses. Fear, or anger, or volition, or moral approbation, or any individual state of the internal consciousness, is as much an object of intuition as a sound, or a colour, or an odour; and is equally capable of being represented in an image or conceived under a general notion. Neither do we make any difference between the real and the imaginary, between the mentally and the physically possible. A centaur is as conceivable as a horse or a man, whether the actual existence of such a creature is physically possible or not. I may imagine or conceive a stone remaining suspended in air or water, or mounting upwards instead of

quæ notionem rei distinctam ingrediuntur, ea singula ad perceptiones rerum in cognitione intuitiva locum habentes referre tenemur, etsi ad notionem eidem respondentem non attendamus, quod eadem ex crebro usu satis intelligere arbitremur. Quamobrem *operatio intellectus prima in cognitione symbolica præsupponit operationem ejusdem primam in intuitiva.* Hæc probe notanda sunt, ne demus sine mente sonos, nobisque persuadeamus nos notionem rei habere, dum vocabula recensere valemus, etsi *cognitionem symbolicam ad intuitivam reducere* minime valeamus : quæ reductio in eo consistit, ut ideam alicujus individui in nobis excitemus, sive sensuum, sive imaginationis ope, ac attentio nostra successive ad ea dirigatur quæ in re percepta insunt, atque deinde vocabula ad eadem referantur, prout singulis, vi significatus quem obtinent alias, subinde etiam vi etymologiæ ac compositionis, denotandis apta deprehenduntur, quatenus scilicet in etymologia vel compositione ratio denominandi latet, ad rem vocabulo denotatam manducens, nisi ipsimet vocabula ad ea significanda in cognitione intuitiva transtulerimus, atque hujus facti meminerimus" (Wolf, *Psychologia Empirica*, sec. 329).

falling downwards, though consistently with the natural law of gravitation it can do nothing but sink to the ground.

Conception without an accompanying intuition is only possible, as we have already observed, by means of symbols ; but the thought which accompanies every complete intuition, and by which various presented attributes are regarded as constituting a whole, is an act of similar character, and may therefore properly be called by the same name. Conception may thus be distinguished as of two kinds :—*Symbolical conception*, in which a general notion, represented in language, is regarded as composed of other subordinate notions similarly represented ; and *Intuitive conception*, in which an individual object, present to sense or imagination, is regarded as a whole composed of certain presented parts. By this the object is *thought under a concept;* being thereby separated from the surrounding objects of intuition, and regarded as a whole by itself.* The former kind of conception is based on the latter, and derives its validity from it. It is in the latter, therefore, that the

---

* "The understanding, thought proper, notion, concept, etc., may coincide or not with imagination, representation proper, image, etc. The two faculties do not coincide in a general notion ; for we cannot represent man or horse in an actual image without individualising the universal : and thus contradiction emerges. But in the individual, say Socrates or Bucephalus, they do coincide ; for I see no valid ground why we should *think*, in the strict sense of the word, or *conceive* the

form and laws of conception will be most clearly exhibited. We must therefore analyse the complex act of intuitive conception, in order to detect, in the whole so conceived, the part contributed by the reflective faculty, and the laws under which it operates.

It has been already observed that intuition and thought, the presentative and the representative consciousness, can be distinguished from each other, as actual states of mind, only logically, not really. To the recognition of either, as a fact of consciousness, the presence of both is indispensable. To discern the element contributed by conception to the cognition of an object of consciousness as such, we may revert, for the moment, to the supposition of a being susceptible of a diversity of intuitions, but with no power of discerning wherein that diversity consists. In other words, we must suppose him divested of the faculty of *comparison*. In the exercise of sight, for example, he might at any moment be dimly conscious that he saw something ; he might also be dimly conscious that he had seen something before ; but he would not be conscious whether the two objects were the same or different in species ; for this implies a

individuals which we *represent* " (Sir W. Hamilton, *Discussions*, p. 13). We may go even beyond this, and regard conception as coinciding, not merely with the *imagination*, but with one element of the *perception* of an individual object. For the combination of individual parts into a whole is a cognition of *relations*, and, as such, is properly an act of the understanding, operating by means of concepts.

reflective cognition of each under a separate notion. By the act of conception I discern a particular object as such; and this implies at the same time a consciousness of its difference from something else. The act of reflection has thus added a new element to the phenomena of intuition—namely, a consciousness of their relation to each other. The mere presence of an object affecting the organ of sight does not in itself imply that any other object accompanies or has preceded it; but the recognition of it as this object rather than that, does so. Conception, whether intuitive or symbolical (for the latter is but the substitute for the former), thus implies the cognition of objects under separate notions; and this cognition constitutes the common or formal feature of the act of conceiving, being unaffected by any diversity in the nature of the objects conceived. To ascertain the Laws of Conception, we must therefore ask what this cognition of objects in all cases supposes: in other words, what are the relations implied in the knowledge of an object as such. In the first place, the object is *discerned,* or separated from all others; and this separation implies two relations, *identity* and *diversity.* The consciousness of identity is at the same time the consciousness of difference: I discern a thing by knowing it as what it is, and by distinguishing it from what it is not. In the second place, the cognisance of this relation between objects implies also their *mutual relation to a common consciousness.* I am conscious of the distinction of one thing from another, by including both as modes of one continuous conscious existence. Without this, memory would be impossible, and without memory there could be no comparison. We have thus the three forms of Unity, Plurality, and Totality, manifested as the necessary relations with which the mind, in the act of conception, invests the materials furnished by intuition. To conceive any object *A* as such, I must distinguish it from all that is not *A*, and I must regard *A* and *not-A* as constituting between them the universe of my consciousness. These requirements are expressed by the three laws of Identity, Contradiction, and Excluded Middle, which may thus be regarded as the universal or formal conditions of every act of conception as such, in contradistinction from the special or material conditions which are necessary to the conception of this or that particular class of objects only.

From the above exhibition of the laws and forms of thought in general, as manifested in the act of conception, it will be easy to deduce, in a somewhat amended enumeration, those special forms which have been treated by logical writers as distinctive of the concept proper.* The concept is necessarily conceived as *one,* as *one of*

* See Kant, *Logik,* sect. 2. Fries, *System der Logik,* sect. 20. The former places the form of a concept in its universality ; the latter adopts the same view, subdividing universality into extension and comprehension.

many, and as *constituting with the many an universe of the conceivable.* From the last of these three conditions it follows, that the concept must possess a generic or universal feature, by which it is characterised as a concept in general, or a member of the conceivable universe. From the second it follows, that it must also possess a differential or peculiar feature, by which it is distinguished from all others. And from the first it follows, that these two features must be united into a single whole. Hence every concept, as such, must possess in some degree the attributes of *distinctness*, as having complex contents, capable of analysis into genus and difference; of *clearness*, as being by one portion of its contents distinguishable from other notions; and of *relation to a possible object of intuition*, inasmuch as the unity of a complex notion depends, not on a mere juxtaposition of terms, but upon its being the representative of one object.* These three forms may be otherwise denominated (for the difference is merely verbal) *comprehension, limitation*, and *extension.* As having complex contents, every concept *comprehends* certain attributes; as distinguishable from others, it is *limited* by its specific difference; and, as representative of a class of possible objects,

---

* Arist. *Metaph* vi. 12 : 'Επὶ μὲν γὰρ τοῦ ἄνθρωπος καὶ λευκὸν πολλὰ μέν ἐστιν, ὅταν μὴ ὑπάρχῃ θατέρῳ θάτερον, ἓν δέ, ὅταν ὑπάρχῃ καὶ πάθῃ τι τὸ ὑποκείμενον ὁ ἄνθρωπος · τότε γὰρ ἓν γίγνεται καὶ ἔστιν ὁ λευκὸς ἄνθρωπος. *Ibid.* vii. 6 : 'Ο δ' ὁρισμὸς λόγος ἐστὶν εἰς οὗ συνδέσμῳ καθάπερ ἡ Ἰλιάς, ἀλλὰ τῷ ἑνὸς εἶναι.

it has a certain field over which it is *extended*. The forms of the concept proper may thus be indifferently enumerated, as Distinctness, Clearness, and Relation to an object ; or as Comprehension, Limitation, and Extension.

We have thus exhibited the general laws of thought in their relation to those objects with reference to which the thinking act is usually distinguished as Conception. But though no conception is possible, except in conformity with these laws, it must not therefore be concluded that conception is possible in all cases in which they are not transgressed. An object may be inconceivable in two ways,—*essentially* or *formally*, because the attempt to conceive it involves a violation of the laws of thought ; and *accidentally* or *materially*, because of the absence of certain preliminary conditions, whose existence must be presupposed before thought comes into operation. By the laws of thought, a concept must have distinctive contents ; it must not comprehend two contradictory elements ; and it must be contained under one or the other of the contradictory notions which constitute the universe of thought. Where these conditions are not observed, the object is formally or essentially inconceivable. Thus pure Nothing, which has no contents, and also the indefinite notions indicated by the terms Being, Thing, Existence in general, which have no definite contents, are formally inconceivable, as violating the law of identity : They are not an *A* as distinguished from a *not-*

A. So, again, we are formally unable to conceive the same surface as both black and not-black, which involves a violation of the law of contradiction; nor yet can we conceive it as neither one nor the other; for this is prohibited by the law of excluded middle. But the accidental or material inconceivability of objects depends on other conditions. The materials of thought are furnished by the phenomena of the senses or of some other intuitive faculty; and hence, when the intuition is wanting, conception is impossible, as having no data upon which to operate. Thus, a blind man can form no conception of colours, and a deaf man can form no conception of sounds,—not because sounds and colours are in themselves inconceivable, but because the preliminary intuition which should furnish the materials of the conception is deficient. And so likewise any man, though in the full possession of his senses, is unable to form a conception of a colour which he has never seen, or of a sound which he has never heard, or of a savour which he has never tasted; or, at least, he can form only such an imperfect conception as may be furnished by its supposed likeness to some object of his actual experience,— a conception necessarily defective, as not containing the specific difference which characterises the object as such, and which actual experience alone can furnish. Objects accidentally inconceivable may be divided into two classes :—those which are deficient in the *matter* of the intuition, and those which are deficient in the *form;* for it must be remembered that the form of intuition becomes part of the matter of thought; and that both these classes are therefore, so far as conception is concerned, inconceivable *materially* or *accidentally.* The form of intuition is to be found in the general conditions of space and time, which are common to all external or internal intuitions respectively, as such: the matter is to be found in the special affections of this or that mode of external or internal sense, by which one object is distinguished from another. Upon the necessary relations of space and time are founded the two sciences of geometry and arithmetic; and a notion which violates the principles of either of these may be classified as inconceivable from a defect in the form of intuition. Thus it is impossible to conceive a figure bounded by two straight lines, or an odd number which is the sum of two even ones; because the two straight lines cannot be perceived or imagined as occupying such a position in space as is necessary before we can include them under the general concept of a figure; and the two even numbers cannot occupy such a succession in time as is necessary to the formation of the concept of an odd number. These notions are not, as some writers have supposed,* logically

* Among others may be mentioned Leibnitz, *Théodicée,* sect. ii. p. 480, ed. Erdmann; Stewart, *Elements,* part ii. ch. i.; and Whately, *Logic,* appendix on Ambiguous Terms, *v. Impossibility.*

self-contradictory, and therefore formally inconceivable : they are not inadmissible in their general character as thoughts, but in their special character as thoughts about figures or numbers.   In one respect they differ considerably from the other class of materially inconceivable objects, in which the impossibility arises only from a deficiency in actual experience of the matter of intuition, such as has been supposed in the case of an unknown colour or sound.   The latter may become conceivable by a mere extension of experience, without any change in our bodily or mental constitution.   The former, being dependent on the subjective conditions of intuition, could not become conceivable without a change in the constitution of our intuitive faculties.   This difference will be more fully examined when we come to treat of the distinction between necessary and contingent truths.

Before concluding this part of our subject, it will be necessary to say a few words on the controverted question of the processes usually regarded as subsidiary to conception, namely, Abstraction and Generalisation.   The account usually given of these processes by writers on logic cannot be regarded as accurately exhibiting the psychological phenomena connected with the passage from intuition to thought ; and the question derives additional interest from the controversy which has been raised by philosophers of eminence concerning the reality of the processes themselves.

The ordinary logical account is to the following effect :—We examine, it is said, a number of individual objects, agreeing in some features and differing in others ; we *abstract* or separate the points in which they agree from those in which they differ ; and we *generalise,* or construct a common notion, represented by a common name, out of the features of similarity so separated from the rest ; which common notion becomes thus indifferently applicable to all the individuals from which it was derived. The process, as thus described, appears to presuppose the very act of conception to which it is represented as giving rise. If, for example, I am to form a general notion of *man* by examining the individuals Peter, James, and John, and by separating the accidents of complexion, stature, expression of countenance, etc., from the human form which is common to all, it is obvious that I must previously have formed general notions of the parts so separated from each other. Before I can say, this man has blue eyes and that man has black, and the colour of the eyes may therefore be set aside as accidental ; I must have discerned, by means of concepts, the eyes as such from other features, and the colours blue and black from other visible qualities. If these concepts, according to the above theory, are formed by means of a previous abstraction, the same difficulty is repeated. Conception supposes abstraction, and abstraction again supposes conception, and the explanation thus runs in a constantly recurring circle.

The error of the theory consists in supposing that the individual is discerned *as such* before the universal. In the confused consciousness, if it can be called consciousness at all, which alone would be possible in an act of sensation unaccompanied by thought, we could not be said to discern either likenesses or differences. We should not be able to distinguish one individual from another, or to compare them together as like or unlike. As soon as thought is awakened, the general notion is perceived in and along with the individual which is discerned under it · and it is impossible to distinguish an individual as such from others, without at the same time being conscious of the notion which that individual exemplifies. Indeed, properly speaking, every collection of individual attributes is potentially the representative of a class ; for there is nothing in the attributes themselves to prevent their being exhibited by more than one object. In one sense, indeed, it might be said that our cognition of the class is prior to that of the individual. For, in the development of consciousness by the aid of language, resemblances are noticed earlier than differences; and even the names distinctive of individuals are at first associated only with their generic features. Children, says Aristotle, at first call all men *father*, and all women *mother*, but afterwards they distinguish one

person from another.*   By the aid of language, our first
abstractions are in fact given to us already made, as we
learn to give the same name to various individuals presented to us under slight and at first unnoticed circumstances of distinction.   The name is thus applied to different objects long before we learn to analyse the growing powers of speech and thought, to ask what we mean
by each several instance of its application, and to correct
and fix the signification of words at first used vaguely
and obscurely.

The nature of the general notion or concept itself has
been no less a point of controversy among philosophers
than the process by which it is formed.   According to
Locke,† the general idea of a triangle is an imperfect
idea, "wherein some parts of several different and incon-
sistent ideas are put together."   As limited to no particular kind of triangle, but including all, it must be
"neither oblique nor rectangular, neither equilateral,
equicrural, nor scalenon ; but all and none of these at
once."   The general idea, as thus described, Berkeley
easily perceived to be self-contradictory, and the doctrine
suicidal.   "I have a faculty," he says, "of imagining or
representing to myself the ideas of those particular
things I have perceived, and of variously compounding
and dividing them.   I can imagine a man with two heads,

* *Phys. Ausc.* i. 1.
† *Essay*, b. iv. chap. vii. sec. 9.

or the upper parts of a man joined to the body of a horse. I can consider the hand, the eye, the nose, each by itself, abstracted or separated from the rest of the body. But then, whatever hand or eye I imagine, it must have some particular shape and colour. Likewise the idea of man that I frame to myself must be either of a white, or a black, or a tawny, a straight, or a crooked, a tall, or a low, or a middle-sized man. To be plain, I own myself able to abstract *in one sense,* as when I consider some particular parts or qualities separated from others, with which, though they are united in some objects, yet it is possible they may really exist without them. But I deny that I can abstract one from another, or conceive separately, those qualities which it is impossible should exist so separated ; or that I can frame a general notion by abstracting from particulars in the manner afore-said."* On these grounds, the bishop maintains that things, names, and notions, are in their own nature par-ticular, and are only rendered universal by the relation which they bear to the particulars represented by them.

The remarks which have been made above, on the distinction between intuitive and symbolical knowledge, and on the office of language in promoting distinctness of intuition as well as of conception, may assist in plac-ing this controversy on a more satisfactory footing. The error of Locke, as Berkeley clearly perceived, consisted

---

* *Principles of Human Knowledge,* Introduction, sec. 10.

in regarding abstraction as a positive act of thought, instead of the mere negation of thought. Abstraction is nothing more than non-attention to certain parts of an object : we do not positively think of the triangle as neither equilateral, nor isosceles, nor scalene ; but we think of the figure as composed of three sides, without asking the question whether those sides are equal or unequal. On the other hand, Berkeley, in maintaining that all notions are in their own nature particular, has overlooked the fact, that thought, and, through thought, language, is necessary to distinguish the particular as particular, no less than the universal as universal ; and that we are thus enabled, both in intuitive and in symbolical cognition, to discern generic attributes, and to constitute them an object of conception, without being conscious of the particulars by which they are accompanied. I see a man at a distance, and I know him to be a man ; here is intuition and conception combined. But I am not near enough to discern either his stature or his complexion ; and though, if my attention is called to the point, I cannot help admitting that he must be of a certain size and a certain colour ; yet the visible object presents neither the one nor the other ; and it is not necessary that my attention should be called to them at all. It is true that the visible object, as a surface, is coloured ; but this colour does not enter into my notion of the thing represented. The faint blue tint that marks a distant object is not included in my conception of the object as a man, and my sight is too feeble to enable me to supply any other. Here, then, is a distinct cognition of generic attributes as such—attributes which are indeed perceived as existing in an individual, but which contain no distinctive feature by which the individual can be recognised as such. The abstraction becomes still greater when the conception is purely symbolical; as we are thus enabled to think of the attributes without being at the moment conscious of their coexistence in any individual whatever. Berkeley mistakes the test of conception for the act of conception itself. Conception is not identical with imagination; though the latter process is so far the test of the former, that nothing can be conceived as constituting a class, which is absolutely and in its own nature incapable of being imagined as existing in an individual.

The length to which our remarks have run on the subject of conception will enable us to be more brief in our treatment of the remaining operations of thought, which are nothing more than the same faculty of comparison applied to different objects.

OF JUDGMENT.

Judgment, in the limited sense in which it is distinguishable from consciousness in general, is an act of comparison between two given concepts, as regards their relation to a common object.   Omitting those judgments which involve merely the enumeration of the attributes comprehended in a concept (the *analytical* or *explicative judgments* of Kant), which may be more properly classified as acts of conception ; and confining ourselves to those in which the contents of the given concepts are distinct from each other (the *synthetical* or *ampliative judgments* of Kant, we may distinguish the Form from the Matter of judgments,—the part contributed by the act of judging itself, from the pre-existing materials on which it operates,—as follows.   The concepts being distinct from each other in contents, their relation to a common object cannot be ascertained by any mere examination of those contents : this relation, therefore, as well as the concepts themselves, must be given prior to and out of the act of comparison.   In other words, the relation between the two concepts must be given in an act of intuition, pure or empirical, imaginary or real, before we can decide by an act of judgment that such a relation does or does not exist.   For example : in order to form the judgment "two straight lines cannot inclose a space," I must not only know the meaning of the terms employed, but I must also, by the aid of imagination, construct a representation in my mind of two actual straight lines and their actual positions in space. I must perceive that these two straight lines are incapable of inclosing a space, before I pronounce the universal judgment concerning straight lines in general. Here the relation between the two concepts is presented in a *pure* or *à priori intuition*—*i.e.* in an intuition containing no adventitious element external to the mind itself. Again, in order to form the judgment "gold is heavy," supposing that my conception of gold does not in itself include the attribute of weight, I cannot, by merely thinking of gold as a hard, yellow, shining body, determine what effect it will produce when laid upon the hand. I must actually place an individual piece of gold upon my hand, and ascertain by experience the fact of its pressure. Here the relation between the two concepts is presented in a *mixed* or *empirical intuition; i.e.* in an intuition caused by the presence of a body external to the mind itself. The examination of these constituent elements will enable us to distinguish between the matter and the form of thought as exhibited in the act of judgment.

If I poise a piece of gold in my hand, in order to ascertain whether it is heavy, the presented phenomena belong to distinct acts of sensation. The evidence of sight attests the presence of a round, yellow, shining body ; the evidence of touch, or rather of muscular pressure, attests its weight. To unite these attributes, as belonging to one and the same thing, is an act, not of sensation, but of thought. The mere sensation aided by the concepts, presents us with three things—the body which is seen, the pressure which is felt, and a certain temporal and local juxtaposition of the two.   To combine the presented attributes as belonging to one thing; to pronounce that it is *the gold* which is heavy, is an act of thought, constituting a judgment.   Here, then, we have one form of judgment, expressed in the copula, " gold *is* heavy ;" this indicates the identification of two concepts as related to a common object; an identification usually known as the *quality* of the judgment.

The same is the case with the *quantity* of judgments. I see a number of balls lying on a table, and pronounce at once that they are all white ; I see another collection, and assert in like manner that some are white and some black.   Here the senses, even when aided by the concepts in distinguishing the balls as such, yet present to us only individual objects   *This, this,* and *this* are within their province ; but they know nothing of *all* or *some.* It is by an act of thought that the several individuals are regarded as constituting a whole, and a judgment pronounced concerning that whole or a portion of it.

A third form of the judgment, as indeed of all thinking, is *limitation.*   In predicating one notion of another, I at the same time necessarily exclude everything to which that predicate is opposed, and thereby limit the subject to one alone of those contradictory determinations which make up the universe of thought.   In asserting, for example, that gold is heavy, I as much exclude it from the class of imponderables as I include it within that of bodies possessing weight. The canon that *predication is limitation* is now, indeed, universally admitted as an axiom in philosophy;[*] and the various metaphysical systems of modern Germany, since the days of Kant, may be briefly described as so many attempts to evade the consequences of this principle by constructing a philosophy of the unlimited on a basis independent of logical predication.

These three forms of the judgment, like those of the

---

[*] See, for example, among others, Fichte, *Ueber den Grund unseres Glaubens an eine göttliche Weltregierung*, p. 16 (*Werke*, v. p. 187); *Gerichtliche Verantwortung*, p. 47 (*Werke*, v. p. 265); *Bestimmung des Menschen* (*Werke*, ii. p. 304). Hegel, *Logik*, p. i. b. ii. chap. 2; p. ii. chap. 2, *Encyklopädie*, sec. 28 (*Werke*, iv. p. 26; v. p. 70; vi. p. 64).

[†] Kant (*Kritik der r. V. Transc. Anal.* B. i. Abschn. 2; *Logik*, sec. 20) admits four forms of the judgment,—quantity, quality, relation, and modality. The two first have been admitted above. That of relation, under which head Kant classes the division of judgments into categorical, hypothetical, and disjunctive, is based on a very questionable position of the ordinary logic. If, as appears to be the case, hypothetical and disjunctive judgments, so far as they are judgments at all, are reducible to categoricals, relation, instead of being a special form of judgment, becomes a term equivalent to judgment in general. As regards modality, it may perhaps be more accurately referred to the matter than to the form of the judgment. The only judgments necessary *as thoughts* are those in which the subject logically contains the predicate : the only judgments impossible *as thoughts* are those in which the one term contradicts the other. These, as analytical judgments, have been above classed under the head of conception. All other judgments, *as thoughts*, are contingent, and become necessary or impossible only as thoughts about

concept, may be regarded as special manifestations of the three conditions of thought in general—unity, plurality, and totality. As *one*, the judgment possesses *quality*, exhibited in its copula, by which as a connecting-link, it is constituted a single act of thought: as *one out of many possible judgments*, it is *limited* by its predicate ; and as *a whole composed of parts*, it represents an object of thought, which, whether it be one individual or many, contains in itself the several attributes indicated by the terms. This relation to an object is expressed by the *quantity* of the judgment, whereby one, some, or all of the members of a class are pointed out as an object possessing various attributes and combining them into a whole.

The three highest laws of thought are likewise operative in the act of judging, as in that of conceiving. This may be shown by ascertaining what are the universal conditions under which the judgment, *as a thought*, is possible. Of course we have nothing to do with the material conditions under which this or that judgment is possible *as a fact*. The latter conditions are special, not general, and apply to this or that particular judgment in its relation to its objects ; not to all possible judgments in their relation to the thinking subject. As

this or that particular object. It is not logic nor metaphysics, but geometry, which tells us that the angles of a triangle *must be* equal to two right angles.

far as the laws of thought are concerned, it is indifferent whether we assert that the earth goes round the sun, or the sun round the earth; the latter proposition being logically as valid as the former, however incompatible with the facts of astronomy. The universal conditions of the possibility of any judgment as a thought may be ascertained by the following question :—Given any concept A, under what conditions may another concept B be predicable of it? The particular objects signified by A and B are supposed to be unknown; the question of the logical validity of the thought being thus kept free from all admixture of material elements. In the first place, the concept B must have definite contents: it is to be a predicate limiting A. It is therefore a portion, and a portion only, of the universe of possible concepts distinct from A. This is expressed by the law of Excluded Middle : "Every concept distinct from A is either B or not-B." In the second place, the concept B must contain no attribute logically incompatible with A. This is expressed by the law of Contradiction. In the third place, the concepts A and B, when united in a judgment, must be regarded as representing one and the same object: that which is A is also B. This is expressed by the law of Identity. A in becoming B remains identical with itself. This apparent paradox of identity in diversity constituted one of the earliest puzzles in metaphysics, and gave rise to a scepticism which, refusing to admit without explanation the laws of thought themselves, consistently denied the possibility of uniting two notions in a judgment.* Whether the doubt thus suggested can be satisfied by Ontology, is a question which cannot be considered at present. In a psychological point of view it is sufficient to say that such is the form which thought necessarily assumes. The office of Psychology is to exhibit the laws of thought as they actually exist: it cannot undertake to vindicate them, or to explain why the human mind is constituted as it is.

OF REASONING.

The third operation of thought, Reasoning, is likewise an act of comparison between two concepts; and only differs from judgment in that the two concepts are not compared together directly in themselves, but indirectly by means of their mutual relation to a third. As the concept furnishes the materials for the act of judging, so

---

* Plato, *Theat.* p. 201: Ἐγὼ γὰρ αὖ ἐδόκουν ἀκούειν τινῶν ὅτι τὰ μὲν πρῶτα οἱονπερεὶ στοιχεῖα, ἐξ ὧν ἡμεῖς τε συγκείμεθα καὶ τἆλλα, λόγον οὐκ ἔχοι· αὐτὸ γὰρ καθ᾽ αὑτὸ ἕκαστον ὀνομάσαι μόνον εἴη, προσειπεῖν δὲ οὐδὲν ἄλλο δυνατόν, οὔθ᾽ ὡς ἔστιν οὔθ᾽ ὡς οὐκ ἔστιν. *Sophist.* p. 251 : Εὐθὺς γὰρ ἀντιλαβέσθαι παντὶ πρόχειρον ὡς ἀδύνατον τά τε πολλὰ ἓν καὶ τὸ ἓν πολλὰ εἶναι, καὶ δή που χαίρουσιν οὐκ ἐῶντες ἀγαθὸν λέγειν ἄνθρωπον, ἀλλὰ τὸ μὲν ἀγαθὸν ἀγαθόν, τὸν δὲ ἄνθρωπον ἄνθρωπον. Arist. *Metaph.* vi. 29 : Διὸ Ἀντισθένης ᾤετο εὐήθως μηθὲν ἀξιῶν λέγεσθαι πλὴν τῷ οἰκείῳ λόγῳ ἓν ἐφ᾽ ἑνός. Simplicius *in Arist. Phys.* f. 20 (Scholia ed. Brandis, p. 330) : Οἱ δὲ ἐκ τῆς Ἐρετρίας οὕτω τὴν ἀπορίαν ἐφοβήθησαν ὡς λέγειν μηδὲν κατὰ μηδενὸς κατηγορεῖσθαι, ἀλλ᾽ αὐτὸ καθ᾽ αὑτὸ ἕκαστον λέγεσθαι, οἷον ὁ ἄνθρωπος ἄνθρωπος καὶ τὸ λευκὸν λευκόν (Cf. Zeller, *Philosophie der Griechen,* ii. p. 115).

the judgment furnishes the materials for the act of reasoning. The Matter of the Syllogism thus appears in the several propositions of which it is composed, and which vary in every different instance; its Form appears in the manner in which those propositions are, in the act of reasoning, connected together as premises and conclusion. This connection consists in the recognition of a relation of identity or contradiction between the terms given in the antecedent and those connected by the reasoning act itself in the consequent. The forms and laws of reasoning may thus be ascertained by the following question :—Given two judgments (no matter what may be their material signification), what relations must exist between them, to warant us in inferring a third judgment as their consequent?

In the first place, the premises and the conclusion must stand to each other in the relation of condition and conditioned. As the predicate of a judgment limits and determines the subject, so the premises of a syllogism must limit and determine the conclusion. *Limitation* is thus a form of reasoning, as of all thinking, and exhibits, as has been shown in the case of judgment, the operation of the law of Excluded Middle. The conclusion, to be determined, must be one of two contradictory possibilities. In other words, the premises must be so related to each other as to necessitate *some* *conclusion*. If the connection between A and B, as exhibited in the premises, be such that, *as far as those premises are concerned*, we are not necessitated to infer that A is either B or not-B, there is no determination of a conclusion, and consequently no reasoning.

In the second place, since the concepts A and B are not compared together directly, but through the medium of a third, it is necessary that this third concept should be successively compared with each of the others. This comparison results in a relation either of identity or contradiction ; the subjects of the two concepts being pronounced identical whenever the premise is affirmative, and contradictory whenever it is negative ; and a similar relation being consequently inferred to exist between the concepts compared together in the conclusion. Hence the reasoning in all affirmative syllogisms is governed by the law of Identity, and in all negative syllogisms by that of Contradiction. Thus, when we reason "All C is (some) B ; all A is (some) C : therefore all A is (some) B ; " the law which determines the conclusion is, that whatever is identical with a portion of C is identical with a portion of that which is identical with all C. Here is the Principle of Identity : "Every portion of a concept is identical with itself." Again, when we reason " No C is (any) B ; all A is (some) C : therefore no A is (any) B,"* the law which determines

---

* In expressing the quantity of the predicate in our propositions, we have adopted the rule laid down by Sir W. Hamilton as the basis of a

the conclusion is, that whatever is identical with a portion of C cannot be identical with that which is contradictory to all C. Here is the Principle of Contradiction : " No portion of a concept can contradict itself." The Forms which the syllogism exhibits, as exemplifying the above laws, are those of *mood* and *figure*, affirmative or negative, which show what relations of identity or contradiction in the premises of a syllogism may legitimately determine a similar relation in the conclusion. Here, again, we see a special exemplification of the three general forms of Unity, Plurality, and Totality ; the middle term, in its two-fold capacity of self-identity and double comparison, constituting the syllogism both a single thought and a whole composed of parts ; while the determination of a definite conclusion and the exclusion of others indicates its limited character as one thought out of many.*

The further examination of the syllogistic forms belongs to the province of Logic. Before dismissing this

new analytic of logical forms—viz. *to state explicitly what is thought implicitly*. The particular instances selected, however, only express the rules of the ordinary logic, which tell us that the predicate is distributed always in negative propositions, and never in affirmative ; *i.e.* that it is actually thought as universal in the one case and particular in the other.

* In the Kantian logic, which adopts the ordinary classification of syllogisms, the categorical syllogisms are referred to a modified form of the laws of identity and contradiction, which Kant treats as one law ; while hypothetical syllogisms are regarded as dependent on the principle

portion of our subject, however, it may be necessary to say a few words in defence of the character which throughout the preceding pages has been assigned to the general laws of thought ;—that of identical judgments, in which the predicate expresses the same notion that is already given in the subject. The reader who remembers the contemptuous chapter of Locke on Trifling Propositions,* or the equally contemptuous observations of Stewart on the Aristotelian Logic,† may be astonished to find these despised propositions elevated to the character of laws of mind, and placed at the head of all thought. In truth, however, the position thus assigned to them is not only justified by the analysis of the act of thought, but is a necessary consequence even of the doctrines of Locke himself. Supposing that the act of thinking is governed by general laws at all (and that it is so, is manifest from the inability to conceive absurdities), such laws can clearly impart nothing in the way of instruction or the discovery of new truths.

---

of sufficient reason, and disjunctives on that of excluded middle. But Kant too hastily accepted the ordinary logical classification. If, as I believe to be the case, all hypothetical and disjunctive reasonings, so far as they are reasonings at all, may be reduced to the categorical form, it follows that all syllogisms will depend on the laws of identity and contradiction, and, in a subordinate manner, on that of excluded middle. The principle of sufficient reason, in its logical form, is, properly speaking, not a law of thought, but only a statement that all thought must be governed by some law or other.

    * *Essay*, b. iv. chap. viii.   † *Elements*, part ii. chap. iii.

A new truth is in its very nature partial ; it is new only because it is partial—because it is the discovery of the particular attributes of some particular thing or class of things.   In a psychological point of view, the determination of the laws of thought (be their character as judgments what it may) is as much a new truth as any other, being the discovery of a particular fact in the constitution of the human mind.   But when we consider the same laws logically, in their application to the products of thought, how is it possible for any new truth to be determined by them?   As general laws, they have no special relation to this object of thought rather than that ; and it is upon such special relations that the discovery of every new truth must depend.   Material knowledge arises from the observation of differences ; the essential features of laws of thought must be abstraction from all differences.*   A necessary law of all thinking, which shall at the same time ascertain the definite properties of a definite class of things, is a contradiction in terms ; for it is optional, and therefore contingent, whether we shall apply our thoughts to that particular class of things or not.   But if all men have been thinking, some on this thing, some on that, but all under one code of laws, what marvel if, when their attention is called to those laws, they should recognise them as what they have all along virtually acknow-

* See Kant, *Logik*, Eintleitung, vii.

ledged. Herein lies at once the explanation and the justification of the so-called frivolity of principles of this kind. They can determine only the general attributes common to all objects of thought as such; and, as every object of thought is such from the moment we are able to think of it at all, these attributes must constitute the very identical judgments which logic has been so much decried for offering. To this it may be added that Locke, who denies the existence of innate ideas, and maintains that man cannot by any power of thought invent or frame a new simple idea,* is the very last philosopher who should have condemned the laws of thought as conveying no instruction. For if the principles of pure thought are competent to add anything to the matter already given, the act of thought can in so far invent or frame a new idea; and this brings us back of necessity to the theory of innate ideas. If, on the other hand, the reflective faculty can only modify the materials already given to it, it follows that identical judgments are not mere verbal frivolities, but fundamental laws of the human mind.

OF THE ASSOCIATION OF IDEAS.†

The laws of thought, properly so called, indicate the

---

* *Essay*, b. i. chaps. ii. iii. iv. ; b. ii. chap. ii.

† For the history of the doctrine of mental association, on which our limits will not allow us to enter, the reader is referred once for all to the

necessary conditions under which one thought suggests another, as involved in it *à priori*, and in its own nature, irrespectively of the particular experience of individual thinkers. These conditions may be reduced to the two relations of Identity and Contradiction; and the principles in which these relations are expressed may be called necessary or *à priori* Laws of thought as thought. We have now to consider another connection, by virtue of which one thought accidentally suggests another, as associated with it in the past experience of this or that individual thinker. The conditions under which this suggestion most frequently takes place may be exhibited as the general conditions of the phenomenon usually known as the Association of Ideas; and the laws in which these conditions are expressed may be called contingent or empirical Laws of Thought in its accidental relations. The phrase *association of ideas* seems to be now so completely established in philosophical language, that it is hardly possible to put it aside in favour of a more accurate expression; but in retaining it, we must, to avoid misapprehension, point out that it is in many respects defective. In the first place, the term

admirable note of Sir William Hamilton, Reid's *Works*, p. 889. The illustrious writer has triumphantly vindicated the claims of Aristotle to be regarded as the earliest, and, even to this day, the most accurate and complete expositor of the whole theory, and has supplied some interesting facts in its later history from authors almost unknown to ordinary readers.

association expresses only a very limited portion of the phenomena,—those, namely, in which the elements associated together are consciously distinguished from each other, and equally correlative ; whereas in many of the most important phenomena of this class the combined elements are so completely fused together that the constituent ingredients can with difficulty, if at all, be detected in the compound ; and in others the relation is almost entirely on one side,—the first element suggesting the second far more strongly than the second suggests the first. In the second place, to speak of the associated objects as *ideas* naturally tends to limit the relation to modes of cognition, to the exclusion of desires and feelings.* On this account it would be better to describe the phenomena in question, in more general language, as those of *related modes of consciousness,*—a phrase which is indifferently applicable to equal and unequal correlatives, and to all the states of mind which are capable of connection among themselves and with each other.

In one sense, indeed, our whole consciousness may be said to be dependent, not indeed on the *association,* which term implies a previous separate existence of the objects associated, but on the *coexistence* or *relation* of

* See the criticisms of Reid, *Intellectual Powers,* Essay iv. chap. iv. ; of Sir James Mackintosh, *Dissertation* (section vi. on Hartley) ; and of Sir William Hamilton, Reid's *Works,* p. 907.

ideas or modes of consciousness to each other. For
consciousness is only possible as an apprehension of
differences ; and this apprehension is only possible by
the simultaneous cognition of the objects distinguished
from each other. I can perceive, for example, a particular colour only by its contrast to some other colour
or to a surrounding darkness. I can be conscious of a
state of pleasure or pain only by its contrast to some
other mental state preceding it; and this contrast
implies a juxtaposition of the two states at the moment
of the transition from one to the other. Consciousness is only realised under the condition of space or
time ; and space and time can only be discerned by
means of the relation between objects contiguous in the
one or successive in the other. These general relations,
as the conditions of all consciousness, have been already
noticed in the preceding pages, and need not be again
examined here.

Nor yet is it necessary to dwell on those special
relations which are necessary to the existence of any
particular mode of consciousness as such, and do not
merely regulate its subsequent reproduction. Our *complex ideas*, as they are called (and all ideas are in some
degree complex), are instances of this class of relations.
My perception of a horse, for example, is compounded
of a certain colour, shape, and arrangement of parts,—
all of which are simultaneously presented to the eye, and

form the conditions of my cognition of the horse as such. This, again, is not a case of suggestion or association, since none of the ideas thus given in combination can be regarded as the cause or antecedent condition of the rest.

Nor, again, should we include under the head of association the logical consequence of one notion from another,—a consequence intrinsic and essential to the thoughts themselves, and not dependent on the experience of a particular thinker. These consequences are all reducible to the relations of identity and contradiction, and imply, not the suggestion of one notion by another, but the analysis of a notion already given into the parts which it implicitly contains, and which are virtually given along with it. Under this class will come those relations which Sir William Hamilton has specified as *logical* or *objective* trains of thought,—in which "thoughts, though denoted by a single and separate expression, implicitly contain a second; which second the process of thinking explicates, but does not determine to succeed."* Such is the case with all terms which in their signification are essentially relative to each other. The thought of a parent is relative to that of a child; that of a greater to a less; that of a cause to an effect. But then the term *parent*, in itself, means parent of a child; the term *greater* means greater than a less; the term *cause* means cause of an effect. Hence,

Reid's *Works*, p. 911.

as Sir W. Hamilton observes, it is improper to say of such terms that they are *associated* or mutually *suggestive*, since the thought of both is already given in the thought of each.

These being discarded, there remain to be considered those relations of thought which, in the language of Sir W. Hamilton, are distinguished as indicating a *psychological* or *subjective* consecution,—a connection, that is to say, established between two phenomena of consciousness, owning to some accidental juxtaposition in the mind of the person connecting them.   Phenomena of this class belong entirely to the Reproductive or Representative Consciousness ; for, though the suggesting antecedent may be an intuition presented from without, the suggested consequent, not being given with it, is called up by the action of the mind itself ; and thus the connection between the two is an act of Representation or Thought. The phenomena of Association, in this limited sense, may be comprehended under two principal classes :—1. Those of Direct Remembrance or Memory, in which the occurrence of any mode of consciousness at a certain time suggests the fact of the same mode having been experienced at a previous time.   2. Those of Indirect Remembrance or Reminiscence, in which the occurrence of any mode of consciousness at a particular time suggests the recollection of a different mode of consciousness, which at some previous time was experienced along with it. Hence arise the two general laws distinguished by Sir

W. Hamilton* as those of Repetition and Redintegration;
namely, *Thoughts coidentical in modification, but differing
in time, tend to suggest each other :* and, *Thoughts once coidentical in time, are, however different as mental modes,
again suggestive of each other, and that in the mutual order
which they originally held.* The first of these laws must
be extended to include not merely total identity of the
mental modification, but also that partial identity which is
the basis of resemblance or analogy. Thus, for example,
I may see a man, and recognise him as the same person
whom I met a few days ago. Here there is a complete
identity of two mental modifications, differing only in
point of time, as earlier and later. But again, I may see,
not the man himself, but his portrait ; and this may re-
mind me of the original. Here there is a partial identity
of the mental modifications ; the man and the picture
being in certain features the same, however different in
other respects. Or again, the metaphorical use of the
term *man*, as applied to the figures on a chess-board, or
to the cairn on the top of a mountain, may suggest the
object from which the metaphor was derived. Here,
however little there may be of visible resemblance be-

---

* Reid's *Works*, p. 912. The latter of these laws has been usually
regarded by modern philosophers as the sole general law of association.
See, for example, Hobbes, *Leviathan*, chap. iii. ; Leibnitz, *Nouveaux
Essais*, l. ii. chap. xxxiii. ; Mill, *Analysis of the Human Mind*, chap.
iii. The former law may perhaps have been hinted at by Aristotle, but
its distinct recognition and enunciation are due to Sir W. Hamilton.

tween the objects, there is still one point in which they are identical—namely, that both are denoted by the same word.* The second law is of still wider application. Not only homogeneous modes of consciousness,—two cognitions, two feelings, two desires,—but heterogeneous modes,—a cognition and a feeling, or a feeling and a desire. which have at any past time been associated together,—may on future occasions mutually suggest each other. The sight of a place may recall to mind an event which has taken place there, and the feeling of joy or sorrow which that event occasioned to ourselves.† The

---

* In some cases the association may depend on mere identity of name, without any other point of similarity or analogy. Thus Alexander the Great may suggest Alexander the Coppersmith. On the influence of language as a principle of association, see Hobbes, *Human Nature*, chap. v. ; Stewart, *Elements*, chap. v. part i. sect. 2 ; Mill, *Analysis of the Human Mind*, chap. iii. Not only identity of names, but even of letters, is noticed by Stewart, as in the case of ideas in poetry suggested by alliteration.

† This is beautifully described by Shelley in a passage from which we can only quote a small portion :—

" You are not here ! the quaint witch Memory sees
　In vacant chairs your absent images,
　And points where once you sat, and now should be,
　But are not.—I demand if ever we
　Shall meet as then we met ;—and she replies,
　Veiling in awe her second-sighted eyes,—
' I know the past alone—but summon home
My sister Hope, she speaks of all to come.'
　But I, an old diviner, who know well
　Every false verse of that sweet oracle,
　Turned to the sad enchantress once again,
　And sought a respite from my gentle pain,
　In acting every passage o'er and o'er
　Of our communion."

sight of the surgeon who has performed a painful operation upon us may recall vividly an image of the agony which we suffered at his hands, and create a feeling of dislike at his presence.* The food which we have tasted during illness, or the syrup in which a bitter medicine was administered, may ever afterwards convey to the mind an impression, in some cases almost amounting to an actual repetition, of the suffering which we felt, or the bitterness which we tasted.†

But the above laws, being the most universal principles of association in general, are not sufficient to account for the special instances included under each. They explain why certain associations of ideas *may* take place ; but they do not tell us why this particular association actually takes place in preference to others of the same kind. Any two modes of consciousness which have once been coexistent in experience have a tendency to suggest one another ; but this does not explain why the tendency is realised in certain instances and not in others. To account for these special phenomena, we must have recourse to a third law,—that of Preference. *Thoughts are suggested, not merely by force of the general subjective relation subsisting between themselves; they are also suggested in proportion to the relation of interest (from whatever*

---

* See the anecdote narrated by Locke, *Essay*, b. ii. chap. xxxiii. sec. 14.

† See the instance mentioned by Vives, quoted by Sir W. Hamilton, Reid's *Works*, p. 893.

source) *in which these stand to the individual mind.** The grounds of this predominant interest may be of various kinds. Sometimes the frequent occurrence of certain experiences may impress the association which they convey indelibly on the mind, and serve to recall it on the slightest occasion. At other times the intensity of the feeling connected with the occurrence may atone for its comparative rarity, and an event which has occurred but once in a lifetime may haunt the memory incessantly during the remainder of our existence. In some instances, in which the repetition is frequent and the suggested consequent of greater practical importance than the antecedent which suggested it, the latter disappears entirely from the consciousness, and the result of association becomes transformed apparently into that of immediate apprehension. A striking instance is furnished by those phenomena of the senses which have been already described under the name of Acquired Perceptions ; such as the apprehension of the distance and unity of objects by the eye, in which the immediate and proper objects of sight, the rays in contact with the two retinæ, have been dropped out of consciousness, and the distant luminous body is to all appearance directly visible. Something similar to this may be observed in less familiar instances, in which we are conscious of the existence of a train of suggested thoughts remotely con-

* Sir W. Hamilton, Reid's *Works*, p. 913.

nected with each other, but overlook the intermediate
and less important links. Such, for example, is the often-
quoted instance mentioned by Hobbes.* "In a discourse
of our present civil war, what could seem more imperti-
nent than to ask, as one did, what was the value of a
Roman penny? Yet the coherence to me was manifest
enough. For the thought of the war introduced the
thought of the delivering up the king to his enemies;
the thought of that brought in the thought of the delivering up of Christ; and that again the thought of the
thirty pence which was the price of that treason." It is
probable, as Stewart has remarked upon this passage,†
that had the speaker himself been interrogated about the
connection of his ideas, he would have found himself at
first at a loss for an answer.

The three above-mentioned laws, of repetition, redintegration, and preference, will, in many cases, act in
combination with each other; ideas, once associated by
similarity, being afterwards further connected by the
fact of that juxtaposition, and acquiring a preferential
claim by the frequency of the recurrence. Thus the
sight of the picture of a man may suggest the original;
and afterwards the thought of the man may suggest the
thought of his picture, as having been seen at a former
time in connection with it. Here the elements of similarity and diversity are combined together in the same

* *Leviathan,* part i. chap. iii. † *Elements,* part ii. chap. ii.

association, as identical modifications of thought at diverse times, and again as diverse modifications of thought at the same time.* To the two first laws may also be reduced the four heads of association enumerated by Aristotle—viz. Proximity in Time, Similarity, Contrast, and Coadjacence.†

The phenomena of mental association, if in modern times they have been too much neglected by some philosophers, have unquestionably been exalted to an extravagant degree of importance by others. If Locke, on the one hand, appeals to this principle chiefly to explain some extravagances and prejudices of individual minds, later writers have, on the other hand, made far more than sufficient amends, by attributing to the power of association results which it is utterly incapable of producing or explaining. According to Hartley and his

* An ingenious, though quaint illustration of this is given by Coleridge, *Biographia Literaria*, chap. vii. :—"Seeing a mackerel, it may happen that I immediately think of gooseberries, because I at the same time ate mackerel with gooseberries as the sauce. The first syllable of the latter word being that which had coexisted with the image of the bird so called, I may then think of a goose. In the next moment the image of a swan may arise before me, though I had never seen the two birds together. In the first two instances, I am conscious that their coexistence in time was the circumstance that enabled me to recollect them ; and equally conscious am I that the latter was recalled to me by the joint operation of likeness and contrast. So it is with cause and effect ; so too with order."

† See Sir W. Hamilton's note, Reid's *Works*, p. 899, where the classification of Aristotle is examined and compared with those of Hume and others.

follower Priestley, "Not only all our intellectual pleasures and pains, but all the phenomena of memory,
imagination, volition, reasoning, and every other mental
affection and operation, are only different modes or
cases of the association of ideas; so that nothing is
requisite to make any man whatever he is, but a sentient principle, with this single property."* In a like
spirit, Sir James Mackintosh, in language in which some
allowance must perhaps be made for the rhetoric of a
public lecture, affirmed that the law of association was
the basis of all true psychology; and that Hartley, by
his exposition of this principle, stood in the same relation to Hobbes as Newton to Kepler; the law of association being that to the mind which gravitation is to
matter.† Condillac, a few years before Hartley, had
testified to the same effect, asserting that all the operations of the mind are engendered from perception alone,
and that the investigation of this process was of more
value than all the rules of the logicians.‡ Accordingly,

* See Priestley, *Hartley's Theory*, Introductory Essays, p. xxiv.

† Lecture delivered at Lincoln's Inn ; quoted by Coleridge, *Biographia Literaria*, chap. v. In his dissertation, Sir James's judgment of
Hartley is more discriminating.

‡ *Origine des Connoissances Humaines*, section seconde. This work
was published about three years before Hartley's *Observations on Man*.
The theory of the latter, however, seems to have been formed independently, and is far more complete and elaborate, as regards association,
than that of the former. Some remarks in comparison of the two will
be found in Sir James Mackintosh's Dissertation, section vi.

in Hartley's theory, as well in that of Condillac, not only our desires and affections, and the phenomena of memory and imagination, but even the universal laws of thought, and the necessary principles of mathematical reasoning, and the immutable judgments of the moral faculty, and the self-determinations of the will, are derived with equal readiness from this prolific law acting on the material furnished by the senses. Association in Psychology becomes, like the adverb in Grammar, entitled to the appellation of the universal recipient, in which is swallowed up every mode of consciousness, and every faculty of the mind.* That the foundation is not always able to bear the weight of superstructure placed upon it, may be suspected at the outset from the amount of transformation which, in the systems of Condillac and Hartley, the sensible materials have to undergo, during the process of association, and of association only. Like "compound medicines," to use the simile of Hartley himself, "the several tastes and flavours of the separate ingredients are lost and overpowered by the complex one of the whole mass; so that this has a taste and flavour of its own, which appears to be simple and original, and like that of a natural body."† Thus the sensation of bodily pain

* "Adverbium Stoici πανδέκτην vocant ; nam omnia in se capit, quasi collata per satyram concessa sibi rerum varia potestate" (*Charisii Ars Grammatica*, lib. ii. De Adverbio).

† Hartley, *Observations on Man*, prop. xii. cor. 1.

becomes by association the emotion of fear ; the pleasure of sucking, and other sensible enjoyments bestowed by the same person, become the affection of the child for its mother ; and the restraint imposed upon actions by prohibition and punishment is gradually metamorphosed into the ideas of right, wrong, and obligation. The advocates of this kind of mental chemistry appear to have overlooked the fact that ideas have not, like chemical substances, a distinct existence and properties of their own, but exist and operate only as modes of the conscious mind. Consequently, the changes effected, even granting in all cases the assumed affiliation of consequent on antecedent, must be due to a transforming power or natural faculty of the mind itself, not to a mere working of sensible impressions in combination with each other. But this admission amounts to a confession that sensation is not the source of the derived ideas, but only furnishes the occasion on which the mind exercises a power of its own, thereby framing additional ideas, or elements of ideas, which sensation does not contain and cannot supply. To this it must be added, that the power of associating ideas at all implies a consciousness of their difference from, and mutual relation to, each other ; and that thus association presupposes thought, instead of thought being the offspring of association.*

* In the above remarks we have considered Hartley's system only with reference to the doctrine of association, omitting the mechanical

But the failure of Hartley's theory is most conspicuous in reference to the phenomena which we have next to consider,—the existence, namely, in consciousness of *necessary truths.*

OF NECESSARY TRUTHS.

It is a fact of consciousness to which all experience bears witness, and which it is the duty of the philosopher to admit and account for, instead of disguising or mutilating it to suit the demands of a system, that there are certain truths which, when once acquired, no matter how, it is impossible, by any effort of thought, to conceive as reversed or reversible. Such, to take the simplest instances, are the truths of arithmetic and geometry. By no possible effort of thought can we conceive that twice two can make any other number than four, or that two straight lines can inclose a space, or that the angles of a triangle can be greater or less than two right angles; nor yet can we conceive it possible that, by any future change in the constitution of things, even by an exertion of Omnipotence, these facts can hereafter become other than they are, or that they are otherwise in any remote part of the universe. It is this characteristic of a certain class of judgments which

hypothesis of vibrations, on which that doctrine is founded. A valuable criticism of the whole theory will be found in Coleridge's *Biographia Literaria,* chaps. vi. and vii.

the theory of association altogether fails to explain ; for it does not appear in those instances in which, according to that theory, we ought to expect it. Probably no man, even of those acquainted with geometry, reads Euclid every day ; and many pass several days together without thinking of mathematical relations at all. Consequently, the conviction that day and night must succeed one another once in every twenty-four hours, ought, as far as it depends on association, to be more fixed and certain than that the angles of a triangle are equal to two right angles, or that seventeen and eight make twenty-five. Whereas, in point of fact, while the two latter propositions are conceived as possessing an eternal and absolute necessity, which no exertion of power can change,* the former is regarded as one out of many possible arrangements, which has no other necessity than the will of the Creator, which might be changed at any moment by an exertion of the same will that produced it, which does not hold good in other parts of the uni-

---

* Le Clerc (*Logica*, p. ii. cap. iii.) enters into a defence of the canons of logic against certain theologians who maintained that the Divine power could make two contradictory judgments simultaneously true. But even this intrepid assertion of apparent absurdity does not amount to maintaining that *we can conceive* such an exertion of power ; and this is all with which, as psychologists, we are concerned. So Descartes maintained that mathematical relations are dependent on the will of God, while admitting that we cannot conceive them as capable of being other than they are. (See *Responsio ad Sextas Objectiones*, and *contra*, Malebranche, *Recherche*, 8ème éclaircissement.)

verse, nor even in certain regions of our own globe. Again, on the theory of association, our conviction of the truth of mathematical propositions should be more certain in proportion to the number of instances in which we have seen them verified. That two and two make four, or that two straight lines do not inclose a space, should be admitted at first with doubt and hesitation, and asserted with more confidence as our experience of its truth increases. Here, again, the fact is at variance with the theory. A single enunciation of an axiom, or a single demonstration of a theorem, in mathematics, is as valid as a thousand; and the conviction once gained is gained with an absolute certainty which no subsequent evidence can increase.

The judgments which appear to possess this character of absolute necessity in thought, which no theory of mere association can explain, may be classified under the following four heads.—1. Logical Judgments, in which the predicate is identical with the whole or a part of the attributes comprehended in the subject; as that every triangle must have three angles, that the sums of equal things must be themselves equal, or that all men must be animals. 2. Mathematical Judgments, which express a necessary relation between two distinct notions concerning quantity, continuous or discrete; as that two straight lines cannot inclose a space, that the angles of every triangle must be equal to two right angles, or that seven and five must make twelve. 3. Moral Judgments, which state the immutable obligation of certain laws of conduct, whether actually observed in practice or not; as that ingratitude or treachery must at all times and in all persons be worthy of condemnation. 4. Metaphysical Judgments, expressing an apparently necessary relation between the known and the unknown, between the sensible phenomenon and the supersensible reality; as that every attribute belongs to some substance, and that every change is brought about by some cause. The necessity in all these four classes of judgments is essentially different from that manifestation of the laws of nature which is sometimes distinguished by the name of physical necessity. The laws of nature, if by *nature* is meant unconscious agents only, express nothing more than an observed fact in its highest generalisation; and of that fact we can only say that it is so, and that it might have been otherwise. This is the case even with those phenomena whose relations may be exhibited by mathematical formulæ; for though the mathematical portion of the reasoning may have an *à priori* necessity, its application to the facts in question is empirical, and, as far as thought is concerned, contingent. Thus, that a body in motion, attracted by a force varying inversely as the square of the distance, will describe a conic section, is a matter of demonstration; but that the earth is such a body, acted upon by a force of this description, is a matter of fact, which might have been otherwise had the Creator been pleased so to appoint. Necessity is the result of law; and law implies an agent whose working is regulated thereby.* But it is a law only to that which works under it: to an observer, who sees the results of the law without being subject to its influence, it is no more than a fact of experience. The laws of nature may be a sufficient reason why certain phenomena must take place in a certain way; but they furnish no reason at all why I must think so. As it is optional with me to study the phenomena in question, it is optional with me to become acquainted with their laws; and I can become acquainted with them as facts only. To know a law as such, I must know it as an obligation binding upon myself as a thinker; and this alone can give rise to a necessity of thought. When I speak of the alternations of day and night as consequent on a *law* of nature, I mean no more than that the alternations have invariably been observed to take place; and when I resolve such alternations into the *law* of the earth's rotation, I mean only that the earth does revolve on her axis once in twenty-four hours. *My belief* in the continuance of the observed order of natural phenomena may be perhaps explained by some law of my mental

* "All things that are have some operation not violent or casual. That which doth assign unto each thing the kind, that which doth moderate the force and power, that which doth appoint the form and measure, of working, the same we term a law" (Hooker, *E. P.* i. 2).

constitution ; but, as thus explained, it is a law of mind and not of matter.

Of the four classes of judgments above distinguished as necessary in thought, the first, or Logical Judgments, do not require much explanation. Any notion, however, empirical in its origin, must, when once acquired, be analysed in accordance with the general laws of thought ; and the result will exhibit that formal necessity which implies no more than the harmony of a thought with itself. Judgments of this character, affirmative and negative, are only particular instances of the two great laws of Identity and Contradiction, and have been already sufficiently explained in our previous remarks on the operations and laws of thought. Thus the axiom, that the sums of equal things are equal, may be expressed, representing the first pair of equals by A, and the second by B, in the form of the identical judgment, $A + B = A + B$. The analysis of a complex notion into its constituent parts, as in the assertion that all men are animals, or that every triangle has three angles, is only a special application of the identical judgment " A is A ;" or, "any particular specimen of a class has the general attributes of the class to which it belongs."

Mathematical Judgments may be divided into two kinds,—indemonstrable or axiomatic judgments, whose necessity is self-evident ; and demonstrable judgments, whose necessity depends on some previous assumption.

The necessity of the latter is derived from that of the former, so that the indemonstrable judgments alone require a special examination. Under this class are comprehended the axioms of geometry, properly so called*—viz. the original assumptions concerning magnitudes in space as such, and the propositions belonging to the fundamental operations of arithmetic—addition and subtraction.† The necessity of these judgments results from the existence in the mind of the *à priori* forms of intuition—Space and Time. The axioms of geometry are self-evident statements concerning magnitudes in space; such as that two straight lines cannot inclose a space. Their self-evidence or necessity is to be explained by the circumstance that the presented intuition, as well as the representative thought, is derived from within, not from without. For geometrical propositions are primarily necessary, not as truths relating to objects without the mind, but as thoughts relating to

* Under this head are included the tenth, eleventh, and twelfth *axioms*, as they are called in the modern editions of Euclid (*postulates* is Euclid's own term), with several other geometrical assumptions employed in the subsequent demonstrations, though not distinctly expressed. The remaining *axioms* of the modern editions (the *common notions* of Euclid himself) are logical, not geometrical principles, and depend solely on the laws of thought.

† " Though in some things, as in numbers, besides adding and subtracting, men name other operations, as *multiplying* and *dividing*, yet are they the same; for multiplication is but adding together of things equal; and division but subtracting of one thing as often as we can " (Hobbes, *Leviathan*, p. i. chap. 5).

objects within : their necessity, as regards real objects, is only secondary and hypothetical. If there exist any-where in the world two perfect straight lines, those lines cannot inclose a space ; but if such lines exist nowhere but in my imagination, it is equally true that I cannot think of them as invested with the contrary attribute. This necessity of thought is dependent on a correspond-ing necessity of intuition. The object of which pure geometry treats is not dependent on sensation, but sen-sation on it : it is a condition under which alone sensible experience is possible ; and therefore its characteristics must accompany all our thoughts concerning any pos-sible object of such experience ; for, however much we may abstract from the attributes of this or that parti-cular phenomenon of experience, we are clearly incom-petent to deprive it of those conditions under which alone, from the constitution of our minds, experience itself is possible. We can perceive only as we are per-mitted by the laws of our perceptive faculties, as we can think only in accordance with the laws of the under-standing. If, then, by a law of my perceptive faculty, I am compelled to regard all objects as existing in space, the attributes which are once presented to me as the properties of a given portion of space, such as the pair of straight lines now present to my sight or imagination, must necessarily be thought as existing in all space and at all times. For to imagine a portion of space in which such properties are not found, would not be to imagine merely a different combination of sensible phenomena, such as continually takes place without any change in the laws of sensibility :—it would be to imagine myself as perceiving under other conditions than those to which, by a law of my being, I am subjected. But a condition, though potentially existing in the original constitution of the mind, is actually manifested only in conjunction with that of which it is the condition. Space, therefore, and its laws, are first made known to consciousness on the occasion of an actual phenomenon of sense. Hence the twofold character of geometrical principles : empirical, as suggested in and through an act of experience ; necessary, as relating to the conditions under which alone such experience is possible to human faculties.

Arithmetic is related to Time as Geometry to Space ; and the necessity of its propositions may be explained upon similar principles. The two sciences, however, present some important features of distinction. Most of the propositions of geometry are deductive : it contains very few axioms, properly so called, and its processes consist in the demonstration of a multitude of dependent propositions from the combination of these axioms with certain logical principles of thought in general. On the other hand, the fundamental operations of arithmetic,—addition and subtraction,—present to us a vast number of independent judgments, every one of which is derived immediately from intuition, and cannot, by any reasoning process, be deduced from any of the preceding ones.[*] Pure geometry cannot advance a step without demonstration, and its processes are therefore all reducible to the syllogistic form. Pure arithmetic contains no demonstration; and it is only when its calculus is applied to the solution of particular problems that reasoning takes place, and the laws of the syllogism become applicable. It is not reasoning which tells us that two and two make four; nor, when we have gained this proposition, can we in any way deduce from it that two and four make six. We must have recourse, in each separate case, to the senses or the imagination, and by counting up an individual succession corresponding to each term, intuitively perceive the resulting sum. The intuition thus serves nearly the same purpose as the figure in a geometrical demonstration; with the exception that, in the latter case, the construction is adopted to furnish premises to a proposed conclusion; while in the former it gives us a judgment which we have no immediate intention of applying to any further use.

The intuition in the case of arithmetic is furnished by the consciousness of successive states of our own

[*] Subtraction may be demonstrated from addition, if all the results of the latter are supposed to be given, or *vice versa*; though it is simpler to regard subtraction as an independent process of *denumeration*, as is done by Condillac, *Langue des Calculs*, chap. i. But no result of either can be derived from a preceding result of the same operation.

minds.   Setting aside all other characteristics of those states, save that of their succession in time, we have the immediate consciousness of *one, two, three, four*, etc.   A purely natural arithmetic would consist in carrying on this series, with no other relation between its members but that of succession, until the memory became unable to continue the process.   The artifical methods by which calculation is facilitated and extended, such as that of a scale of notation, in which the series recommences after a certain number of members, vastly increase the utility of the calculus, but do not affect its psychological basis.   To construct the science of arithmetic in all its essential features, it is only necessary that we should be conscious of a succession in time, and should be able to give names to the several members of the series ; and since in every act of consciousness we are subject to the condition of succession, it is impossible in any form of consciousness to represent to ourselves the facts of arithmetic as other than they are.

The necessity of propositions in geometry and arithmetic is thus derived from their relation to the universal forms of intuition—Space and Time.   We can suppose the possibility of beings existing whose consciousness has no relation to space or time at all.   This is no more than to admit the possible existence of intelligent beings otherwise constituted than ourselves, and consequently incomprehensible by us.   But to suppose the existence of geometrical figures or arithmetical numbers such as those with which we are now acquainted, is to suppose the existence of space and time as we are now conscious of them, and therefore relatively to beings whose mental constitution is so far similar to our own.   Such a supposition necessarily carries with it all the mathematical relations in which space and time, as given to us, are necessarily thought. For mathematical judgments strictly relate only to objects of thought as existing in my mind, not to distinct realities existing in relation to my mind. They therefore imply no other existence than that of a thinking subject, modified in a certain manner.   Destroy this subject, or change its modification, and we cannot say, as in other cases, that the object may possibly exist still without the subject, or may exist in a new relation to a new subject ; for the object exists only in and through that particular modification of the subject, and, on any other supposition, is annihilated altogether.   Thus it is impossible to suppose that a triangle can, in relation to any intelligence whatever, have its angles greater or less than two right angles, or that two and two should not be equal to four ; though it is quite possible to suppose the existence of intelligent beings destitute of the idea of a triangle or of the number two.   This is *necessary matter* in the strict sense of the term ; a relation which our minds are incapable of reversing, not merely positively, in our own acts of thought, but also negatively, by supposing others who can do so.

A somewhat similar consideration will explain the necessity of Moral Judgments also. The fact of duty, whether in conformity or not with an absolute standard of morality, is in each case intuitively presented to me as an act in relation to a law of whose obligation on myself I am immediately conscious. It thus essentially differs from the phenomena of external nature, whose laws I do not intuitively perceive, but only infer them from the observed recurrence of certain facts. The moral sense, like the intuitions of space and time, is thus an *à priori* condition of my mind, not determined by experience as it is, but determining beforehand what experience ought to be ; and, though manifested in consciousness on the occasion of experience, does not arise from experience as a fact, but is given by nature as a law,. which, like other natural gifts, grows with our growth, and develops itself in a certain way, whatever may be the experience to which it is subjected. Its nature, like that of the tree, cannot be changed by the soil in which it is planted, though its growth may be advanced or stunted by this or other accidental circumstances.* But the immediate consciousness of law

---

* Arist. *Eth. Nic.* vi. 11. Διὸ καὶ φυσικὰ δοκεῖ εἶναι ταῦτα, καὶ φύσει σοφὸς μὲν οὐδείς, γνώμην δ' ἔχειν καὶ σύνεσιν καὶ νοῦν. Σημεῖον δ' ὅτι καὶ ταῖς ἡλικίαις οἰόμεθα ἀκολουθεῖν, καὶ ἥδε ἡ ἡλικία νοῦν ἔχει καὶ γνώμην, ὡς τῆς φύσεως αἰτίας οὔσης.

carries with it a consciousness of necessity and immutability in relation to the agent who is subject to it. For to suppose the law reversed in relation to myself, to suppose that it can ever become *my duty* to do what it is now my duty to forbear, is to suppose my whole mental constitution to be reversed, my personality still remaining unchanged;—a supposition which destroys itself; since my present mental constitution is included in the idea of my personality. Hence I cannot conceive myself as subjected to a different law of moral obligation from that of which I am conscious ; nor yet can I conceive other beings so subjected ; for I can only conceive their obligations at all by regarding their mental constitution in this respect as identical with my own. But I have no difficulty in supposing the existence of creatures who have no conception of duty at all (though even in this case I cannot distinctly conceive the nature of their consciousness) ; just as I can suppose the existence of creatures who have no conception of mathematical relations ; and such a supposition is indeed actually made with regard to the lower animals. This explanation is sufficient to account for the necessary character of morality, regarded as a subjective obligation of the personal conscience. Its objective character, as indicating a standard above conscience, belongs to another branch of metaphysical inquiry.

The Principles of Substance and Causality likewise

depend for their necessity as thoughts on a previous necessity of intuition ; but, in relation to both, it is requisite to distinguish between the necessary thought itself and the accidental associations by which it is accompanied. As regards material substances, for example, what do we mean when we say that extension, figure, colour, hardness, etc., are the attributes of *something* extended, figured, coloured, hard, etc.? Are we compelled to think that, besides the sensible qualities, where exists a distinct imperceptible thing to which those qualities belong ; or can the language which apparently conveys this meaning be explained in any other sense? We are not now inquiring into the real existence of this supposed substratum ; which is a question of Ontology, not of Psychology : we are only asking, Do we, as a mental fact, really suppose it to exist : and, if so, how can that supposition be accounted for? Are we, as a matter of fact, compelled to think that, besides the properties which we perceive by the senses, there exists also an insensible substratum, in which they inhere, to use the simile of Coleridge,* like pins sticking in a pin-cushion and hiding it? Consciousness surely tells us nothing of the kind ; but what it does tell us is sufficient to explain how its testimony has been thus perverted. In the first place, it tells us that no sensible quality can be perceived or conceived

* *Aids to Reflection*, Conclusion.

by itself; but that each is necessarily accompanied by an intellectual apprehension of its relation to space, as occupying it and contained in it. Colour cannot be perceived without extension; nor extension without solidity; and solidity is not a single attribute, but includes in its comprehension the three special dimensions of length, breadth, and thickness. In the second place, it tells us that all sensitive perception is a relation between self and not-self; that all sensible objects are apprehended as occupying space, and thus as distinct from the apprehending mind, whether distinct or not from the bodily organism. Every attribute is thus intuitively perceived, and consequently is also reflectively conceived, as accompanied by other attributes, and as constituting, in conjunction with those attributes, a *non-ego* or sensible thing: but of an insensible substratum consciousness tells us, and can tell us, nothing; nor do we feel any necessity of believing in its existence, when the question is distinctly put before us, disentangled from its usual associations.

But does not the use of language, it may be asked, imply a real, though perhaps a confused consciousness of something more than this? Does not the name of each attribute separately denote relation, not merely to other attributes, but to a substance? Does not extension imply a thing extended, and colour a thing coloured, not merely a coloured extension or an extended colour?

What, in short, is the difference denoted by the use of
abstract and concrete terms, except that qualities are
universally apprehended as really inhering in a subject,
though logically distinguishable from it? An explanation of this may, we think, be furnished, partly by a fact
of the sensitive consciousness, and partly by an association derived from another source. The fact is to be
found in the distinction which has been pointed out in
the preceding pages between sensation and perception.
Any material phenomenon may be regarded in two
points of view : First, by itself, as a particular affection
of the nervous organism, distinguishable as such from
any other, and present to consciousness as a mode of the
sentient subject. Secondly, in conjunction with the
apprehension of space, as extended, consisting of parts
out of each other, and constituting one element of the
complex phenomenon, which is conceived as an object.
The former point of view is indicated by the abstract, the
latter by the concrete term. In the former we contemplate
the sensible affection alone, as a state of the *ego*, without
attending to the necessary accompaniment of its relation
to space. In the latter we contemplate it in the opposite
relation, as forming one element of the material *non-ego*,
or sensible object existing in space. The association
which has contributed to a different interpretation of
these terms is furnished by the opposite class of intuitions,
those, namely, of internal preception or self-consciousness.

Modes of mind differ from modes of body, in being immediately given in relation to a common subject. While colour, and figure, and hardness, and other sensible qualities, are united together only by their coexistence in space, sensations, emotions, volitions, and other affections of mind are manifested in consciousness as modes of existence of one and the same indivisible self,—the subject of all, and yet identical with none. The personal self is neither a mode of consciousness nor the aggregate of many modes, but a substance, distinct from all its affections, though discerned in consciousness in conjunction with them. This one presented substance, *myself,* is the basis of the other notions of substance which are thought representatively in relation to other phenomena.* When I look at another man, I do not immediately perceive his consciousness; but I can mediately and reflectively transfer to another that of which I am directly cognisant only in myself. Beyond

---

* "Ex iis vero quæ in ideis rerum corporalium clara et distincta sunt, quædam ab idea mei ipsius videor mutuari potuisse; nempe *substantium,* durationem, numerum, et si quæ alia sint ejusmodi" (Descartes, *Meditatio Tertia*). From this was probably borrowed the similar remark of M. Royer-Collard (see Jouffroy's translation of Reid, vol. iv. p. 350) :—"Le moi est la seule unité qui nous soit donnée immédiatement par la nature; nous ne la rencontrons dans aucune des choses que nos facultés observent. Mais l'entendement, qui la trouve en lui, la met hors de lui par induction, et d'un certain nombre de choses coexistantes il crée des unités artificielles." (See also Maine de Biran, *Œuvres Inédites,* iii. p. 346.)

the class of conscious beings I have only a negative idea of substantiality, except in so far as it is synonymous with the occupation of space.* Some imperceptible bond of union between the phenomena of matter may exist, or it may not ; but if it does exist, it exists in a manner of which I can form no conception ; and if it does not exist, my faculties do not enable me to detect its absence. But the immediate knowledge, which consciousness gives me, of my own presented unity, is sufficient to explain the association which has led to its representation in other objects.

The principle of Causality, as well as that of Substance, has been disguised by associations which do not properly belong to it. In the first place, we must separate the special judgment from the general ;—the assertion that this particular event is dependent on this particular cause, from the assertion that every event is dependent on some cause. The belief in the uniformity of nature is not a necessary truth, however constantly guaranteed by our actual experience. We are not compelled to believe that, because A is ascertained to be the

---

* "Una est cujusque substantiæ præcipua proprietas, quæ ipsius naturam essentiamque constituit, et ad quam aliæ omnes referuntur. Nempe extensio in longum, latum et profundum substantiæ corporeæ naturam constituit; et cogitatio constituit naturam substantiæ cogitantis. Nam omne aliud quod corpori tribui potest, extensionem præsupponit, estque tantum modus quidam rei extensæ ; ut et omnia, quæ in mente reperimus, sunt tantum diversi modi cogitandi" (Descartes, *Principia,* i. 53).

cause of B at a particular time, whatever may be meant by that relation, A must therefore inevitably be the cause of B on all future occasions. This conviction may amount to a moral certainty; we may act upon it without hesitation in the affairs of life; but it has no such necessity that we are unable to conceive the contradictory.* But to conceive it possible that B may at one time be caused by A and at another by C, and that A may at one time produce the effect B and at another D, the other circumstances being in all the cases exactly alike, is very different from conceiving it possible that B may exist without being produced by any cause, and that A may exist without producing any effect. In the second place, therefore, we must ask what is the exact meaning of the assertion, that every event must be produced by *some cause*. In one sense, this judgment is unquestionably necessary. If *cause* be interpreted to mean no more than *temporal antecedent*, the assertion that every event must have a cause, implies only that no event can be conceived as the beginning of all existence, but in every case we are compelled to think

---

* Into the controversies concerning the origin of this belief it is unnecessary to enter. Whether it be derived from association, or from an intuitive law of the mind, or from any other source—whether it be conceived as absolutely certain, so long as the present constitution of the world lasts or not—is immaterial. At any rate, it is not conceived as a law which in no imaginable world, and by no possible exertion of power, could be otherwise than it is : and this is sufficient to exclude it from the class of necessary truths which we are now considering.

that it has been preceded by some other. This is the necessary consequence of the subjection of our intuitions to the law of Time. I can be conscious of an event only as taking place in time, and I can be conscious of time only in conjunction with a succession of events taking place in it. It is therefore impossible to conceive an absolutely first occurrence. The principle of Causality is thus derived from the intuition of Time, as that of Substance is from Space. To this necessary notion of *some antecedent* is afterwards united by association the empirical notion of the uniformity of nature; and the conception of cause thus assumes the form in which Hume and Brown, from different points of view, both regard it; namely, that of the invariable antecedent of a particular change. The law of time compels us to believe that there *must be* some antecedent phenomenon or aggregate of phenomena; experience, and the anticipations to which experience gives rise, tell us that this antecedent *is* invariable; and the complex judgment is apparently invested with the absolute necessity which of right belongs to one of its ingredients only.

But the causal judgment, as usually understood, appears to contain something more than the idea of antecedence. The cause is supposed, not merely to precede the effect, but to have *power* to produce it. Whether the notion of *invariable recurrence* is included or not, it seems at least to be regarded as certain that, *upon any* *one occasion*, the effect is so far completely dependent upon the cause that, the latter being given, the former *cannot but* take place. The explanation of this impression may, we think, be found in another association, derived from the personal causality manifested in volition. In the exercise of an act of will, I am intuitively conscious of two things :—First, that I am acted upon, though not necessitated by, motives : secondly, that I act upon my own determinations as their producing cause. In the first relation I am conscious of a choice between two alternatives ; that is to say, that from certain given antecedent motives, a particular consequent may or may not follow, as I choose to determine. In the second relation I am conscious of an exercise of power ;* the final determination being called into existence by an act of my own will. To this intuition may be traced the origin of the idea of power and of causation, in a sense distinct from that of mere temporal antecedence. The power of which I am presentatively conscious in myself I transfer representatively to other

* Those philosophers who derive the idea of causation exclusively from the succession of phenomena, are bound in consistency to regard the idea of power, as distinct from that of succession, as a pure delusion. And this is directly asserted by Hume, *Inquiry concerning Human Understanding*, sec. 7 ; *Human Nature*, part iii. sec. 14 ; by Brown, *Inquiry into Cause and Effect*, p. 18 ; and by James Mill, *Analysis of the Human Mind*, vol. ii. p. 256. Unfortunately, this theory does not inform us how, consistently with the laws of the imagination, such a delusion could have originated.

agents whom I suppose to be similarly constituted to myself; and thus I regard other men as being, like myself, the efficient causes of their own determinations, and, through their determinations, of their actions. But beyond the range of conscious beings, this representation of cause, like the corresponding one of substance, is inadmissible. The connection between the antecedent motive and the consequent determination is regarded as contingent, so long as a voluntary exercise of power is interposed between the two. But where consciousness, and consequently volition, is excluded, I can no longer regard the relation between the antecedent and consequent phenomena as contingent. Contingence in a single succession* is only conceivable under the form of *choice*, by the interposition of the *ego*, the only given substance, between two successive phenomena. When this is excluded, the phenomena become coadjacent; there is, no choice, and consequently no conceivable contingence in the succession. The apparent necessity of the causal relation in every single instance is thus

* It is necessary to specify *in a single succession;* as, in another sense, those phenomena may be called contingent which do not uniformly, in various successions, follow from a given antecedent. But in this case the antecedent is not regarded as the cause of the consequent at all. But, in the case of any single occurrence, we are compelled to conceive that there is some antecedent or other on which it is dependent, and which being given, the occurrence could not but take place, *unless it is the result of an act of free will.* This conviction, with the exception, is the phenomenon to be explained.

explicable as a negative idea. It is not so much a positive conception of necessity as an inability to conceive the opposite. But this inability does not depend on a law of thought. It is not an essential, but an accidental inconceivability, dependent, according to the classification made in a previous page,* on a defect in the matter of intuition. The contingency is in this case inconceivable, because contingency can only be conceived at all in the form in which alone it is presented to intuition —namely, as a conscious choice between two alternatives.† If this explanation of the apparent necessity of

---

* See above, p. 211.

† In this reduction of the apparent necessity of the causal judgment to an impotence caused by the absence of the data for thought, I must acknowledge my obligations to the corresponding portion of the theory of Sir W. Hamilton, *Discussions*, p. 609. This acknowledgment is the more necessary, inasmuch as, except in so far as regards the condition of relativity in time, I am compelled to dissent from the views of that eminent philosopher. His statement of the causal judgment, as an inability to think that the complement of existence has been either increased or diminished, is open to various objections. In the first place, I am not conscious of any such inability. Existence is only conceivable under the conditions of plurality and difference, as existence in this or that particular form ; not in the abstract, as pure existence or undeveloped potentiality. I have therefore no difficulty in conceiving that the amount of existence in the universe may at one time be represented by A, and at another by A + B. It is true that I cannot conceive nothing becoming something ; for I cannot conceive nothing *per se ;* but neither, on the other hand, can I conceive A, or any part of A, becoming B, while A remains at the same time undiminished. But the *result* is perfectly conceivable, though the *process* is not so, and cannot on any hypothesis become so. In the second place, whether we represent the new appear-

the causal judgment be admissible, it will lead to some important consequences as regards the question of free-will and determinism. But this controversy belongs rather to Ontology than to Psychology.

The above inquiry into the nature and origin of necessary truths will enable us to throw some light on the controverted question concerning the existence of innate ideas—a question which should be discussed, not where Locke placed it, at the beginning of mental philosophy, but at the end ; for its answer depends on an examination of the actual features of the phenomena of consciousness, and thus presupposes the facts of Psychology, instead of being presupposed by them. Setting aside, as irrelevant, those arguments which are little better than quibbles on the word *innate*, such as Locke's appeal to the consciousness of new-born child-

ance as a *change* or as a *creation*, we are equally compelled to suppose a cause of its taking place. To say that B previously existed under the form of A, is not to explain the causal judgment ; for we have still to ask why A became B. In the third place, the theory fails to account for the origin of the idea of *power*, which, whether rightly or wrongly, all men instinctively attribute to the supposed cause. To represent it as a delusion is not sufficient : unless it can be shown how, consistently with the limits of thought, such a delusion could have originated. I regret, however, that Mr. Calderwood, with some of whose criticisms I concur, should have charged the above theory with pantheism. If ever there was a philosopher whose writings from first to last are utterly antagonistic to every form of pantheism, it is Sir William Hamilton. Pantheistic his theory certainly is not, for it represents the pantheistic hypothesis as the result of a mere impotence of thought, exalting its own inability to think into the measure of all possible existence.

ren the real point to be determined is this :—Are there any modes of human consciousness which are derived, not from the accidental experience of the individual man, but from the essential constitution of the human mind in general, and which thus naturally and necessarily grow up in all men, whatever may be the varieties of their several experiences?* The previous analysis of consciousness will furnish an answer to this question. Every phenomenon of consciousness consists of two elements—a matter, derived from experience; and a form, dependent on the original constitution of the mind. But the matter and the form are given in conjunction, and require an effort of analysis, aided by language, to separate them. This analysis may or may not be performed by this or that man, according to the circumstances in which he is placed. The forms of consciousness in general, and of its several modes— personality, space, time, unity, plurality, totality—may or may not be represented by the mind in their abstract

---

* " Innate," says Lord Shaftesbury, "is a word he (Locke) poorly plays upon : the right word, though less used, is *connatural.* For what has birth, or progress of the fœtus out of the womb to do in this case ? The question is not about the *time* the ideas entered, but whether the constitution of a man be such, that, being adult or grown up, at such or such a time, sooner or later (no matter when), the ideas of order, administration, and a God, will not infallibly, inevitably, necessarily grow up in him." The latter part of the criticism is not decisive ; for Locke cites the adult savage to show that these ideas do not necessarily grow up. The true answer is, that experience itself is partly innate.

character, as ideas or notions embodied in language; and the necessary truths based upon them may or may not be consciously discerned in the same character. A savage may never have contemplated the notions, *one, two, three, four,* etc., in the abstract : he may not know as an universal truth that two and two make four. But he knows the difference between a man and a tree, and he knows the difference between one man and many; and his knowledge contains the same ideas in the concrete. He embraces various sensible phenomena under the single notion of a man, though he has never asked himself the abstract question, How can the one be many and the many one? Locke is, therefore, in one sense, right in denying the existence of innate ideas; for no idea can be formed independently of experience, and no idea need consciously be separated from the empirical accompaniments with which it is first manifested in consciousness. But precisely in the same sense, we may deny the existence of ideas of sensation; for sense alone could distinguish no two ideas from each other, without the co-operation of the understanding, which invests the materials furnished by sensation with certain universal and necessary forms. Instead of attempting. to classify the actual phenomena of consciousness under one or the other head,—instead of saying that certain ideas are wholly empirical and certain others wholly innate,—we should rather say that every phenomenon of consciousness contains an adventitious and a native element; and that, without the union of these two, no consciousness is possible. The criterion of universality and necessity marks the native or *à priori* element; but this criterion cannot be applied to the complex phenomena of any complete act of consciousness, but only to the element, when separated by an act of analysis, and embodied in that symbolical form which is not consciousness itself, but a substitute for it.

Cognate to this is another question of far greater importance :—What are the Limits of Thought? Is the mind capable of transcending the boundaries of all possible experience : and is such a power manifested by its possession of necessary truths? for necessity is not the result of experience. Experience tells us *what is*, but not *what must be*. Here, again, we must distinguish between the complete facts of consciousness and the several elements which are logically distinguishable from each other. If by *experience* is meant all that is presented in any mode of intuition, matter and form included; and if the question is understood to mean, Can we contemplate in thought any object which has never been presented as an element in any mode of intuition ? the answer must undoubtedly be given in the negative. But experience in this sense contains a necessary as well as a contingent—a formal as well as a material element. Either of these may be contemplated in thought, apart from the other ; and either may be contemplated in relations in which experience has never presented it. We have never seen a straight line, except as part of a surface ; nor a surface, except as composed of some material, such as wood, or slate, or paper. But when thought, assisted by language, has enabled us to distinguish these concomitant phenomena from each other, we may reproduce in imagination the straight line as a modification of pure space, and contemplate its necessary relations in that character. Thought is so far dependent on experience, that where experience is impossible, thought is impossible likewise ; it is so far independent of experience, that it can contemplate apart from each other the native form and the adventitious matter, which experience always presents in conjunction.

"The dominion of man," says Locke, " in this little world of his own understanding, is much-what the same as it is in the great world of visible things ; wherein his power, however managed by art and skill, reaches no further than to compound and divide the materials that are made to his hand ; but can do nothing towards the making the least particle af new matter, or destroying one atom of what is already in being. The same inability will every one find in himself, who shall go about to fashion in his understanding any simple idea, not received in by his senses from external objects, or by reflection from the operations of his own mind about them."* The preceding remarks will show with what modifications this statement should be received. It is true, in so far as it asserts that nothing can be represented in thought which has not, separately or in conjunction with other phenomena, been presented in intuition; but it is incorrect, in so far as it overlooks the fact that intuition has a necessary element, derived from the constitution of the mind, as well as a contingent element, derived from the phenomena of sensation and reflection.

But whether we regard the objects of consciousness as presented in intuition, or as represented in thought; whether we look to the necessary or to the contingent elements of which they are composed; there is one limitation which the very conception of Consciousness as a relation between a subject and an object, necessarily implies, and to which in all its modes it must inevitably submit. Nothing can be presented in intuition, or represented in thought, except as *finite*. So long as the relation between subject and object exists in consciousness, so long each must limit the other. The subject is distinct from the object, and the object from the subject, and neither can be the universe. Nay, · the object itself can only exist, as such, under the conditions of limitation and difference : it can be discerned

* *Essay,* b. ii. chap. ii. sec. 2.

only as one out of many ; as implying the existence of other things besides itself ; and hence, again, as a finite portion of the universe.   The infinite cannot be an object of human consciousness at all ; and it appears to be so only by mistaking the negation of consciousness for consciousness itself.*   *The infinite,* like *the inconceivable,* is a term which expresses only the negation of human thought :—nay, the two terms are, in fact, synonymous, for conception is limitation.   But the limits of possible thought are not the limits of possible existence. The infinite may—nay, must—exist though we cannot conceive it as existing ; for the denial of its existence involves a contradiction, as well as the assertion of its conceivability.   Hence we learn the important lesson, that the provinces of reason and faith are not coextensive ; that it is a duty, enjoined by reason itself, to believe in what we cannot comprehend.

From the above examination of necessary truths, it may be shown that no matter of fact can be a matter of demonstration in the highest sense of the term.   For it is essential to demonstration that its object should be such as we can construct from within, out of the forms inherent in our own mental constitution ; and it is essential to the existence of a fact, as such, that it should be presented to us from without.   A fact, as

* See on this point the admirable remarks of Sir W. Hamilton, *Discussions,* p. 12.

such, must exist independently of my thinking about it : an object of demonstration, as such, exists only in and by the act of conceiving it. This consideration is sufficient to explain the failure of all attempts to demonstrate, *à priori*, the being and attributes of God —a failure which should rather be a matter of rejoicing than of regret to the believer. If we can demonstrate the attributes of those objects only which we have constructed for ourselves, it follows that a demonstrated God is a creature of the human imagination. Such a demonstration is not, indeed, incompatible with the real existence of the Deity ; as the demonstrations of geometry are not incompatible with the existence in nature of perfect geometrical bodies ; but it adds not one tittle to the evidence of his existence ; and it encumbers theology with arguments too pretentious not to provoke criticism, and too feeble to endure it. " Mischief," says Waterland, "is often done by pretending to strict and rigorous *demonstrations*, where we have no occasion for them, and where the subject is too sublime to go far in, with clear and distinct ideas. Such attempts serve only to make that become a matter of *question*, which before was *unquestionable*, while standing only on *reasonable* presumption or *moral* proof."* The triumph over a weak defence of a truth is too often regarded as a

---

* *Dissertation on the Argument* à priori *for proving the Existence of a First Cause* (*Works*, vol. iii. p. 371).

triumph over the truth itself; and we may therefore rejoice that theology, in the hands of its best exponents, has wisely abstained from resting its claims to belief on the evidence of rigid demonstration.

Lastly, we may observe that the distinction which various schools of philosophy, under various names, have attempted to establish between the Understanding and the Reason, as separate faculties of thought, is, on the above principles, unnecessary, and therefore untenable. Whether, with the ancients, we distinguish between νοῦς and διάνοια, the intuitive and the discursive thought, the faculty of principles and the faculty of deduction from principles; or, with the moderns, especially in Germany, between understanding, as the faculty of generalisation from the intuitions of consciousness, and reason, as the faculty which endeavours, intuitively or discursively, to apprehend the supreme conditions on which consciousness itself depends; we alike divide that which is one and indivisible, and attribute to the faculty of thought an operation which it never performs. The function of thought is in all cases the same—namely, to represent reflectively what is presented intuitively; and the existence of necessary as well as contingent principles in thought, is to be explained, not by a double operation of the thinking faculty, but by the existence of a corresponding distinction between necessary and contingent facts in intuition. The hypothesis of a faculty of reason distinct from understanding may indeed be necessary, as an assumption, to support the systems of those philosophers who aim at constructing a philosophy of the absolute and the infinite ; for intuition, and therefore thought, as described in the preceding pages, takes cognisance only of the relative and the finite. But this assumption, consistently carried out, involves the annihilation of consciousness itself. But the mention of the absolute and the infinite reminds us that we are entering on the domain of the second portion of Metaphysics—Ontology, or the Philosophy of Being.

ONTOLOGY ; OR THE PHILOSOPHY OF THE
REALITIES OF CONSCIOUSNESS.

THE term Ontology, or the Philosophy of Being, has become, in the estimation of no inconsiderable class of critics, a mere synonym for barren and useless logomachy. And it must be confessed that the manner in which this field of inquiry has been frequently cultivated has gone far to explain, if not to justify, the contempt into which it has fallen. The philosophy which attempts to deduce a science of realities from the most abstract and general conception of Existence must, from the necessity of the case, deal with words, and not with things. It has been already observed, in the preceding pages, that the human mind possesses no positive notion answering to the term *existence* or *being* in general; and it follows that there can be no law of the human reason which can indicate any necessary results involved in such a notion, and no fact of human experience which can give rise to a corresponding intuition. Every existence which we can perceive is definite and particular, limited and related ; and every existence of which we can think is definite and particular, limited and related likewise. It must therefore needs be that a science which starts from the assumption of Being in the abstract (which is not a conception, but an equivocal term, capable of relation to many distinct conceptions), and attempts, by pure deduction and division, to reason down to the concrete existences which alone are objects of positive thought, must end by delivering, not differences of things, but distinctions of words. And this must be admitted to be the case with the speculations of Ontology in much of their ancient and mediæval, and in some stages also of their modern development. The science was divorced from Psychology; and was therefore destitute of facts, and compelled to supply their place by the signs of facts. Reversing the law of all reasoning, that of proceeding from the known to the unknown, it endeavoured to arrive at the truths which are immediately known in consciousness by commencing with the unknown and unknowable beyond it. But, profitless as such attempts ever have been, and ever must be, there were not wanting circumstances in the history of philosophy calculated to invest them with an apparent importance, and to engage acute and subtle intellects in the hopeless investigation. The science of mathematics was almost completed, in the essential features of its pure and abstract character, as the science of the relations of number and magnitude, at a time when its most important applications to the explanation of the phenomena of the material world were but dimly conceived, and not at all executed. With the triumphs of this science—the earliest the clearest, the most rigorous in its reasonings, the most unassailable in its conclusions, before their eyes—the patriarchs of philosophy might be justified in believing that, in the law of intellectual progress, the abstract and rational must precede the concrete and empirical,—that the necessary relations of things in general must be determined prior to the investigation of the actual attributes of things in particular. But though the relation of mathematical to physical science presents, in some respects, an analogy to that between the rational and empirical philosophy of mind, the analogy unfortunately fails in the very feature that is most essential to scientific progress.

OF DOGMATIC OR DEMONSTRATIVE METAPHYSICS.

The demonstrations of geometry are due to the possession by that science of concrete as well as abstract axioms—of à priori intuitions of objects, as well as analyses of notions. Had the geometer been confined to such general and abstract principles as, that the whole is greater than its part, or that the sums of equal things are equal,—principles which indicate merely the logical analysis of thoughts, not the geometrical intuition of

magnitudes ;—had he been debarred, as some theorists
have wished to debar him, from the use of the axiom of
parallel lines, and the assumption that two straight lines
cannot inclose a space, and other similar principles,
many of which are implied, though not expressed, in all
geometrical reasonings,*—his science would have remained to the end of time a science of words only.
Yet it is upon the model of the merely logical principles
that the majority of deductive metaphysicians have
framed their fundamental assumptions.† Definitions of
Being in various senses of the term, and of the attributes
coextensive with Being ; divisions and subdivisions, with
explanations of each, and analyses of the contents of the
several notions ; have constituted, for the most part, the
entire apparatus of ontological reasoning—a reasoning
which, being based entirely upon the logical conditions
of thought, can attain to no other truth than that which

* It is with reference to these axioms that Kant proposes, as preliminary to all metaphysics, the question—"How are synthetical judgments à priori possible ?" For the general axioms are merely analytical
judgments, in which the predicate contains nothing more than is already
implied in the conception of the subject. The special axioms are the
only ones in which an additional attribute is asserted of the subject ;
and, consequently, the only ones that can be considered as in any sense
a statement of real relations.

† "Etenim Euclides demonstrationes suas in principia ontologica re-
solvit, quæ instar axiomatum absque probatione sumit ; veluti quod totum,
sit majus qualibet sua parte, quod æqualia eidem tertio sint æqualia
inter se" (Wolf, Ontologia, sec. 9). In the same passage these axioms
are called "principia quæ mathesis pura ex ontologia mutuatur."

is implied in the formal harmony of one thought with another, and the consequent consistent use of the language in which thoughts are expressed. And, accordingly, Ontology, thus treated, obtained the name, more suited to its performances than to its pretensions, of a *lexicon of philosophical terms.** It is manifest, however, that such a method involves, however little its professors may be aware of the fact, a virtual abandonment of the problem which Ontology undertakes to solve. That problem, as has been before observed, is to determine the relation which exists between the necessities of thought and the constitution of things. But a science which starts with a definition of Being in general, commences with one member only of this relation, the notion of *being as conceived by us.* To verify this conception, by showing that being as it corresponds to being as we conceive and define it, it is necessary that the conception should be compared with something distinct from itself; and the data for this comparison cannot be supplied by a merely logical development of one notion from another.

In point of fact, the speculations of Demonstrative Ontology accomplished far less than this. The analysis of a thought may be complete as a logical process, whether answering to reality or not, provided that its fundamental assumption represents at starting a posi-

* Wolf, *Ontologia*, sec. 25.

tive and intelligible conception. But the fundamental assumption of Ontology, that of *ens* or *being in general*, represents nothing of the kind. What is being in general, apart from the special modes of being which are manifested in consciousness? When, in the crucible of abstraction, self and not-self, the factors of consciousness, and every special modification of either, have evaporated, what remains as the residuum? Absolute zero; a mere word with no thought answering to it; a being which is neither my being nor that of anything else, and which is therefore removed from all the conditions under which being is, or can be, made known to us. I have no conception of being in general which is not some being in particular; and to assume that the various modes of being which consciousness reveals to us are but subordinate species of one and the same genus, is to assume a fact which consciousness does not testify, and which, if it can be proved at all, must be the conclusion, and not the premise, of the science that deals with it. Deductive Ontology, by assuming Being as its starting-point, necessarily abandons thought to juggle with words.*

* The following summaries, extracted from the works of two eminent metaphysicians of the seventeenth and eighteenth centuries, may enable the reader to form some notion of the treatment of ontology in systems prior to the criticism of Kant. The contents of Burgersdyk's *Institutiones Metaphysicæ* are enumerated as follows :—" De natura metaphysicæ—De communi entis notione—De eo quod est medium inter ens et nihil in genere—De privatione et denominatione externa—De ente rationis—De relatione—De modis entium—De principiis incom-

OF THE SUBDIVISIONS OF DOGMATIC METAPHYSICS.

A Metaphysic of Being in general, even if successful in its aim, can only be regarded as a preparation for a more special philosophy. Even if it could solve its own problem, it would answer none of the important questions which connect metaphysical inquiries with the in-

plexis sive essentia et existentia—De principiis metaphysicæ complexis —De entis affectionibus in genere—De unitate et multitudine in genere —De unitate numerica et formali, de que principio individuationis—De unitate universali—De specibus et gradibus unitatis—De diversitate sive distinctione et convenientia—De oppositione—De ordine—De veritate et falsitate—De adjunctis veritatis—De bono et malo—De localitate, temporalitate et duratione—De toto et parte—De causa et causato in genere—De causa materiali—De causa formali—De causa efficiente— De fine—De subjecto et adjuncto—De eo quod est necessarium, impossible, contingens et possible—De potentia et actu—De perfecto et imperfecto, sive perfectibili et perfectione." The contents of Wolf's *Ontologia* are of a similar character :—DE NOTIONE ENTIS IN GENERE ET PROPRIETATIBUS QUÆ INDE CONSEQUUNTUR—*De principiis philosophiæ primæ*— De principio contradictionis—De principio rationis sufficientis—*De essentia et existentia entis, agnatisque nonnullis notionibus*—De possibili et impossibili—De determinato et indeterminato—De notione entis —*De generalibus entis affectionibus*—De identitate et similitudine—De ente singulari et universali—De necessario et contingente—De qualitate et agnatis notionibus—De ordine, veritate, et perfectione—DE SPECIBUS ENTIUM ET EORUM AD SE INVICEM RESPECTU—*De ente composito*—De essentia entis compositi—De extentione, continuitate, spatio et tempore— De qualitatibus et magnitudine entis compositi—De motu—*De ente simplici*—De differentia entis simplicis et compositi—De modificatione rerum præsertim simplicium—De finito et infinito—*De respectu entium ad se invicem*—De dependentia rerum earumque relatione—De causis—De signo.

U

terests and destinies of man ; it would satisfy none of the yearnings which compel men to undertake the study of them. The ideas of God, of Freedom, and of Immortality, are too special to be elicited by the processes of general Ontology, except in the form of Pantheism, which disposes of them by annihilating them altogether. The idea of God becomes merged in that of the sum total of existence ; that of freedom is destroyed by representing this quasi-deity as the sole real agent ; that of immortality is exchanged for an absorption of the phenomenal self into the real universe. To preserve the heirlooms of human reason intact, it was necessary for philosophy to descend from the region of pure abstraction into one in which the conception of being could assume a more definite form. And here, at least, the investigations of the metaphysician had the advantage of starting from the testimony of consciousness. Every act of consciousness is given to us as a relation between *self* and *not-self*. These two elements, as mutually related, are necessarily viewed as modifying and limiting each other. But the consciousness of the relative and the limited suggests, by inevitable association, the notion of the absolute and the unlimited as its contrast. Hence arise the three fundamental ideas which underlie the whole fabric of ontological speculation—conditioned existence, manifested in the two relative and finite forms of the *ego* and the *non-ego ;*

and unconditioned existence, implied in the suggestion of the absolute and infinite. The investigation of these ideas has given rise to three branches of metaphysical philosophy—Rational Psychology, Rational Cosmology, and Rational Theology :—the *ego* being identified with the human soul, regarded as a substance distinct from its phenomenal modifications ;* the *non-ego* with the reality which manifests itself in the sensible world ; and the absolute or unconditioned with the Deity.† But, in the prosecution of these inquiries, metaphysicians committed the same error which has been already noticed as vitiating the theories of Being in general. They deserted the facts of consciousness, to take refuge in abstractions, of which we are not, and cannot be conscious. Let it be granted that every phenomenon im-

---

* The character of rational psychology, as distinguished from empirical, is thus stated by Wolf :—" Definio *psychologicam empiricam* quod sit scientia stabiliendi principia per experientiam, unde ratio redditur eorum quæ in anima humana fiunt . . . . . In psychologia rationali ex unico animæ humanæ conceptu derivamus à priori omnia quæ eidem competere a posteriori observantur et ex quibusdam observatis deducuntur" (*Philosophia Rationalis Disc. Prœlim.* sec. 111, 112). Compare Herbart, *Allgemeine Metaphysik*, sec. 29.

† These three objects of metaphysical inquiry—God, the World, and the Soul,—answer to Kant's three ideas of pure reason ; but he arrives at them in a different way ; namely, by regarding them as all alike intimations of the unconditioned, suggested by the three kinds of logical syllogism ;—a derivation fanciful and extravagant, and which nothing but the profound genius of its author could have rescued from utter absurdity.

plies a corresponding reality; that the phenomena of the *ego* indicate the existence of the human soul; and the phenomena of the *non-ego*, that of a substantial universe; and the relation between the two, that of a being who is beyond relation;—still, in no fact of consciousness is the reality given apart from the phenomena which are related to it. The notions of an abstract Self, modified in no particular manner; of an abstract World, isolated from the special phenomena of sense; and of an abstract Deity, apart from those finite attributes by which he is manifested in relation to the finite consciousness of mankind, can be given in no phase of consciousness; for if they were, the relation and succession which constitute consciousness would be annihilated. Whether these three metaphysical ideas all stand on the same footing within the domain of consciousnes itself, is a question which we shall have to ask hereafter; but, assuming for the moment that they do, and assuming that in each there is a legitimate passage from the phenomena presented in consciousness to the ultimate realities beyond, it is clearly begging the whole question, and anticipating the inquiry which philosophy has not yet commenced, to start with the abstract notions of such realities, as if the problem had been already solved, and the passage found. Hence, like Ontology in general, the three branches of Ontology, if deductively treated, will deal with words and not with things. Unable to

verify their fundamental assumptions by an appeal to
the facts of consciousness,—unable even to determine
whether those assumptions represent thought or the negation of thought—they can but torture words under
the name of analysing notions, and arrive at conclusions
which indicate no more than a consistent use of language. Thought itself, in its bare and unmixed form,
cannot be handled in any mental process. It must be
contemplated either in the words which represent it, or
in the things which it represents, or in the union of the
two ; and the whole difference between reasoning and
logomachy depends upon a single criterion :—Can the
relations of language, which our process exhibits as representing thought, be verified by an appeal to the facts
of consciousness, of which thought itself is the representative ? Such an appeal is manifestly impossible to
those who commence their inquiries by assuming an
abstraction of which consciousness does not and cannot
take cognisance.

Thus, to illustrate our remarks by special instances,
the aim of Rational Psychology is to frame definitions
exhibiting the essential nature of the soul and its properties, as realities conceived by the intellect, under-
lying and implied by the phenomena presented in
consciousness ; and to prove by a demonstrative process
that the notions thus defined necessarily flow one from
another. Psychology is thus raised from a science of

observation to one of demonstration ; and its objects are transformed from phenomena presented in experience to realities contemplated by the intellect. The soul, by virtue of its essential nature as a simple substance, is shown to possess, of necessity, certain attributes as rationally conceived and defined—such as sense, imagination, intelligence, will, spirituality, indestructibility, and so forth; and the same conclusions are even demonstrated of other spiritual natures which partake of the generic attributes of the human soul.* The weakness of the whole process is, that it tacitly postulates as its starting-point a principle which is neither evident in itself, nor such as can be made evident by any process of thought. It assumes, that is to say, a transcendental definition of the real nature of the soul, beyond and above those facts and relations which are manifested

* The following table of the contents of Wolf's *Psychologia Rationalis* will exhibit a brief summary of this method :—" *De anima in genere et facultati cognoscendi in specie*—De natura et essentia animæ—De facultate sentiendi, sive sensu—De imaginatione et memoria—De attentione et intellectu—*De facultate appetendi*—De appetitu sensitivo et aversatione sensitiva atque affectibus—De appetitu et aversatione rationali, seu de voluntate et noluntate—*De commercio inter mentem et corpus*—De systematis explicandi commercium inter mentem et corpus in genere—De systemate influxus physici—De systemate causarum occasionalium—De harmonia præstabilita—*De variis animæ attributes, spiritu in genere, et animabus brutorum*—De spiritu in genere et spiritualitate animæ in specie—De animæ ortu, unione cum corpore, et immortalitate—De animabus brutorum." Compare Kant, *Kr. der r. V. Trans. Dial*, B. ii. H. 1. Hegel, *Encykl.* sec. 34.

in consciousness. But how is the truth of such a definition to be guaranteed? Of the soul as a simple substance, apart from its particular modifications, consciousness tells us nothing. Its permanent existence is known only in conjunction with and by means of its successive modifications. How, then, is this abstract conception of the nature of the soul to be verified? It cannot be self-evident; for self-evidence is nothing more than the instantaneous assent of consciousness; and the assumption in question cannot be submitted to the judgment of consciousness at all. It cannot be demonstrable; for it could only be demonstrated by the assumption of a higher notion of the same kind, concerning which the same question would then have to be raised. It cannot be generalised from experience; for experience deals with the facts of consciousness only, and tells us not of what *must be*, but only of what *is* or *seems to be*. Unable to verify his fundamental definition by any reference to the reality which it is supposed to represent, the metaphysician is compelled to confine himself to the relations of the language by which it is represented.

The case is still stronger as regards the other two branches of deductive metaphysics. Cosmology, as exhibited by Wolf, professes to deduce, from ontological principles, a demonstration of the nature of the world and the manner in which it is produced from simple

substances.* The world, according to this method, is
represented as an absolute whole, or entire system of
causes and effects, which cannot be conceived as itself a
part of any greater whole ;† and the office of Cosmology
is to deduce, from the abstract principles of being in
general, the necessary relations which the world, as a
compound being, must exhibit. It is thus based, not on
an examination of the mundane phenomena as they
actually exist in the present system of nature, but on
the general conception of the world, as a possible system, under which the actual system is included, as an
individual under a species.‡ Cosmology, as thus exhibited, can contain nothing more than an analysis of
general notions, and can lead to no conclusions but such
as the philosopher has himself virtually assumed in his
premises. The abstract notion of the word contains
implicitly whatever attributes we choose to assume as
its constituents ; and the metaphysical or logical analy-

---

* Wolf, *Cosmologia Generalis*, secs. 2, 7. The following are the
questions discussed by Wolf in this work, as constituting a metaphysical
theory of the material world:—*"De notione mundi seu universi*—De rerum
nexu et quomodo inde universum resultet—De essentia mundi et ejus
attributis—*De notione corporum ex quibus mundus componitur*—De
essentia et natura corporum—De clementis corporum—De ortu corporum ex clementis—de legibus motus—*De natura universa et perfectione mundi*—De natura universa in genere, itemque naturali et super-
naturali—De perfectione mundi—De ordine mundi atque naturæ."

† Kant, *Leçons de Metaphysique traduites par Tissot*, p. 144.

‡ Wolf, *Cosmologia*, sect. 49.

sis of that notion can contain no more. For the world, as a possible system of realities, and not as an actual system of phenomena, is not an object of intuition, pure or empirical; and, without intuition, it is impossible to connect the concepts of the understanding with a single attribute beyond those which they contain in their original comprehension.*

This criticism is still more applicable to the system of Rational Theology, In this science, we are supposed to start from a nominal definition of the Deity, as the most perfect being, containing in his nature the sum of all possible realities in an absolutely perfect degree.† But here again the question arises—How do we know that our conception at all corresponds to the nature of the being whom it professes to represent? The object,

---

* "Cosmology," says Hegel (*Encyklopædie*, sec. 35), " treated of questions concerning the contingency or necessity of the world, its eternity or limitation in space and time, and the formal law of its changes ; together with those concerning human freedom, and the origin of evil. It contemplated its object, however, not as a concrete whole, but only according to abstract definitions. Thus, for example, it discussed such questions as, whether the world is subject to chance or necessity ; whether it is eternal or created." A portion of the questions here mentioned were sometimes transferred to other branches of metaphysics ; but the method in all cases was the same, and the results equally barren.

† The following are the matters treated of in the second or *à priori* portion of Wolf's *Theologia Naturalis*,—" De notione entis perfectissimi et ejus existentia—De intellectu Dei—De voluntate Dei—De creatione, providentia, et potentia Dei—De atheismo—De fatalismo,'deismo, et naturalismo—De anthropomorphismo, materialismo, et idealismo—De paganismo, manichæismo, spinozismo, et epicuræismo."

which the conception represents, is either given in some fact of consciousness, or it is not. If it is not given, I cannot compare the conception with its object: for comparison is itself an act of consciousness, and cannot be applied to anything of which I am not conscious. If it is given, it must be given, like all other facts of consciousness, in the form of an object related to myself. By what right, again, do I venture to transcend that relation, and assume that what is given in relation to me is identical with that which exists out of all relation? We are not, be it remembered, discussing the sufficiency of the religious consciousness for the spiritual wants of man : we are only examining the claim of the metaphysician to found thereon a system of absolute and necessary truths. Such a system claims, in its very conception, a right to transcend consciousness. The form of consciousness is *myself*, and the facts of consciousness postulate my existence as their condition. By what warrant am I justified in reasoning from the relative to the absolute—in identifying that which depends on me with that on which I depend? A conception of the Deity, in his absolute existence, appears to involve a self-contradiction; for conception itself is a limitation, and a conception of the absolute Deity is a limitation of the illimitable.

OF THE CRITICAL PHILOSOPHY OF KANT.

The above method of dogmatic metaphysics, of which the most complete specimen is furnished by the writings of the celebrated Leibnitzian philosopher, Wolf, received its death-blow from the criticism of Kant. The fundamental position of the Wolfian dogmatism consisted in the assumption that the realities of the intelligible world constitute a system of immutable truths, which furnish the reason and the explanation of the phenomena of the world of sense. The counter-theory of Kant consisted in showing that the conceptions of the understanding and the ideas of the reason are equally phenomenal and relative with the intuitions of sense. The whole field of consciousness, reflective as well as sensitive, he argued, is the product of an objective and a subjective element, and can in no case be regarded as the exact representation of an extra-mental reality. We can perceive only as the laws of our intuitive consciousness, exhibited in the forms of space and time, permit : we can think only as the laws of our reflective consciousness, manifested in the categories of the understanding, permit. The product, in both cases alike, is not a *thing in itself,* but a *phenomenon,* or thing such as the laws of our mental constitution determine it to appear to us. The object, in one mode of consciousness as much as in another, is coloured by the medium through which it passes to reach the mind ; and, in bringing the phenomena of sense before the tribunal of intellectual conceptions, we are not comparing the phenomenal with the real, the representation with the thing represented ; we are only comparing one class of phenomena with another, and judging the representations of the human senses by the representations of the human understanding. Even the ideas of the reason, which correspond to the three great objects of metaphysical inquiry—God, the world, and the human soul—are not representations of objects actually discerned in their own nature, but regulative principles of thought, fallaciously invested with an objective existence. A necessity of thought manifestly indicates a law under which we must think ; but it does not therefore guarantee the existence of a corresponding reality out of thought. The true *thing in itself*, the *being*, as distinguished from the *phenomenon*, is not the object such as we are compelled to conceive it, but the object out of all relation to our faculties ; and, as such, it is manifestly unknown and unknowable. To perceive a thing in itself would be to perceive it neither in space nor in time ; for these are forms furnished by the constitution of our perceptive faculties, and form an element of the phenomenal object of intuition only. To think of a thing in itself would be to think of it neither as one, nor as many, nor under any other category ;* for these, again, depend upon the constitution of our understanding, and form an element of the phenomenal object of thought. The phenomenal is the product of the inherent laws of our own mental constitution, and, as such, is the sum and the limit of all the knowledge to which we can attain.

The logical result of Kant's speculative philosophy (of his practical philosophy we can say nothing at present), was to prove that real being cannot be an object of human thought ; and, consequently, that a system of Ontology, in the highest sense of that term, is unattainable by human reasoning. But, partly in consequence of the inconsistencies of Kant himself, and partly because of the sweeping scepticism to which his method at last appeared to lead, it was almost inevitable that his successors should attempt to reconstruct on a surer basis the dogmatic metaphysics which his criticism had overthrown. The Kantian philosophy had confined itself too much to negative results : it had demonstrated the inconclusiveness of the earlier systems of metaphysics : it had exhibited in the clearest light those apparent self-contradictions of the human reason which make metaphysics, in some form or other, an intellectual necessity to man ; but it had not attempted to solve the contradictions it exhibited : it had neither pointed out the way to a surer metaphysical system, nor placed the

* For a list of the Kantian categories, see above, p. 193.

reason in a position to dispense with metaphysics altogether. Kant had only succeeded in showing that the
household of human consciousness was divided against
itself : he had neither been able to merge the contradiction in a higher principle of unity, nor to show that
contradiction itself is an evidence of truth and reality.
The want which a philosophy of the real attempts to
satisfy still remained ; and to meet that want it was
necessary to reconstruct metaphysics by another method.
Kant had proved that the real, in its highest sense,
could not be an object of consciousness : his successors
accepted the conclusion, and consistently attempted to
construct a philosophy of the real which should be
above consciousness. Kant had proved it to be impossible to bring the object in itself within the grasp of the
subject: there remained the yet wilder attempt to ex-
pand the subject to the immensity of the object—an
attempt which necessarily ended in the identification
and consequent annihilation of both.

OF THE SYSTEMS OF FICHTE, SCHELLING, AND HEGEL.

The philosophy of Fichte furnished the transition
from a destructive criticism to a new form of construc-
tive dogmatism. The primitive fact of consciousness is
that of a relation between the *ego* and the *non-ego*, between *myself*, the conscious subject, and an object of

which I am conscious. But, thus manifested, self and not-self are correlative terms, existing for each other only under the conditions of human consciousness ; that is to say, as *phenomena*, in Kant's sense of the term. To attain to a philosophy of the real, it was necessary to merge this primitive relation between the subject and object of consciousness in a higher relation between the entire world of phenomena revealed by consciousness, and the ultimate reality beyond it. And this was partly accomplished by the theory of Fichte. Commencing with the mere existence of consciousness in some mode or other, he endeavours to reduce this existence to its simplest and most abstract form, by the discovery of some principle which necessarily lies at the basis of all consciousness and is independent of any empirical modi-fication. Such a principle, as regards its form, is found in the logical law of identity, *A is A.* But to give this principle a real as well as a formal necessity, to raise it from a logical to a metaphysical axiom, we must regard its terms as signifying something which unques-tionably does exist, and whose identity with itself is therefore not merely hypothetical but absolute. Such an unquestionable existence is found in the *ego.* For in thinking that A is A, I, the thinker, necessarily exist; and the judgment, *I am I,* has thus an absolute neces-sity in matter, no less than in form.* The fact of con-

* *Grundlage der gesammten Wissenschaftslehre*, sect. 1.

sciousness thus implies the existence of a conscious subject; and this subject, though manifested in consciousness as modified in a particular manner, must be supposed to have an independent existence distinct from any special modification. Hence the first postulate of philosophy is that of the existence of an absolute *ego* or unconscious subject, susceptible potentially of all modes of consciousness, but actually modified by none. The first formula of Fichte's system, "A = A," or the *ego* posits itself, may thus be interpreted to mean, " the fact of a necessary thought implies the existence, not only of an actual thinker, but of a real subject, capable of becoming a thinker." But this real subject, though existing independently of consciousness, becomes aware of its own existence only in and by consciousness. And consciousness, as a particular phenomenon, depends upon something by which the impulse is given to the subject, whereby it determines itself to become conscious. Hence the *ego,* in becoming conscious of its own existence, supposes at the same time, though it is not conscious of, the existence of a *non-ego.* And this is expressed by the second formula "$-A \neq A$; or, the *ego* implies a *non-ego.*" But this implied *non-ego* is merely supposed by an act of thought, in order to account for the fact of the *ego* becoming conscious of itself. Hence arises the third formula of Fichte's system—"The *ego* and the *non-ego* are both posited by the *ego* itself;" in other words, the relative and conscious *ego*, and its counterpart, the *non-ego* implied by consciousness, both owe their existence to the fact that the absolute *ego* becomes conscious of itself. Hence these are posited in and by the absolute *ego*.

The absolute *ego* is thus the one primitive existence, and, as such, must be absolutely free. Hence, in becoming conscious, the *ego*, by a free act, creates the whole contents of its consciousness—the modified *ego* and the *non-ego* together. The *non-ego* of Fichte thus assumes the position which in the Kantian philosophy was occupied by the *thing in itself*, being not the object of consciousness, but the supposed reality beyond ; and this supposed reality is itself shown to possess only a secondary and derivative existence, being postulated to account for the fact of consciousness ; which fact itself is the result of the self-determination of the absolute *ego*.

The error of this system (an error shared by most of the subsequent developments of German metaphysics) is, that it attempts to explain and account for the primitive dualism of consciousness, instead of accepting this fact as the principle from which the explanations of philosophy must take their start. Hence we have the contradictory ideas of an *ego* absolutely free, and yet compelled to posit the existence of a *non-ego*. The *ego*, we are told, strives to realise its own freedom. How came that freedom ever to be impaired or to need realisation? Does anything ever freely operate to its own deterioration? Or rather, we may ask, does not freedom itself imply consciousness? Is it not a self-contradiction to suppose a free agent unconscious of its own freedom? The philosophy which starts from the single being of God is presumptuous enough, and deals sufficiently with the incomprehensible. But Fichte's system, in making *the ego* the first principle of all things, leaves no room for the distinct existence of a Deity ; and hence Fichte is compelled to confess that he knows no other God than the moral order of things.* In this unsatisfactory position, the absolute *ego* is compelled to give way to a higher idea ; and thus Fichte's later philosophy, while retaining its original terminology, virtually passes over to a new position, in which he had been already anticipated by Schelling.

The rival theories of Schelling and Hegel present the most perfect specimens, from two opposite points of view, of a system of metaphysics constructed, not merely independently of, but in direct opposition to, the laws of consciousness. The *ego* and *non-ego* of Fichte, in their original form, were entities beyond consciousness, but not necessarily antagonistic to it :—on the contrary, they were rather represented as harmonising with and ex-

---

* *Ueber den Grund unseres Glaubens an eine Göttliche Weltregierung. Werke*, vol. v. p. 186.

plaining consciousness itself. But as thus implied by, and yet not given in, consciousness, they necessarily remained unknown and unknowable. Consciousness might, perhaps, justify the inference *that* they are ; but it could not possibly inform us *what* they are. The entities of Fichte were thus, though arrived at by a different process, virtually the same as those of the older metaphysicians—the unknown subjects or causes of sensible or intellectual phenomena. To make the Real an object of science, it was necessary that it should be directly given or revealed to intelligence :—there must be an absolute Knowing to answer to the absolute Being. Philosophy must postulate, not merely an object of knowledge beyond consciousness, but a manner of knowledge above it ; and this was attempted in two ways—by Schelling, from the side of the presentative faculties ; and by Hegel, from that of the representative. The former based his philosophy on the fiction of an intellectual intuition emancipated from the conditions of space and time ; the latter, on that of a logical reason emancipated from the laws of thought.

In the philosophy of Schelling, the *ego* is stripped of even the small remnant of personality which it retained in the original scheme of Fichte. That which in Fichte's system appears as an abstract *self*, modified in no particular manner, but susceptible of modification in any, becomes, from Schelling's point of view, abstract intelligence in general, having no personality, but capable of becoming personal. In Fichte's system, the absolute *ego* creates the several modes and objects of its own consciousness. In Schelling's, the absolute intelligence, by a free act, creates its own personality with its modes on the one side, and the material world or system of nature on the other.* Thus the object, which in Fichte's system is posited by the subject, becomes in Schelling's identified with it ; subject and object being merged in the Absolute, which in its own nature is the indifference of the two, and which creates the distinction by becoming conscious of itself.† The system is thus at the same time realism and idealism : the world of things and the world of thought are but two opposite aspects of one and the same being, manifesting itself without or with consciousness.‡ The human reason is identical with the divine ; and philosophy is the reproduction of creation, or rather is creation itself ; for the philosophy of the absolute is above the condition of time : it is not an imitation or repetition of the divine thought, but the divine thought itself developed into consciousness.

It is obvious to ask how such a system, admitting it to be possible or even true, can be known to be possible or true. Can the individual man, supposing him·to be

* *Ideen zu einer Philosophie der Natur,* p. 9, sqq. (2d edition); *Bruno,* p. 57, sqq. (2d edition).

† *Ideen,* p. 67, sqq. ; *System des transcendentalen Idealismus,* p. 480.

‡ *Ideen,* p. 64 ; *System des tr. Idealismus,* p. 17.

a phenomenon and not a reality, become conscious of his own nonentity? The first testimony of consciousness is to the existence of the conscious subject : the idea of reality and existence arises in and by that testimony. Can I then, existing in consciousness, be at the same time conscious that I do not exist? Can I be conscious and not conscious, substance and accident, reality and phenomenon, personally existing and merged in the absolute, at one and the same instant, in one and the same act? This Schelling's theory virtually declares to be possible ; and the means by which it is accomplished is Intellectual Intuition. This intuition is the instrument and the method of philosophy : it is the process by which the absolute becomes conscious of itself, by which the philosopher becomes conscious of his identity with the absolute.* It is an act out of time, and by which time is constituted ; an act which is distinct from and above ordinary consciousness ; which cannot be described in language or apprehended in conception ; whose results cannot be communicated to ordinary consciousness, and, of course, cannot be verified by it.†

Let us grant for an instant such an abnormal state to be possible. Let us grant even that, the state being above conception, it is no argument against it that its conception is self-contradictory and annihilates itself. What even then would be proved, save that one portion

* *System des tr. Idealismus*, p. 50, sqq.   † *Ibid.* pp. 59, 471.

of our knowledge is at variance with another, and that there is no arbiter to decide between them? *Cogito, ergo sum;*—the act of knowledge is an act of personal existence:—this is the testimony of the normal consciousness. *Cogito, ergo non sum;*—the act of knowledge is an act in which personal existence disappears in the absolute:—this is the testimony of the abnormal intuition. Neither of these can judge the other; for neither testimony can be translated into the language or represented in the thought of the other. It is mere idle boasting for the would-be philosopher to assert the superiority of his instrument over that employed by the rest of mankind; for superiority implies comparison, and comparison is an act of relation, and relation annihilates the absolute as such.* The controversy must remain undecided, until a third faculty shall be discovered, which, being, in one and the same act, normal and abnormal, conscious and not conscious, existent and non-existent, may embody

---

* The acute and decisive criticism of Schelling's theory by Sir W. Hamilton, is too valuable to be omitted in this place. "We cannot at the same moment be in the intellectual intuition and in common consciousness; we must therefore be able to connect them by an act of memory—of recollection. But how can there be a *remembrance* of the absolute and its intuition? As out of time, and space, and relation, and difference, it is admitted that the absolute cannot be construed to the understanding. But as remembrance is only possible under the conditions of the understanding, it is consequently impossible to remember anything anterior to the moment when we awaken into consciousness; and the *clairvoyance* of the absolute, even granting its reality, is thus, after the crisis, as if it had never been" (*Discussions*, p. 23).

in one process the results of intellectual intuition and ordinary consciousness, and examine them on common principles before a common tribunal.

Something like this union of all contradictories is proclaimed in the Logical Idea of Hegel, the supreme principle of all truth and of all reality.* The method of Hegel commenced by attempting to justify the assumption of Schelling, and ended by superseding it. While admitting, as substantially true, the fundamental principle of Schelling's philosophy, the unity of subject and object in the Absolute, Hegel protests decidedly against the method by which, according to Schelling's theory, this principle is apprehended. The intellectual intuition, which is demanded as the condition of all philosophy, is a faculty which any individual may or may not possess. The philosophy of Schelling thus appears to demand, as its condition, a special artistic talent

---

* In the words of Hegel himself, " Die Idee kann als Subjekt-Objekt, als die Einheit des Ideellen und Reellen, des Endlichen und Unendlichen, der Seele und des Leibs, als die Möglichkeit, die ihre Wirklichkeit an ihr selbst hat, as das, dessen Natur nur als existirend begriffen werden kann u.s.f. gefasst werden, weil in ihr alle Verhältnisse des Verstandes, aber in ihrer unendlickken Rückkehr und Identität in sich enthalten sind " (*Encyklopädie*, sec. 214). In the words of his disciple and expositor, Michelet :—" Die Idee ist als Werden, die Einheit von Sein und Nichts, als Unendliches, die Einheit des Etwas und seines Andern ; Wesen und Erscheinung, Form und Materie, Inneres und Aeusseres, Möglichkeit und Wirklichkeit, Allgemeines und Besonderes, u.s.f. sind ebenso darin zur Identität gekommen " (*Geschichte der letzten Systeme der Philosophie*, vol. ii. p. 745).

or genius, an accidental gift of good luck. But philosophy must, from its nature, be capable of becoming common to all men; for it is based upon thought, and thought is the characteristic of man as man.* But the logical process which Hegel announces as common to all men is at least as far removed from the conditions of normal intelligence as the extraordinry endowment demanded by Schelling. The postulate upon which the entire system rests—the identity of thought and being—is constantly asserted, but never proved; and this assumed identity necessitates a conception of thought not only distinct from, but at variance with, the evidence of consciousness. Thought in consciousness is manifested in the form of successive modifications of the personal self—relative, determinate, special states of my individual existence. Thought in the system of Hegel is represented as an impersonal, absolute, indeterminate, universal, unconscious substance, determining itself in opposed and yet identical modifications, becoming all things, constituting the essence of all things, and attaining to consciousness only in man. Consciousness is thus the accident, not the essence, of thought; and the unconscious process of the idea in nature is regarded as fundamentally one with the conscious development of human intelligence. Hegel's famous theory of the identity of contradictions derives its whole plausibility

* *Geschichte der Philosophie.* *Werke,* vol. xv. p. 592.

from a twofold confusion—of thought with being, and of identity with coexistence. In consciousness, two identical thoughts are undistinguishable from each other ; and as consciousness is only possible as a cognition of differences, it follows that a system of identical determinations of consciousness is tantamount to the annihilation of all consciousness. The possibility of consciousness, therefore, implies the coexistence of opposites ; but, for the very reason that there is coexistence, there is not identity. Any special modification of consciousness is discerned to be that which it is by being distinguished from that which it is not ; and in this manner consciousness is only possible on the condition of a relation, not merely between subject and object, but between a plurality of objects opposed to each other. But, in order that these opposite objects should be regarded as identical, or rather as constituent elements of one and the same reality, it is necessary that the *notion* or *thing in itself* should be represented, not as a single object of consciousness, but as an unperceived substratum, which underlies the relation between the two opposed objects, and out of which they mutually spring as distinct sides of one and the same reality. Being is thus no longer identical with thought :—or rather the term *thought* is used in an equivocal sense, to denote consciousness and unconsciousness at the same time. But it is nowhere explained how this abstract thought can exist independently of a thinking mind; nor how, supposing it to exist, and supposing the philosopher to become conscious of its existence, his consciousness is thereby identified with the object of which he is conscious.

The method of Hegel is sometimes described as an attempt to *re-think the great thought of creation ;* * the philosopher being supposed to place himself at the point at which the Divine mind developed itself into finite existences, and to repeat that development in the process of his own system. This supposition is sufficiently presumptuous; but, as usually understood, it by no means expresses the full pretensions of Hegel's theory. Creation, in the Hegelian point of view, does not imply a creator, nor thought a thinker. Instead of commencing with God, as the beginning of all existence, this philosophy commences with zero. The *notion*, whose development constitutes the process alike of existence and of thought, is pure Being, which is identical with pure Nothing.† The union of being and nothing

---

* "Den grossen Gedanken der Schöpfung noch einmal zu denken." Such, according to Hegel's editor, Michelet, is the true business of philosophy. "In der That," he continues, "was können wir Anderes wollen, wenn wir über die Natur philosophiren, als das intelligible Wesen der Natur, die zeugenden Ideen derselben, aus dem Innern unseres Geistes denkend zu reproduciren?" (Hegel's *Werke*, vol. vii., Editor's Preface.)

† "Das Seyn, das unbestimmte Unmittelbare ist in der That Nichts, und nicht mehr noch weniger als Nichts. . . . Nichts ist dieselbe Bestimmung, oder vielmehr Bestimmungslosigkeit, und damit überhaupt

constitutes Becoming;* and from becoming proceeds all determinate existence. The Hegelian process may thus be described as a creation of the Deity no less than of the world; for it recognises the existence of no Deity distinct from the world. But the philosopher, though aspiring to construct the universe, is virtually compelled to assume a prior universe as his foundation. Though he will not postulate a mover, he is compelled to postulate motion. The pure being, which is also pure nothing, has a power of self-development.† How this process takes place; or how pure nonentity can contain a principle of self-development; or how, if being and nothing are absolutely one and the same, they can at the same time be two elements united together; or how the union of the identical with the identical can form a compound distinct from its factor or factors— these points Hegel has omitted to explain.

There is a germ of truth in Hegel's opening paradox, "pure being is pure nothing," if it be understood as applied, where alone we have any data for applying it, to the necessary limitations of human thought. The

dasselbe, was das reine Seyn ist" (Hegel, *Logik*, b. i. chap. 1; Cf. *Encyklopädie*, sec. 87).

* "Das Nichts ist als dieses unmittelbare, sich selbstgleiche, ebenso umgekehrt dasselbe, was das Seyn ist. Die wahrheit des Seyns, so wie des Nichts, ist daher die Einheit beider; diese Einheit ist das *Werden*" (*Encykl.* sec. 88; Cf. *Logik*, b. i. c. i.)

† See the criticism of Trendelenburg, *Logische Untersuchungen*, vol. i. c. ii.

conceptions of man are limited to the finite and determinate ; we can conceive existence only under the conditions of relation and difference, as this particular kind
of existence, distinguished from others.　The conception
of being in general which is no being in particular, is
thus, to human intelligence, no conception at all : it
indicates only the absence of any definite object of
thought, and consequently of any power of thinking.
But to convert this negation of the relative into an
affirmation of the absolute, is to go beyond the ancient
sophist, to make man's ignorance, instead of his knowledge, the measure of all things, and thus to dogmatise
on no other grounds than the absence of all materials
for dogmatism.　And even this apotheosis of human
impotence does not guarantee the fundamental assumption of the system; for if being is the same as non-
being, and if being and thought are one, thought is also
identical with the negation of thought ; and the absolute
thinking, which is absolute existence, is, by the same
argument, no thinking at all.

OF THE SYSTEM OF HERBART.

The Idealist Systems of Fichte, Schelling, and Hegel,
while differing considerably in their details, were
characterised by one common principle.　They all
sought to escape from the phenomenal and relative
character of the products of consciousness, by placing

real being in an unity above consciousness. In antagonism to these, another offshoot of the Kantian criticism, the Realism of Herbart, sought to attain the same end by means of a plurality below consciousness. The one attempted to generalise beyond the limits of thought; the other, to individualise beyond the limits of sense. According to Herbart, all the original notions which we form of the objects presented to us by experience, whether as regards external or internal phenomena, are, upon examination, found to involve contradictions, and thus to condemn themselves as inconceivable. The office of Metaphysics is so to modify these notions as to remove the contradictions, and thus to reconcile the testimony of experience with the requirements of thought.* To attain this end, Herbart has recourse to a modified form of Leibnitz's theory of monads.† The phenomena of experience are regarded as dependent on the mutual relations of a number of real or absolute beings, simple, unextended in space, and subject to no succession in time, and thus without parts and without

---

* "Die Metaphysik hat keine andre Bestimmung, als die nämlichen Begriffe, welche die Erfahrung ihr aufdringt, denkbar zu machen" (*Lehrbuch zur Einleitung in die Philosophie*, sec. 149).

† "Herbart, says Trendelenburg, "has recourse, on the one side, to the Eleatics, and, on the other, to Leibnitz. From the former he acknowledges the pure conception of existence, but denies that existence is one. From the latter he accepts the plurality of existences, but refuses to endow the monads with a plurality of attributes" (*Ueber Herbart's Metaphysik*, p. 5).

change. We are thus, he thinks, enabled to avoid the fundamental contradiction of experience, with which all philosophy has to struggle—the antagonism between the One and the Many; we escape from the paradox of maintaining that the same *thing* can consist simultancously of various elements, or exist successively in various states. Every real being is simple in itself, though different one from another : the world of sensible experience is but an aggregate of phenomena, resulting from the mutual attraction and repulsion of insensible units ; and the principle which pervades the whole is the effort of each unit for self-conservation.

Among many merits of detail, it is impossible to overlook the weakness of Herbart's fundamental assumption. His system, by deriving the known world of relations from an unknown world of absolute beings, postulates ignorance as its starting-point, and makes philosophy dependent on an assumption whose only guarantee is, that we have no means of verifying it. The existence of the supposed world of realities is unknown ; for it confessedly lies beyond the limits of experience ; and mere thought does not prove the reality of its object. Its relation to the world of phenomena is unknown ; for the knowledge of a relation implies the knowledge of both correlatives. Its existence is assumed in order to solve certain supposed contradictions ; and the assumption itself introduces other contradictions; for the conceptions of extension composed of unextended elements, and of attraction and repulsion out of time and space, are in appearance no less contradictory than those which they pretend to explain, and labour under the additional difficulty that they are not even apparently warranted by experience. The real world of Herbart is thus reduced to the condition of an occult cause—an *ens rationis*— which might perhaps be shown to exist had we the faculties requisite for discerning it; but which, upon the same supposition, might equally be shown not to exist; and which, to our present faculties, is eucumbered with apparent contradictions which render the latter conclusion the more probable of the two. The theory solves none of the difficulties which give rise to it, but only conjectures that, under certain possible conditions of superhuman knowledge, they might be soluble;—a very legitimate position, if it were proposed as resting, not on reason, but on faith—not as explaining difficulties, but as bidding us rest content without explanation—not as the basis of a theory, but as a reason why theories are inadmissible. Let us grant, for the moment, Herbart's assertion that our intuition of objects in space and time is at variance with the laws of thought. It is no solution of the contradiction to reply that there may possibly be a superhuman intuition of objects out of space and time, and that, if we had such an intuition, there might perhaps be no variance. For we do not know that such an intuition is possible ; and we do not know that, if it were possible, it might not present still greater variance. And so long as there is variance, what right has one of the adverse faculties of our nature to demand the submission of the other. Why should experience give way to thought, rather than thought to experience ? "Which is the wiser here—justice or iniquity ?" Which element of our nature testifies to the real, and which to the phenomenal ?

OF THE PHILOSOPHY OF THE ABSOLUTE IN GENERAL.

This brief survey of the principal ontological systems of modern Germany, the only country in which the study of Ontology proper has been zealously pursued in recent times, may, it is hoped, be of some use in clearing the field of discussion, and in bringing the great problem of philosophy under certain definite conditions, under which alone its solution can be attempted with a reasonable hope of success. In abstruse speculations of this character we learn almost as much from the chart which tells us of rocks and shoals to be avoided, as from the compass which points out the direction in which we ought to steer ; and the study of the Philosophy of the Absolute is at least serviceable in eliminating elements foreign to the investigation of the truth, and in teaching us, as Hegel himself said of the Newtonian optics, the manner in which metaphysical inquiries ought not to be pursued. Various and conflicting as are the theories of modern German philosophy, one common error may be detected as pervading all of them—that of identifying Reality with the Absolute or Unconditioned. Instead of examining the conception of the real as it is formed under the necessary conditions of human thought, and inquiring what is the object which corresponds to the conception so conditioned, they assume at the outset that real existence means existence dependent upon nothing but itself, and that the conception of real existence is a conception determined by no antecedent. Ontology is thus the absolute knowledge of absolute being; and, from this point of view, being and knowledge are necessarily one and the same thing; for if the object known is distinct from the act of knowing, the latter, to be valid, must conform itself to the nature of the former, and thus becomes relative and subject to conditions. Absolute knowledge is thus possible only on the condition that the mind, in the act of thought, creates the objects about which it thinks;—or rather, that the act of thought itself creates its own object and subject; for we clearly renounce *in limine* all pretension to absolute knowledge, if we admit that the act of knowing is in any degree dependent on the prior constitution either of a mind which thinks, or of a thing

Y

about which it thinks. The Philosophy of the Absolute thus admits of a twofold refutation; in the consequences to which it leads, and in the premises from which it starts. In its consequences it admits of no alternatives but Atheism or Pantheism; atheism, if the absolute reality or creative thought is identified with myself;—pantheism, if it is identified with anything beyond myself. Subjective Absolutism, or *Egoism*, postulates self as the primitive reality on which all things depend, and acknowledges no God distinct from self and its modifications. Objective Absolutism regards personality itself as a phenomenal manifestation of some higher reality, which alone is truly existent, and to which it gives the name, but not the nature, of God. Religion is equally annihilated under both suppositions; for if there is no God, whom are we to worship? and if all things are God, who is to worship him? Morality is equally annihilated under both suppositions; for if I am the Absolute, I create my own moral duties, and cannot be required to conform to any standard independent of myself; and if I am a mode of the Divine Being my actions flow from the self-determinations of the Deity, and are all equally necessary and equally divine. The premises from which these consequences issue are equally untenable with the consequences themselves. The primary testimony of consciousness affirms the distinct existence of an *ego* and a *non-ego*, related to and limiting each other. I know myself as existing in the midst of certain phenomena, which I did not create, and can only partially control. Pan theism contradicts the first element of consciousness, by denying the real existence of myself. Egoism contradicts the second element, by denying the real existence of anything distinct from myself. But if the testimony of consciousness on this point is false, how can I assume that it is true in any secondary and derived modification? How do I know that the very language of the philosopher of the absolute means what it appears to mean, or that my conviction of the truth of his system is not itself an evidence of its falsehood? Nay, how do I know that there is any philosophy of the absolute at all, or that the book in which, seeming to be myself, I seem to read it, has any contents, or communicates any knowledge, or is addressed to any reader?

OF THE CONDITIONS NECESSARY TO THE EXISTENCE OF ONTOLOGY.

Philosophy commences with doubt; and doubt is a state of consciousness. It is necessary, therefore, that the object of Ontology, as a branch of philosophy, should be one to whose existence, at least in idea, consciousness bears positive testimony. This is not the case with the Unconditioned, to the existence of which consciousness only negatively testifies, in so far as contradictory notions naturally suggest each other. The conceivable suggests the inconceivable; the real, the unreal; the possible, the impossible; and the conditioned, the unconditioned. To assume from this suggestion alone that we have a distinct conception of the unconditioned, or that there is a distinct reality answering to, or identical with, that conception, is as unwarrantable as to assume on the same grounds the reality of the unreal or the conceivability of the inconceivable. Thought is positive in so far as it represents an actual intuition; and two opposite objects, which can be both presented intuitively, may be both conceived reflectively, whether the terms by which the conceptions are denoted are positive or negative, contrary or contradictory. But, without a corresponding intuition, positive thought is impossible; and the intellectual intuition of Schelling is thus a necessary condition of the existence of any Philosophy of the Absolute. Unfortunately for the Absolute, the intellectual intuition is a state of mind to whose existence consciousness does not and cannot testify;—nay, which it distinctly and positively declares to be impossible.

It is thus indispensable for the metaphysician, before commencing an inquiry into the nature of the Real, to ask what is the actual conception of the Real which consciousness furnishes; and what is the evidence on which we assert the existence of a corresponding object.

It may be that the facts of consciousness present nothing but phenomena, and that the real is merely suggested by language as the negation of the phenomenal; or it may be that some of the facts of consciousness exhibit certain characteristics, which indicate a higher amount of reality than can be assigned to others. Is the notion of the real positive or negative? and if it is positive, in what acts of consciousness do we find the corresponding intuition? When we have answered these questions, we shall have succeeded at least in confining the problem of Ontology within definite limits: we shall have indicated the field of search, if we do not go so far as to discern the object. But the testimony of consciousness is clearer on the negative side than on the positive. It will assist our inquiry considerably, if we can first ascertain, from the decisive evidence of consciousness, what the Real of which we are in pursuit *is not*.

OF THEORIES OF THE REAL NOT FOUNDED ON CONSCIOUSNESS.

In the first place, the Real of Consciousness is not the Kantian *Ding an sich*, or thing as it exists in its own nature, out of all relation to the human mode of perceiving it. Consciousness is given to us as the product of two factors, on both of which it is equally dependent,— the constitution of the person apprehending, and that of the thing apprehended. If either of these were changed the result might be something totally different from its present appearance. In mathematical language, the result of consciousness is a *function* of the subject and the object together, and must be regarded as variable with the variation of either. To attain to a knowledge of a thing in itself out of relation to our faculties, it would be necessary to apprehend the thing with a new set of faculties, retaining at the same time a perfect recollection of our former mental constitution and its results, in order to separate what is relative and dependent on the existing constitution of the human mind from what is absolute and common to other orders of intelligent beings. It is manifest, therefore, that the real, in this sense of the term, represents nothing which can by any possibility be presented in consciousness.

In the second place, the Real of Consciousness is not the Absolute which has reigned supreme in German philosophy since the time of Kant ;—that is to say, an unconditioned first being, which exists in and by itself, and does not imply the prior or simultaneous existence of anything else. This has been already shown in our previous remarks on this theory, which exhibits its antagonism to the primitive dualism of consciousness, in which *self* and not-*self* mutually imply each other, and, consequently, in which neither of them is the absolute. It is also sufficiently shown by the admission of the absolutist philosophers themselves, who, by basing their systems on a supposed form of knowledge beyond, and even contradictory to, consciousness, virtually confess that the absolute has no existence in consciousness. The contempt with which the majority of German critics almost invariably mention the name of Dualism, is a proof, among many others, of the necessity which they feel of lifting the standard of philosophy in opposition to the authority of consciousness.

In the third place, the Real of Consciousness is not the *Substance* or *Matter* of an earlier school of metaphysiciaus; that is to say, the insensible substratum of sensible qualities, viewed by itself, apart from those attributes by which it is made known to experience. We may not commence our inquiries with the assumption that the shape, the colour, the smell, and other sensible qualities of a rose are one thing, and that the rose itself, the thing possessing the qualities, is another. "The idea," says Locke, "to which we give the general name *substance*, being nothing but the supposed, but unknown support of those qualities we find existing, which we imagine cannot subsist *sine re substante*, without something to support them, we call that support *substantia;* which, according to the true import of the word, is, in plain English, *standing under* or *upholding*."* "I perceive," says Reid, "in a billiard ball, figure, colour, and motion; but the ball is not figure, nor is it colour, nor motion, nor all

* *Essay*, b. ii. chap. xxiii. sec. 2.

these taken together; it is something that has figure, and colour, and motion. This is a dictate of nature, and the belief of all mankind."* Without attempting at present to anticipate the necessary inquiry into the validity of that law of belief which apparently compels us to refer a plurality of attributes to a single subject, we may safely assert that the notion of such a subject, as a being distinct from its attributes, is utterly empty and meaningless; and that no such being can be the object of metaphysical research. Consciousness does not testify that such a being exists or is conceivable ;—nay, such a testimony would be impossible without the annihilation of consciousness itself. For consciousness is possible only under the condition of difference. I can be conscious of an object, as such, only by being conscious of it as distinguished from other objects; and this distinction is only possible by means of the special attributes which the object possesses. Deprive the billiard ball of its figure and colour, and all other sensible qualities, and do the same to the table on which it stands; and how is the ball to be distinguished from the table? The residuum, if there is any, is neither the ball as a ball, nor the table as a table, nor any one thing as distinguishable from any other thing, nor an object of consciousness as distinguished from the subject. It is the vague and empty notion of being in general which is no

* *Intellectual Powers*, Essay ii. chap. xix.

being in particular—pure existence, which is identical, so far as human thought is concerned, with pure nothing. Things can be distinguished from each other only by their attributes ; and to be conscious of a thing apart from its attributes, is to be conscious of a difference with no difference to be conscious of. " The knowledge of pure substance distinct from its qualities," says M. Cousin, " is impossible, for the simple reason that no such substance exists. Every real being is of such or such a kind ; it is either this or that. If it is real, it is determinate ; and to be determinate is to possess certain manners of being, transitory and accidental, or constant and essential. The knowledge of being in itself is therefore not only forbidden to the human mind, but is contrary to the nature of things.* Whether the existence of a thing distinct from any and all of its attributes be, as Reid says, a dictate of nature or not ; at any rate, in the instance which he adduces, it is not *presented* as a fact of consciousness, but *inferred* from the presence of the attributes ; and, in maintaining the veracity of the facts of consciousness themselves, we do not therefore maintain the validity of all the inferences to which those facts appear to lead. What is the exact fact upon which this inference is grounded, the principle on which it is made, and the amount of credit due to it, we shall endeavour to show hereafter by an examination of conscious-

---

* *Histoire de la Philosophie Morale au dix-huitième siècle,* Leçon xii.

ness itself.   For the present, it is sufficient to say, that the fact, whatever it may be, is not a direct cognition of the existence of a substratum of material attributes.

It thus appears that the celebrated hypothesis of Bishop Berkeley, so far as it merely denies the existence of matter, is not in any way contrary to common-sense (if by common-sense is meant the direct evidence of consciousness); inasmuch as it only denies that concerning which consciousness offers no evidence at all. For *matter*, in Berkeley's sense, does not mean anything which can be perceived by the senses; but only, as Locke defines it, "the supposed, but unknown support of those qualities we find existing."   " I do not argue," says the bishop, " against the existence of any one thing that we can apprehend either by sense or reflection. That the things I see with mine eyes and touch with my hands do exist, really exist, I make not the least question. . . . If the word *substance* be taken, in the vulgar sense, for a combination of sensible qualities, such as extension, solidity, weight, and the like, this we cannot be accused of taking away.   But if it be taken in a philosophic sense, for the *support of* accidents or *qualities without the mind*, then, indeed, I acknowledge that we take it away, if one can be said to take away that which never had any existence, not even in the imagination."*   And had Berkeley confined himself to

* *Principles of Human Knowledge*, xxxv. xxxvii.

the sceptical side of the question—had he contented himself with maintaining that we have no evidence for asserting that matter, in this sense of the term, has any existence—he would have said no more than the testimony of consciousness fully warrants. But when he went a step beyond this, and not only doubted the existence of matter but asserted its non-existence, he transcended the evidence of consciousness on the negative side, as much as his opponents did on the positive. If consciousness says nothing about the existence of matter at all, we are equally incompetent to affirm or to deny. The sceptic, so long as he remains a mere sceptic, is unassailable ; the dogmatist, whether in affirmation or in negation, equally dogmatises on the ground of his own ignorance. But, in admitting one portion of Berkeley's theory as perfectly tenable, we do not therefore accept his entire system of idealism. It is quite possible to take an intermediate course ; to admit, with Berkeley, that we have no right to assert the existence of any other kind of matter than that which is presented in consciousness ; but to deny his other main position, that we are conscious only of our own ideas. If, in any mode of consciousness whatever, an external object is *directly presented* as existing in relation to me, that object, though composed of sensible qualities only, is given as a material substance, existing as a distinct reality, and not merely as a mode of my own mind. And to this extent the arguments of Reid and his followers, however inaccurate their analysis of consciousness may be in some of its details, are valid against idealism.

The antagonism of the Scottish philosophers to the theory of Berkeley arose more on account of its supposed remote consequences, than of its immediate conclusions. It was supposed to furnish a legitimate foundation for the scepticism of Hume, who argued against the existence of mind on the same grounds on which Berkeley had denied the existence of matter. Within myself, he urged, I am conscious only of impressions and ideas, as in external sensation I am conscious only of extension, figure, and so forth. The substance called *mind* may therefore be a mere fiction, imagined for the support of the internal states of which I am conscious, just as the substance called *matter* is imagined for the support of sensible qualities.* But, in order that this conclusion may legitimately follow from Berkeley's principles, we must concede an additional premise, which Berkeley by no means admits,† namely, that the evidence of consciousness in relation to matter and to mind is of

---

* See *Treatise of Human Nature*, part iv. secs. 5, 6.

† In the third dialogue between Hylas and Philonous, Berkeley expressly says :—" I know or am conscious of my own being ; and that I myself am not my ideas, but somewhat else,—a thinking, active principle, that perceives, knows, wills, and operates about ideas." Here he distinctly denies the position of Locke, and refutes by anticipation Hume's deduction from his own principles.

precisely the same character. If, as Locke maintained, and as the antagonists of Hume allowed, we have no immediate consciousness of *self*, but only of its several modes, the sceptical conclusion necessarily follows ; and Hume, as a professed sceptic, had nothing to do with correcting the received dogmas of philosophy, but only with exhibiting their ultimate consequences. Those consequences can only be refuted if, by a more exact analysis of the facts of consciousness, it can be shown that the personal self, as the one permanent subject of various successive modes, is directly presented in intuition along with its several affections. But this analysis neither Reid nor Stewart attempted ; and the consequence was, that in their hands the sceptical argument remained, in its main positions, unrefuted.

In the fourth place, it may be shown, by the same consideration, that the Real of Consciousness is not the *First Matter* of the peripatetic philosophy ; that is to say, an universal substratum, common to all objects of sense, and subject to the changes of form which constitute this or that definite object.[*] This first matter is, indeed, nothing more than the *matter* of the last hypothesis, stripped of some of its more glaring incongruities, but not thereby made more accessible to consciousness. The theory of a first matter avoids, indeed, the absurdity

---

[*] Aristotle, *Phys. Ausc.* i. 7. Compare Harris, *Philosophical Arrangements*, chap. iv.

of saying that any one particular thing, such as a bil-
liard-ball, is something distinct from its own sensible
qualities ; but the supposition which it assumes instead
—that of a subject which is all things in capacity, and
nothing actually—is only a more logical negation of all
difference, and therefore of all consciousness ; for consciousness is possible only through difference.   The psychological value of the axiom on which this theory
apparently rests—namely, that all things are changed,
and nothing created or destroyed ; so that the quantity
of real matter in the world can never be conceived as
increased or diminished—has been examined in a previous passage ; but even if a greater amount of truth be
assigned to this principle than our previous remarks
have accorded to it—whether it be regarded as a law,
or merely as an impotence of mind—it is at any rate a
phenomenon of mind and not of matter: it can be explained on psychological grounds only ; and it presents
no fact in the constitution of things, but only a mode of
our conceiving them.   Unless the truth of that conception can be guaranteed by a positive intuition of its object, which in this case is impossible, we are not warranted in elevating a mere consciousness of the limit of
our own powers of thought into a measure of the conditions of all possible existence.

In the fifth place, the Real of Consciousness, so far
as the material world is concerned, is not to be found in

the simple Elements into which bodies may be ultimately resolved.   It does not express any metaphysical
distinction to say that what appears to be air is in
reality oxygen and nitrogen ; or that water, ice, and
steam are but different appearances of the same ele-
mentary particles.   This is perfectly true as a physical
fact ; but it contributes nothing towards the solution of
any problem of metaphysics.   The chemical element, as
well as the compound, is an object of sense, and its presence must be tested by sensible criteria.   If, then, there
is any apparent antagonism between sense and thought ;
if there is any room for doubt whether what sense regards as a reality independent of myself, thought may
not resolve into a transitory affection of my own mind ;
such a doubt is equally possible, whether the object
of sense be more or less minute, whether its presence be
manifested by the immediate evidence of sight, or by the
indirect test of experiment.   In one respect, indeed, the
chemical element has less of the character of a real object than the compound into which it enters ; inasmuch
as its presence must frequently be inferred rather than
perceived—detected in its effects on something else, not
in its own proper nature.   There will still remain the
question, What is the *thing itself*, as distinguished from
the test by which we discover its presence on particular
occasions ?

In like manner, it may be shown, lastly, that the

metaphysical question is in no way simplified by any theóry, such as that of Boscovich, which regards the senses as immediately cognisant, not of Matter in itself, but only of the attractive and repulsive Forces which one particle exercises on another. For the ultimate atoms of matter being, upon this hypothesis, never presented in consciousness, could never have given rise to the distinction, which apparently exists in our minds, between the real and the phenomenal. That distinction must be suggested by something of which we are conscious ; and if we are conscious only of forces, it must depend upon some difference in the forces themselves. The forces thus inherit all the metaphysical difficulties of the matter which they represent ; and we must still have recourse to the analysis of consciousness itself, to determine in what manner the metaphysical doubt could have originated, and what are the data available for its solution. To inquire into the truth and value of Boscovich's theory itself, is a question of Physics, not of Metaphysics.

OF THE REAL AS GIVEN IN CONSCIOUSNESS.

Having thus simplified the problem by the elimination of foreign elements, we have next to inquire what is the positive testimony of consciousness itself, as regards the existence of a distinction between the phenomenal and the real, and how far the distinction thus indicated will enable us to ascertain the nature of the respective objects to which it refers? for that the distinction has a foundation in consciousness, however much its meaning may have been misinterpreted, is manifest, if it were only from the existence of such misinterpretation. Rightly or wrongly, men have thought that such a distinction exists—why they have thought so, the examination of consciousness itself can alone explain.

It is necessary, in the first place, to determine clearly what it is of which we are in search. We must know what is meant by *reality*, and what by *appearance*, before we can classify the facts of consciousness as indicating one or the other. For here there is an ambiguity which, if not cleared up at the outset, may confuse the whole subsequent inquiry. It is one thing to distinguish between the real and the phenomenal, as exhibited in the facts of consciousness themselves; it is another to determine what are really facts of consciousness and what are not. There are judgments which are sometimes supposed to rest on the immediate testimony of consciousness, but which, rightly interpreted, are inferences only remotely suggested by it. I think I see a friend at a distance; on a nearer approach he turns out to be a stranger. Here the apparent testimony of sight is in reality an inference pursued through many successive stages. In the first place, I am not really conscious by sight of the presence of a distant object at all, but infer its presence from the consciousness of certain affections of the organ of vision. In the second place, when I have projected by association the impression of a certain coloured surface into a space exterior to my organism, I do not thereby know that this surface is a man ; this is a second inference, implying memory, and comparison, and recognition of certain specific attributes. In the third place, when I have so far obliterated these connecting-links as to fancy that I see a man, I do not thereby know a friend from a stranger ; this is another act of inference, implying memory of certain individual features, and comparison of them with my present impression. Yet all this is performed with such rapidity as to appear an immediate act of perception ; and John or Thomas is, in ordinary apprehension, as much an object of sight as redness or blueness.

This distinction is irrelevant to our present inquiry. When we ask how reality and appearance may be distinguished from each other by the testimony of consciousness itself, it is to be supposed that we have already ascertained what are facts of consciousness, and what are not. But this being granted, a second ground of distinction presents itself. Every fact of consciousness, as such, guarantees the existence of its object, so long as it is actually present. But there are some facts of consciousness which are instinctively acknowledged tó indicate only the relative and transitory existence of their objects, and there are others which are supposed to imply something more than this. An affection of the nervous organism exists only as it is felt, and ceases to exist when it is felt no longer; it has no independent existence of its own, but is a mode of my being, created by the act of consciousness, and ending along with it. But, on the other hand, all men instinctively believe, and will believe in spite of the arguments of the idealist, that we are immediately conscious of an external world, and that that world exists when we are not conscious of it. The impression which the sight of a mountain makes on my optic nerve is destroyed when I shut my eyes; but no man believes that the mountain is destroyed along with it. Consciousness testifies that we have this belief; and on this testimony metaphysical systems have been built, which, however widely some of them may have wandered from the true solution of the question, all alike prove that the question itself is suggested by consciousness.

This latter description properly belongs to Ontology; the former to Psychology; though, in actual discussion, the two have been frequently mixed together. Among the facts, or supposed facts, of consciousness, the impressions of the senses, from the one or the other of the, above points of view, have been, almost from the commencement of philosophy, especially noted as indicating appearance and not reality. The following may be cited among the arguments adduced in proof of this position :—In the first place, sensation is but the result of a transitory relation between the organ and its object; —colour, for example, exists neither in the eye by itself nor in the visible object by itself, but is produced by their temporary juxtaposition.* In the second place, the same object presents different impressions to the same sense, according to the condition of the sensitive organ itself.† A man with the jaundice sees all objects as yellow : one afflicted with colour-blindness sees as blue that which, in a healthy state of the eyesight, appears as red : to a diseased palate the taste appears bitter which a sound palate receives as sweet. But if the abnormal state of the organs of sense produces an impression which is acknowledged to be apparent only, why should the normal state be regarded as giving a knowledge of reality? If the unusual appearance is wholly dependent on an extraordinary condition of the organism, is not the usual appearance equally depend-ent on the ordinary condition? And how can either of them represent a real object, which in itself is unaf-fected by any change in the condition of the person per-ceiving it ? In the third place, the same object presents

---

* Plato, *Theatetus*, pp. 153, 156.

† Plato, *Theatetus*, p. 159. Pyrrho *apud* Laert. ix. 82. Sext. Empir. *Pyrrh. Hyp.* i. 100.

a different quality to different senses. An apple, for instance, is perceived by the sight as yellow, by the taste as sweet, by the smell as fragrant.* If the several objects of sense are distinct realities, the apple is not one, but many; if, on the contrary, the apple is, as we are compelled to conceive it, one, it follows that the impressions of the senses are not real things, but unreal appearances of that which in itself is not diverse but uniform. In the fourth place, the same object presents different impressions to the same sense, according to the different circumstances in which it is placed. A tower, which at one distance appears to the eye as square, at another seems to be round; at one distance it appears larger, at another smaller.† But the tower itself undergoes no change of figure or size. It is manifest, therefore, that one at least of these impressions exhibits not that which is, but that which seems to be; and unless some reason can be assigned for preferring one to the other, we may reasonably conclude that both do so. In the fifth place, the sensible impression may take place without the presence of any external object by which it can be caused. Such is the case in dreams and spectral illusions, in which we appear to see, with all the vividness of actual

---

* Pyrrho *apud* Laert. ix. 81. Sext. Empir. *Pyrrh. Hyp.* i. 90. Cf. Plato, *Sophistes*, p. 251.

† Pyrrho *apud* Laert. ix. 85. Sext. Empir. *Pyrrh. Hyp.* i. 118. Hume, *Essay on the Academical Philosophy.*

sight, things which have no existence except in our own imagination.* But if this actually takes place in some instances, why may it not take place in all? By what criterion are we to distinguish the true from the false ; or how can we be sure that the senses present to us real objects, when their testimony can be so well counterfeited by mere phantoms ?

These difficulties are considerably increased, if we adopt, with the vast majority of philosophers in ancient and modern times, the representative theory of perception, and maintain that like can only take cognisance of like, and therefore that the mind, which is the seat of all consciousness, perceives through the senses, not material objects, but only its own ideas, by which material objects are represented. For how are we to guarantee that the idea has any resemblance to the object which it represents? To know that two things resemble each other, I must compare them together. But the material world, according to this hypothesis, is never perceived at all, and therefore cannot be compared with its sup-

---

* Plato, *Theatetus*, p. 157. Pyrrho *apud* Laert. ix. 82. Sext. Empir. *Pyrrh. Hyp.* i. 104. We have not noticed those arguments which are drawn from the comparison of one man with another, or of men with brutes. We are treating only of the distinctions indicated by consciousness ; and we have no access to the consciousness of any other creature than ourselves. A complete account of the earlier and later tropes of scepticism is given by Sextus Empiricus, *Pyrrh. Hyp.* i. 36, 164. See also Hegel, *Geschichte der Philosophie, Werke*, xiv. p. 491.

posed representative.* And the ideas, whether regarded as immaterial objects distinct from the percipient mind, or as modifications of the mind itself, are called into existence in and by the act of perception, and have no existence except when they are perceived.† On this hypothesis we are not warranted in affirming the existence of that of which we are never conscious ; and the conclusion to which it naturally leads is that which denies the existence of matter, and makes the whole external world a series of phenomena dependent on the action of the mind.

Such are a few of the grounds on which philosophers in all ages have maintained that the senses are the sources of deception, not of truth, and are conversant with appearance only, not with reality. And a more accurate acquaintance with the physiology of the sensitive organs confirms the latter part of this verdict, though it furnishes a defence against the former. The senses do not deceive us with regard to an external world, because, rightly interpreted, they tell us nothing at all about it. We are deceived, not in the facts to

---

* Sext. Empir. *Pyrrh. Hyp.* ii. 74. Berkeley, *Human Knowledge,* part i. sect. 8 ; Cousin, *Cours de* 1829, Leçon 21.

† Berkeley, *Human Knowledge,* part i. sec. 3 ; *Dialogues between Hylas and Phylonous,* Dial. ii. Berkeley goes so far as to deduce from this position an argument for the being of God ; on the ground that the world cannot have a continuous existence, except in some continuously percipient mind.

which the senses bear witness, but in the inferences which we draw from them. The colour and the savour appear different in different states of health, because, in truth, as affections of the nerves of sight and taste, they are different in different conditions of the organism. The sensible qualities of a body are in fact, as they appear to be, distinct affections of the several organs; and it is not sense which tells us that these different qualities constitute a single thing. The tower which appears to change its shape and size as we approach it, is not in reality the same visible object at any two steps of our progress. What we actually see at any moment is nothing but the rays of light in contact with the organ of vision; and every change of position places us in contact with a different complement of rays. The dream or the spectral apparition is as veritable an affection of the optic nerve as the commonest impression of sight; and we err only in inferring the presence of an external object, of which the sight itself in no case tells us anything. But while we may thus defend the senses against the charge of deception, we are in another respect compelled to acknowledge that their objects are not things but phenomena. An affection of the nerves of sense is not a distinct reality existing independently of myself; it is but a transitory mode of my own consciousness, which exists only while I am conscious of it. A real object is not dependent for its being and properties on my being aware of them ; it has an existence and attributes of its own, whether I am at this moment conscious of them or not. But the proper objects of the bodily senses—colours, sounds, flavours, savours, and tactual sensations—exist, as such, only in my consciousness, and cease to exist when my consciousness ceases. They may be caused by some permanent reality or realities independent of me ; but of the existence and nature of this reality the senses tell us nothing.

It is not, therefore, to the senses, properly so called, that we must look for the distinction between Reality and Appearance in the material world. The only attribute of matter which these make known to us is the extension of our own organism ; and, with regard to this, the distinction in question has no place. Were the senses the only channels of communication between mind and matter, we could never have thought of asking how much of that communication is real, and how much phenomenal. Whether my nervous organism exists, as an extended substance, out of the act of perception in which its extension is manifested, is a question which could never have arisen from the act of sensitive perception alone ; for, in order to ask such a question, I must first be enabled to separate in thought the object of perception from the act of perceiving it, and thus to constitute it an extra-organic reality ; and to do this, the extra-organic world must first be presented in some form of intuition. Apart from the associations which the senses derive from this intuition, all modes of perception would be regarded as equally real, or equally phenomenal; for the real and the phenomenal could never have been conceived as contrasted with each other.

The analysis of the facts of external intuition, which has been given in the preceding pages, will enable us to ascertain the meaning of the distinction, and to determine the limits within which the question which it raises can be intelligibly answered. Resistance to the locomotive energy is the only mode of consciousness which directly tells us of the existence of an external world ; and the attributes which are made known to us in that relation are the only ones which are directly given as constituting a material reality. These attributes are *occupation of space*, implying size and figure: and *resistance*, more or less stubborn, implying the impossibility of two bodies occupying the same place. And these are, in fact, the tests of reality to which we instinctively appeal on all occasions, even where the circumstances of the case do not permit their actual application. A body is necessarily conceived as in space, and an external body as in a space exterior to our organism. This implies the occupation of a portion of space, which is size, and the limitation by surrounding space, which is figure. But I may not be able, in particular cases, to verify this conception by any empirical test. I may be placed blindfold against a wall, of which I am not able to feel the extremities. I cannot therefore pronounce empirically, either directly, from contact, or indirectly, from sight, that it is limited in its length and height, or that it is square, or circular, or of any other known figure. But I am compelled to believe that it has a definite size and figure, and that I should be able to feel them if I were in some other position. Again, a volume of smoke may offer no perceptible resistance to the motion of my arm. But here, again, I am compelled to believe that it offers some resistance, which, with more acute faculties, I should be able to perceive; for I cannot conceive myself as placing my hand in the midst of the smoke without displacing the particles with which it comes in contact. The atmosphere, whose ordinary pressure, like the music of the spheres, is unperceived because it is always present, exerts, as is well known, a resistance as great as 15 lbs. on the square inch ; and wherever a body penetrates, it produces during its occupation an atmospheric vacuum. A body, then, is *presented* as real when it actually offers resistance to the locomotive effort; it is *represented* as real when we believe that it would resist if we were in a position to make the attempt. By this test the objects of the senses are instinctively, and often unconsciously, judged. The visible and tangible impressions, which are usually accompanied by the apprehension of resistance, are regarded, first, as signs of the presence of a real object, and afterwards as real objects themselves ; and the sight of the sun in the sky gives us a conviction of its independent existence, as firm as if we could feel it supporting our tread. But that this conviction is indirect, not immediate—the result of association, not of original intuition—is evident from the fact that, when the association is broken, the belief in the reality of the object is instantaneously destroyed. Let an object be given as visible but unresisting, and it is at once acknowledged to exist in appearance only, and not in truth :—

> " Ter conatus ibi collo dare brachia circum ;
> Ter frustra comprensa manus effugit imago,
> Par levibus ventis volucrique simillima somno."*

These lines express the instinctive belief of all mankind in the true criterion of material reality—a belief which is justified and explained by the testimony of consciousness read by the light of psychological research.

OF THE REAL IN COSMOLOGY.

The above observations may furnish materials for a criticism of that branch of Metaphysics known as Cosmology, or the Ontology of the material world. They will serve to point out what are the facts of consciousness which give rise to the conception of such a science,

* Virgil, *Æn.* ii. 792.

and what are the limits within which that conception can be realised. The conception of reality in material objects is derived from the consciousness of extension and resistance in conjunction ; and the philosophy of the real, in this department, has no legitimate field beyond the several conditions and relations of these attributes, as presented in various modes of experience. Its object, therefore, is not a supersensible world lying beyond the facts of consciousness, but the sensible world, in those properties which are primarily and directly made known to us as modes of resistance to the locomotive energy, such as gravity, cohesion, repulsion, motion, and their various subdivisions. Its method is not demonstrative, except in so far as the mathematical attributes of pure extension are applicable hypothetically to extension in conjunction with resistance. In the verification of this hypothesis in any particular case, and in those researches which belong to its own province, it deals with matters of fact ; and matters of fact cannot, as such, be matters of demonstration. This limitation is confirmed, on further consideration, by those facts of consciousness which at first seem to point to a contrary conclusion—the necessary principles and reasonings of geometry. For these have been shown to depend on certain forms or conditions of experience, derived from the constitution of the mind itself, and to imply the existence of nothing but a conscious mind, modified in a certain manner. Of the real existence of its object geometrical reasoning tells us nothing ; but only that, on the supposition of its existence, certain properties may be proved to belong to it ;—the proof, however, being equally valid whether the supposed existence be in fact or merely in imagination. The test of the real existence of matter is resistance, without which extension alone is not conceived as an external reality : and to the modes of resistance, as such, the demonstrations of geometry are not applicable.

The above conception of Cosmology is, it must be confessed, very different from that which metaphysicians in general have attempted to realise. Indeed it may be regarded by some as indicating rather a physical than a metaphysical system; and this charge must be admitted, if the science of Physics is viewed in its most general extent, as embracing the universal properties of matter in general, as well as the special characteristics of this or that body.* But the fault, if it be one, lies, not in the conception, but in the facts of human nature on which it is founded. If our faculties are so limited as to present us only with physical attributes of matter, the Metaphysics of matter can contain nothing more than

---

* According to Aristotle (*De Anima*, i. 1), physical philosophy is concerned with the special operations and attributes of this or that body as such (περὶ ἅπανθ' ὅσα τοῦ τοιουδὶ σώματος καὶ τῆς τοιαύτης ὕλης ἔργα καὶ πάθη). If this definition be accepted, the attributes common to all bodies may be properly referred to a more general branch of philosophy·

the principles and results of Physics in their most general extent.   We may regret, if we please, the limitation, and sigh for a knowledge of a hyperphysical world : but our faculties do not convey such a knowledge, and all our sighing will not make them do so.   The limitation is one which our Creator has thought fit to impose upon us, and, regret it as we may, we cannot escape from it.

But a philosophy which fails to solve, and even refuses to grapple with, certain problems, may vindicate itself by explaining why they are insoluble.   Before quitting the subject of Cosmology, it is necessary to point out in what respects the above sketch falls short of the highest conception of a metaphysical system, and why it does so.   In the first place, it starts from the apprehension of matter as extended, and does not attempt to solve the higher difficulty involved in the notion of extension itself.   Extension cannot be regarded as the unit of material reality ; for it is dependent on a juxtaposition of parts whose reality cannot consist merely in their combination.   Extension is a relation between parts, as exterior to each other ; and a relation implies things related, which must be real in themselves, else no reality could result from their combination.   This difficulty, with all the accompanying paradoxes involved in the infinite divisibility of matter, is abandoned as insoluble: and it is obvious why it is so.   If space is a necessary form of intuition, involved in the laws of our mental constitution, it follows that, to explain the generation of space itself, we must go out of our constitution. To conceive the ultimate reality on which extension depends, I must conceive the non-extended becoming extended—a conception which is impossible; first, because thought is only operative within the limits of possible intuition, and we can have no intuition of unextended matter; secondly, because, to conceive a relation between the unextended and the extended, I must be able to compare them together; and to do this I must be in and out of my mental constitution at the same moment. An ultimate unit of space is thus as inconceivable as a first instant of time; and for the same reason —because both space and time are necessary forms of intuition. In the second place, the riddle which has puzzled the metaphysicians of all ages still remains unanswered :—" How can the one be many, or the many one ?" In other words, " How can a variety of attributes constitute a single object ?" This problem also is insoluble; and for a like reason—because consciousness cannot account for its own laws. If consciousness is limited, the existence of that limit implies the existence of something of which we are not conscious ; and this is equally true of the limits of intuition and of those of thought. Now, it is a necessary condition of conception, as has been already shown, that its object must comprehend a plurality of attributes ;—in other

words, that thought is impossible except under the condition of diversity in unity.*　To explain why this is so
would be to explain why our minds are constituted as
they are ; and this involves a criticism of the laws of
thought themselves.　But such a criticism manifestly
destroys itself ; for it can only be carried on by thought
operating under the very laws whose validity is questioned.　Whatever doubt, therefore, can be raised concerning the object of criticism must likewise affect the
critical process itself.　Wherever, therefore, we fix the
limits of thought, something must remain inexplicable.
From this we cannot escape, except by denying that
thought has limits ; and this denial again annihilates
itself ; for if thought has no limits, nothing is unthinkable ; and if nothing is unthinkable, nothing is absurd ;
and if nothing is absurd, no system of philosophy is
more reasonable than another, and the denial of limits is
not more true than the assertion of them.　In the third
place, metaphysical philosophy is admitted to be concerned, not with matter as it is, but with matter as we
conceive it ; and this admission, too, is a necessary consequence of the laws of consciousness, in its manifestation, as a relation between a subject and an object.　We
cannot compare the object of consciousness with a thing
of which we are not conscious ; for comparison itself is
an act of consciousness ; we can only compare one

* See above, pp. 192, 209.

2 A

object of consciousness with another—the permanent with the transitory, the necessary with the contingent. There still remains the question, "Do things as they are resemble things as they are conceived by us?"—a question which we cannot answer, either in the affirmative or in the negative; for the denial, as much as the assertion, implies a comparison of the two.* If, then, *being* is interpreted to mean the absolute beyond consciousness, and *appearance* the relative within it (an interpretation, however, which is not warranted by the analysis of consciousness itself), it must be admitted that the philosophy of the material world, in its highest form, is not Ontology, but Phenomenology.

OF THE REAL IN PSYCHOLOGY.

This admission, however, cannot be extended to the second branch of the Metaphysics of Being, which deals with the internal consciousness and the personal self; for here the interpretation on which it depends is utterly untenable. Psychology, like Cosmology, cannot transcend the limits of consciousness; but in Psychology it cannot in any sense be maintained that the real is that

---

* Kant maintains that the objects of our intuition *are not* in themselves as they appear to us (*Kritik der r. V.* Transc. Æsth. sec. 8). Here, however, the critic becomes a dogmatist in negation, and contradicts his own fundamental hypothesis; for if things in themselves are absolutely unknown, how can we say whether they are like or unlike anything else?

of which we are not conscious. My own consciousness is not merely the test of my real existence, but it actually constitutes it. I exist in so far as I am a person ; and I am a person in so far as I am conscious. Were it possible, which it is not, to conceive the human soul as a substance of which consciousness is only an accidental mode—which may exist at one time in a conscious, and at another in an unconscious state—such a soul could in no sense of the term be called *myself;* the various modes of its existence could in no sense be called *mine.* The Cartesian *cogito, ergo sum,* is so far from being, as its opponents have maintained, an illogical reasoning from a premise to its conclusion, that its only fault consists in assuming the appearance of a reasoning at all. My consciousness does not *prove* my existence, because it *is* my existence. Descartes does not intend, as Reid imagined,[*] to reason from the existence of thought to the existence of a mind or subject of thought : he intends to state wherein personal existence consists ; and he rightly places it in consciousness.[†] The opinion of Locke,[‡] that

[*] *Inquiry,* chap. i. sec. 3.

[†] See the dissertation of M. Cousin, "Sur le vrai sens du *cogito, ergo sum,*" printed in the earlier editions of the *Fragments Philosophiques,* and in vol. i. p. 27, of the collective edition of his works. The same position is well illustrated by Mr. Veitch in the introduction to his translation of the *Discours de la Méthode,* p. 22. See also *Principia,* p. i. secs. 8, 9, 53. There is a remarkable anticipation of the Cartesian doctrine in St. Augustine, *De Civ. Dei,* xi. 26.

[‡] *Essay,* b. ii. ch. i. sec. 10.

the soul does not always think, is tenable only as a part of that false psychology which regards the soul as a substance projected, as it were, out of consciousness, the unknown substratum imagined as the support of known accidents.* If I am never conscious of myself, but only of my ideas, I can, of course, pronounce nothing concerning the conditions of my real existence; but then, upon the same supposition, I could never have known that *I* am conscious, or that the ideas are *mine*. If there is nothing given in consciousness but ideas, there is no such thing as personal existence; but only a multitude of isolated ideas, each conscious of itself. Put the question in another form: ask what is the evidence that *I exist* at all; and I can only adduce the direct witness of consciousness. The existence of *myself* is a fact of consciousness, not an inference from it; for an *I* must be presupposed to make the inference. The unconscious

---

* Locke's assertion is but partially refuted by Leibnitz (*Nouveaux Essais*, ii. 1), who holds that, in sleep without dreams, the mind is in a state of obscure perception, not amounting to consciousness;—an opinion which is also maintained by Wolf, *Psychologia 'Rationalis*, sec. 59. But the opposite opinion, suggested by Aristotle (*De Somno*, c. i., ἢ συμβαίνει μὲν ἀεὶ καθεύδουσιν ἐνυπνιάζειν, ἀλλ᾽ οὐ μνημονεύουσιν), is adopted by some of the most eminent psychological and physiological writers of modern times, as confirmed both by *à priori* probability and by positive experience. (See Kant, *Anthropologie*, secs. 30, 36; Jouffroy, *Mélanges Philosophiques*, p. 290; Holland, *Chapters on Mental Physiology*, p. 80; Brodie, *Psychological Researches*, p. 147.) Some valuable remarks and illustrations of this position are contained in Sir W. Hamilton's *Lectures on Metaphysics*, Lect. xvii.

substratum of possible ideas may be a *soul*, in some arbitrary and unmeaning definition of that term ; but assuredly it is not *myself*. If we could suppose a human body growing up to maturity without conscious-ness, and a conscious principle afterwards infused into it, the body in its previous condition would be no more a part of myself than the limb which was amputated from me ten years ago, and which is now dissolved into its chemical elements. Yet the inquiry, how far per-sonality is diminished by amputation or increased by corpulence, is not more irrelevant than to ask when consciousness begins in a new-born infant or in the fœtus in the womb. In so far as the rudiments of my body existed prior to the birth of consciousness, in so far they were not parts of myself : and I, as a person, had no existence. I hold that my personality is undimin-ished by the loss of a limb, simply because I am con-scious that it is undiminished ; and for the same reason I refuse to acknowledge that *I* existed in the rudi-mentary fœtus, or in the germs from which it was formed, or in the organism of my remote ancestors.*

* "For aught I know," says Coleridge, "the thinking spirit within me may be *substantially* one with the principle of life and of vital oper-ation. For aught I know, it may be employed as a secondary agent in the marvellous organisation and organic movements of my body. But surely it would be strange language to say that *I* construct my *heart !* or that *I* propel the finer influences through my *nerves !* or that *I* com-press my brain, and draw the curtains of sleep round my own eyes !" (*Biographia Literaria*, vol. ii. p. 158, ed. 1847.)

But when we place the personal existence in consciousness, it is necessary to distinguish between the accidents of consciousness and its essential constituents. A man who has lost his eyesight has in one sense less consciousness than he had before; he has lost that portion which consists in the sensations of vision. But his personality remains undiminished by the loss either of the bodily organ or of the affections of consciousness which that organ communicates. The same may be said of the other bodily senses; each of which may be conceived to be annihilated without any destruction of the personality of the conscious subject. This is the natural testimony of consciousness to the spirituality of man. We cannot help believing that the body and its organs, however necessary during the present life to certain modes of consciousness, however chronologically the occasion of the earliest development of consciousness in general, is yet no part of the conscious subject—is not, in any sense of the term, *myself*. And this instinctive conviction of the untaught consciousness of mankind is further strengthened by all that science tells us of the constitution of the body and its organs. Of the animal body is emphatically true what Heraclitus and the general voice of philosophy after him declared of the objects of sense in general :*—it exists not, but is continually being produced; it no sooner comes into being

* See Plato, *Theatetus*, p. 152.160; Arist. *Metaph.* i. 6 ; xii. 4.

than it ceases to be. At no two successive moments does it consist of exactly the same particles ; and during the course of a long life the entire system is many times destroyed and renewed again. Our whole physical existence is but a series of chemical changes ; "the solid," to quote the words of a recent writer,* "melting into the liquid, the liquid congealing into the solid ; whilst both stand so related to the air, which is the breath of life, that they are continually vaporising into gases." Yet amidst all these changes, the conscious subject, the personal self, continues one and unchanged. A similar distinction between the accidental and the essential must be made with regard to the internal consciousness : the matter of that consciousness is continually changing ; while the form abides permanent and immutable : emotions, thoughts, volitions, succeed one another at every moment : the self—feeling, thinking, willing—is one and the same throughout. It is not necessary to my personal existence that I should feel joy or sorrow, anger or tranquillity ; for the calm man of to-day is the same as the angry man of yesterday ; and he who laughs to-day may weep to-morrow. Nay, more : not only is every special experience which constitutes the matter of consciousness alien to and separable from the personality of the subject ; but even a portion of the form of consciousness must be regarded

* Professor George Wilson, in the *Edinburgh Essays*, p. 313.

as having in this relation only a hypothetical and secondary necessity. The intuition of space, though necessarily accompanying every perception of matter, whether in our own organism or in the exterior world, is yet necessary only so long as we are in the body and conscious by the bodily senses. We cannot positively conceive a state of existence from which space is separated; yet, on the other hand, we are compelled to believe that existence in space is an attribute of body, and not of mind.

But when all these are set aside, there yet remain two conditions which I conceive as essential to my personal existence in every possible mode, and such as could not be removed without the destruction of myself as a conscious being. These two conditions are *time* and *free agency*. To consciousness, in its limited and human form of existence (of the Divine Consciousness we are not entitled to speak), it is essential that there should be a permanent subject with a succession of modifications. The consciousness of any object, as such, is only possible under the condition of change; and change is only possible under the condition of succession. Destroy this condition, and though I am not warranted in saying that no kind of consciousness can exist, I am warranted in saying that such consciousness could not be *mine*. That a being now subject to the law of succession should be identical with one hereafter not so subject, implies a self-contradiction; for it implies a consciousness of the relation of present to past, and the absence of time, the basis of that relation. Succession in time is thus manifested as a constituent element of my personal existence, without which I could not be conscious of that existence; and, as consciousness is in this case reality, without which I could not exist. Again, consciousness in its human manifestation implies an active as well as a passive element;—a power of attending to the successive states of consciousness, as well as a succession in those states themselves. Attention appears to be necessary, not merely to the remembrance, but even to the existence of various states of consciousness as such;—indeed, attention is but consciousness in operation upon some definite object.[*] But in attention we remark, obscurely, indeed, but certainly, the presence, in a more or less obtrusive form, of the power of volition. It is impossible, indeed, to estimate by analysis the exact amount of will, in the strict sense of the term, that is implied in the ordinary cognition of objects; the frequency of the act having obliterated the distinctive marks of its several elements, before we are capable of reflecting upon them; but its presence as a constituent element is not the less surely implied, though it requires some research to disengage it. It is not going too far to say that, without the conscious exercise of volition, the distinction between the

* See above, p. 136.

permanent subject and its transitory modes, between *myself* and *my affections*, could never have arisen in the human mind; and the consciousness of that distinction is even now observed to vary with the fact which gives rise to it, to become more or less vivid in proportion as the consciousness of voluntary action is more or less obvious. *I* am emphatically and prominently present to my own consciousness in the exercise of choice: those acts are peculiarly *mine* which are consciously imputable to me as their cause, and for which I feel myself responsible.* Volition is not, indeed, the whole of personality, but it is one necessary element of it ;— the consciousness of the one rising and falling with the consciousness of the other ; both more or less vividly manifested, as is the case with all consciousness, according to the less or greater familiarity of particular instances ; but never wholly obliterated in any ;— capable at any moment of being detected by analysis, and incapable of being annihilated by any effort of thought. That a conscious being can, under no possible conditions, be a merely passive link in the chain of causation is more than I can venture to assert ; but this much I know, that such consciousness could not possibly be *my* consciousness ;—that *I* could not become such a being, retaining my present personality

---

* See on this point, Kant, *Religion innerhalb der Grenzen der blossen Vernunft*, part i. sec. 1.

unimpaired ; but that I must be destroyed, and a distinct being substituted in my place. The freedom of the will is so far from being, as it is generally considered, a controvertible question of philosophy, that it is the fundamental postulate without which all action and all speculation, philosophy in all its branches, and human consciousness itself, would be impossible.

The task, then, of the metaphysician, in this branch of his science, is to unravel and solve the difficulties which accompany the conception of Personality in its twofold character—that of existence in time, and that of free agency. The fact itself is in both cases equally indubitable : it is as certain, from the testimony of consciousness, that we are free agents, as that our ideas occur in succession, one after another. We are not called upon to account for this ;—which would be to account for our own existence ; every attempt at which must manifestly assume the very fact which it professes to call in question ;—but assuming this as the basis of consciousness, and, in consciousness, of personal existence, we must endeavour to meet the objections to which it is apparently liable, and which will generally be found to arise from a misinterpretation of the testimony of consciousness itself. For instance, it has been asked, How can a real thing exist in time ? and if it does so, how can we be conscious of its existence ? The earlier phases of its being have passed by, and

exist no more ; the future exists not yet ; the present is
perishing as we contemplate it : How can these several
phenomena make one thing? and if they can, how
can we be conscious of it? To know that my past
self is identical with my present, I must compare them
together ; this is impossible, as they cannot be made to
exist together. · Nay, even to compare the thought of
one with the thought of the other, I must contemplate
them successively ; and thus each vanishes as the other
presents itself.* The answer to this objection may be
furnished by a more accurate analysis of the idea of
time itself. The consciousness of time does not simply
imply succession : it implies a permanent subject under
successive modifications. The object of consciousness
can only be presented as successive, on the condition
that the subject is presented as continuous. It is only
when I become an object of consciousness to myself
that I become a member of a successive series ; but in
this case the object is not the presented self, but my
representative conception of that self. *My notion of myself* may alternate in consciousness with my notions of
other things ; but it can do so only on condition that
the *presented self*, the subject, and not the object, of consciousness, remains one and indivisible. The subject, it
is true, cannot be contemplated apart from its modifica-

* See Herbart, *Lehrbuch zur Einleitung in die Philosophie*, sec.
120, sqq. ; *Hauptpuncte der Metaphysik*, sec. 11.

tions ; for this would be to transform it from a subject to an object ; but the two elements are not the less clearly discerned in the relation of consciousness ; though they are discerned only in conjunction with each other. For this reason, the language which implies succession becomes obviously improper when applied to the subject of consciousness. I may speak accurately enough of my earlier and later thoughts or feelings ; but I cannot, with any philosophical accuracy, speak of an earlier and later *self*, even as a merely logical distinction, for the sake of afterwards identifying the two. To identify is to connect together in thought objects of consciousness given nuder different conditions of space or time; as when I pronounce the man whom I met in the street to-day to be the same who called at my house yesterday. But *myself*, the subject of consciousness, is never given under these different relations at all. It is that presentation from which our original notion of numerical identity is drawn, and which cannot be subjected to later and secondary applications of the same idea. These considerations may perhaps throw some light on the vexed question of *personal identity*—a question which can only be asked concerning the represented self, or notion made an object; and which cannot be asked at all without presupposing the presented identity of the subject.

A like answer may be made to the objections against

free-will, drawn from the supposed necessity of a determining antecedent in time.　Consciousness, rightly interpreted, repudiates both the extreme theories ; that of an irresistible determinant, or set of determinants, and that of an arbitrary will, altogether uninfluenced by motives.　Two alternative motives are manifested in consciousness as both influencing, but neither compelling ;　and the freedom of the will consists, not in being absolutely uninfluenced, but in the power of determining which of the two influences shall prevail.　Of a temporal antecedent necessarily determining my volitions, consciousness tells me nothing ;—nay, it tells me the very reverse, that the influence of such an antecedent is not necessary.　It is only when the idea of volition is excluded, and, with volition, that of choice, and, with choice, that of contingence, that the temporal antecedent is transformed into a necessary determinant.*
But this merely negative idea of necessity, which is, in fact, only an inability to conceive contingence, is derived solely from the absence of volition, and is inapplicable where volition is present.　The only positive notion which I possess of *causative power* is that of *myself determining my own volitions.*　This notion presupposes the freedom of the person, and has no existence whatever if that freedom be denied.　To apply this notion in support of the hypothesis of necessity, is not

* See above, p. 270.

only to go beyond, but actually to reverse the testimony of consciousness. It is, in fact, to say that the consciousness of myself having absolute power over my own volitions is identical with the consciousness of something else having absolute power over me.

But if we are conscious that we are free, we are free in reality; for, as regards the personal self, consciousness *is* reality. In this respect the Ontology of the personal self, which stands in the place of the rational Psychology of the pre-Kantian metaphysics, occupies a very different position from the Ontology of the material world, which inherits the unsolved problems of rational Cosmology. The latter science, in its only attainable form, is but a Phenomenology of a higher order. It can distinguish between the permanent and the transitory attributes of matter relatively to consciousness; but it is compelled to admit the possible existence of a further material world of things, of which we are not conscious, and which may or may not resemble the objects of which consciousness, and, through consciousness, philosophy, takes cognisance. But, as regards *myself*, this supposition is inadmissible. I exist as a person only as I am conscious of myself; and I am conscious of myself only as I exist. The consciousness of Personality is thus an Ontology in the highest sense of the term, and cannot be regarded as the representation of any ulterior reality. The neglect of this distinction forms the weak point in the otherwise masterly discussions of Kant on the antinomies of pure reason. Denying the existence of an immediate consciousness of self, and holding, as all who deny this must do, that the freedom of the will is incompatible with existence in time, he endeavoured ·to save liberty itself, and, through liberty, morality, by a distinction between the phenomenal self of consciousness, and a real self, of which we are not conscious. The self of consciousness, he said, is a phenomenon existing in time; and, as such, is necessarily determined by antecedent phenomena. If, then, phenomena were things in themselves, freedom would be impossible. But beyond the field of consciousness there must exist a transcendental self, the ground and support of the phenomena; and to this transcendental subject, as under no conditions of time, we may legitimately attribute a power of self-determination, or free causality. To this attempted solution obvious objections may be raised. In the first place, it may be urged that our real personal existence is the existence of consciousness; and no higher guarantee of reality can be admitted. The self of consciousness is the true self : that which is beyond consciousness, if such can be supposed, is in this case the phenomenon. In the second place, we are not compelled in thought to postulate the existence of any transcendental self at all; for consciousness itself presents the permanent subject of its own phenomena. In the third place, liberty is so far from being incompatible with consciousness, that it is directly given in consciousness itself ; for I am immediately conscious that the temporal antecedents of my volition exercise no coercion upon it. Kant's solution is, in fact, the very reverse of the truth :—it is the self of consciousness which is really free : the hypothesis of necessity can only be maintained by the gratuitous supposition of a law of causality beyond consciousness, by which I am determined without knowing it. Such a perversion of the truth, on the part of so profound a thinker, can only be explained as a consequence of that suicidal position maintained as a canon of psychology by the philosophers of the last century ; namely, that I have no immediate consciousness of myself, but only of my successive mental states—a position which can only be described as one among many pernicious results of that reaction of physical upon mental science which, under the abused name of inductive philosophy, was permitted to poison with its crude analogies the very fountain and source of philosophy itself. The same consciousness which tells me that I am compelled to believe in the existence of a material world when I am not directly conscious of it, tells me also that I am directly conscious of myself, and that I exist in and by that consciousness. To overlook the distinction thus clearly laid before us is to confound with each other the two poles of speculative philosophy, the subject with the object, the necessary with the contingent, the permanent with the transitory, the *ego* with the *non-ego*.

Beyond the attributes manifested by consciousness as essential to personality, the Ontology of the soul has no province. It cannot assume those attributes as the basis of any further demonstration; for the principles of demonstration are inapplicable to real objects. Neither the simplicity of the soul nor its immortality can be demonstrated as a necessary truth; for they are not implied in the conception of personality, and beyond that conception we have no intuition of necessary relations. The favourite representation of the soul as a simple substance, indivisible, and therefore indestructible, is one which, except so far as it is synonymous with continuous existence in time, is either untrue or unmeaning. If interpreted to mean that the conception of personality comprehends only a single attribute, it is untrue; if intended to state that the soul is not composed of parts coadjacent in space, it is unmeaning except on the principles of materialism. A material atom is an intelligible expression, whether the object which it denotes is conceivable as really existing or not. A mental atom is as utterly unmeaning as the opposite expression of a mind composed of atoms.* Immor-

---

* The only legitimate argument from the simplicity of the soul to its immortality is of a purely negative character. We are not authorised to

tality, again, however surely guaranteed upon other grounds, cannot be represented as a necessary attribute of personal existence. That which did not exist once, may, without any absurdity, be supposed not to exist hereafter. The power which was sufficient to create is also sufficient to destroy ; and if man is destined to exist for ever, it is from no inherent immortality of his own, but solely because such is the will of his Maker. That we are designed for a future life, may indeed be inferred from the direct testimony of consciousness, in so far as it reveals the existence within us of feelings and principles which do not find their full satisfaction in this life; but this inference, however legitimate, does not fall within the province of Metaphysics.

OF THE REAL IN THEOLOGY.

In treating of the third branch of Ontology, that of Rational Theology, it is necessary to take a different course from that adopted by the majority of those metaphysicians who have attempted theological reasoning at all. In the number of these, however, we cannot

say that we know the soul to be simple, and that therefore it is indestructible ; but only that we do not know the soul to be compound (indeed, that the epithets *compound* and *simple*, as applied to the soul, have no meaning), and, therefore, that we cannot infer its mortality from the analogy of bodily dissolution. And this is, for the most part, the limit within which the argument is confined by one of the soberest as well as deepest of thinkers, the admirable Bishop Butler. The majority of philosophers, however, have not been so cautious in their reasoning.

include those philosophers, whose systems, however veiled under the language of theism, or even of Christianity, exhibit a conception of the Deity which virtually amounts to pantheism. A personal God cannot be identified with all existence; and an impersonal Deity, however tricked out to usurp the attributes of the Godhead, is no God at all, but a mere blind and immovable law or destiny,* with less than even the divinity of a fetish, since *that* can at least be imagined as a being who may be offended or propitiated by the worshipper. But, however much we may sympathise with the purpose of those philosophers who have endeavoured to demonstrate, *à priori*, the existence and attributes of a personal God, we cannot help feeling that such demonstrations, whatever may be their apparent logical validity, carry no real conviction with them to the believer or to the unbeliever.† And the reason of this is not far to seek. No demonstration from conceptions can prove the real existence of the object conceived; and, till this is done, the demonstration of the attributes of a hypothetical object proves no more than

* See Kant, *Beweisgrund zu einer Demonstration des Daseyns Gottes, Vierte Betrachtung*, sec. 3.

† For a criticism of some of the principal demonstrations of this kind, see Kant, *Kritik der reinen Vernunft*. Abth. iii. B. ii. Hauptst. 3. The same grounds of objection are also applicable to other reasonings of this kind. Compare Waterland's *Dissertation on the Argument* à priori *for a First Cause*.

the connection between certain thoughts in our own minds.* The actual existence of an object can never be shown by thinking about it; for imaginary objects are as capable of being represented in thought as real ones. Reality must be tested, not by thought, but by intuition: we must be able to point to certain facts of consciousness in which the object of which we are in search is actually presented before us; or, at least, which can only be accounted for on the supposition that such an object exists. But this argument from the facts of intuition is not *à priori*, but *à posteriori*: it does not commence with a general conception, in order to exhibit by analysis the subordinate conceptions comprehended in it, or to construct in imagination a corresponding object; but it starts from certain facts of experience, manifested in the outer or inner consciousness, in order to determine the nature of the object which those facts present or point out to us.

We must therefore begin our inquiry by asking, What are the facts of consciousness which appear directly to indicate the existence of a spiritual being superior to ourselves? Two of the intuitions of the internal consciousness appear especially to possess this character:—the *sense of dependence* and the *sense of moral obligation*. To these must be added, as an indirect and collateral witness, the *consciousness of limitation*, which,

* See above, p. 279.

by suggesting, though not immediately presenting, the unlimited as its correlative, serves in some degree to interpret and connect the other two. The argument from causation, through holding an important place among the evidences of natural religion, can hardly be placed among those direct indications of consciousness which come within the legitimate province of Metaphysics. We are immediately conscious, indeed, of the necessity of supposing a phenomenal antecedent to every event; but we are not immediately conscious of a necessity of conceiving that the series of phenomena is limited or unlimited. Nay, rather, we are conscious of two counter inabilities, which hinder us from conceiving either an absolutely first cause, or an absolutely unlimited series of causes and effects.* We have thus two contradictory hypotheses, one of which must be believed, though neither can be comprehended ; and the evidence of reason being thus neutralised, we are bound to adopt that alternative which is most in harmony with the remaining testimony of consciousness.

* The counter arguments on either side are exhibited by Kant, in his first antinomy of pure reason. The same conclusion, however, is evident without argument, from the direct testimony of consciousness. For to conceive an absolutely first member of the causal series is to conceive a beginning of all time, and thus to be conscious of a relation of time to an object out of time, and therefore out of consciousness ; and to conceive an infinite series of causes and effects, we must carry our thought through an infinite succession of objects—a process which would require an infinite time to accomplish it.

But in so doing, we obey a moral, not an intellectual obligation ; and our conviction, as far as the argument from causation alone is concerned, is not that of reason, but that of faith. The conclusion from the evidences of design in the works of creation, which is but a special form of that from causation, is likewise not an immediate suggestion of consciousness, but the gradual product of experience and comparison, arguing by analogy from what we have learned concerning the works of man, to what we may infer concerning the works of God. Such arguments have great value in their own place, as illustrative of, and auxiliary to, the convictions forced upon us by our religious and moral instincts ; but they are based upon reflection, not upon intuition ; and, though they may serve to enlarge our conception of the Deity when once formed, they do not explain its origin and formation.

The province of the metaphysical theologian is confined to those evidences which belong to the direct testimony of the intuitive consciousness, as manifested in the feelings of dependence and moral obligation. The feeling of dependence is something very different from the mere recognition of the relation of subject to object in consciousness, and of the consequent limitation of the one by the other.* It is a feeling that our welfare and

* In consequence of not distinguishing between these two, Schleiermacher (*Der Christliche Glaube*, sec. 4) has fallen into the error of repre-

destination are in the hands of a superior Power ; not of an inexorable fate or immutable law, but of a Being having at least so far the attributes of personality that He can show favour or severity towards those dependent upon him, and can be regarded by them with the feelings of hope, and fear, and reverence, and gratitude, and be addressed in the words of prayer and praise. It is a feeling similar in kind, though higher in degree, to that which is awakened in the mind of the child by his relation to his parent, who is first manifested to his mind as the giver of such things as are needful, and to whom the first language he addresses is that of entreaty. With the first development of consciousness, there grows up, as a part of it, the innate feeling that our life, natural and spiritual, is not in our own power to prolong or to sustain ; that there is One above us on whom we are dependent, whose existence we learn, and whose presence we realise, by the sure instinct of prayer. That this feeling is natural to us, is manifested by the universal practice of mankind ;—every nation, however degraded may be its form of religion, having some notion of a superior being, and some method of propi-

senting our relation to the world as a feeling of partial dependence, and our relation to the Deity as one of absolute dependence. Thus represented, God can no longer be conceived as a person, but is nothing more than the world magnified to infinity ; and the feeling of absolute dependence becomes the annihilation of our personality in the being of the universe. Of this feeling, the intellectual exponent is pantheism.

tiating his favour. We have thus, in the sense of dependence, the pyschological foundation of one great element of religion—the fear of God.

But the mere consciousness of dependence does not in itself exhibit the character of the Being on whom we depend. It is as consistent with superstition as with true religion—with the belief in a malevolent as in a benevolent deity ; it is as much, if not more, called into exercise by the painful and terrible aspects of nature as by the pleasing and encouraging. It indicates the power of God, but not necessarily his goodness. This deficiency, however, is supplied by the other psychological element of religion, the consciousness of moral obligation. It is impossible to maintain, as Kant has attempted to do,* the theory of an absolute autonomy of the will; that is to say, of an obligatory law resting on no basis but its own imperative character. The will, or practical reason, with its law of immutable obligation, is in itself a fact of the human constitution, and it is no more. Kant's fiction of an absolute law, binding upon all rational beings whatever, has only an apparent uni-

---

* See *Metaphysik der Sitten* (Abschn. ii. pp. 61, 71, ed. Rosenkranz). Thus refusing to acknowledge an intuition of God as a moral lawgiver, Kant is compelled to rest the evidence of the existence of the Deity on an assumed necessity of rewarding men according to their deserts, a necessity which implies an all-wise judge who can estimate merit in every degree. For an able criticism of Kant's theory, see Müller *On the Christian Doctrine of Sin* (vol. i. p. 73, of the English translation).

versality, because we can only conceive other rational beings by identifying their constitution with our own, and making human reason the measure and representative of reason in general. Why, then, has one part of my constitution, as such, an imperative authority over the remainder? What right has one part of the human consciousness to represent itself as duty, and another merely as inclination? There is but one answer possible. The moral reason, or will, or conscience—call it by what name we please—of man, can have no authority, save as implanted in him by some higher spiritual being, as a law emanating from a lawgiver. Man can be a law unto himself only on the supposition that he reflects in himself the law of God. If he is absolutely a law unto himself, his duty and his pleasure are undistinguishable from each other; for he is subject to no one, and accountable to no one. Duty itself becomes, in this case, only a higher kind of pleasure—a balance between the present and the future, between the smaller and the larger gratification. We are thus compelled, by the consciousness of moral obligation, to postulate a moral Deity, and to regard the absolute standard of right and wrong as constituted by the moral nature of that Deity.* The conception of this

* The theory which places the standard of morality in the *Divine nature* must not be confounded with that which places it in the arbitrary *will* of God. On the latter, see the remarks of Sir James Mackintosh, Second Dissertation, *Encyclopædia Britannica*, 8th edition, vol. i. p. 312;

standard in the human mind may indeed be faint and fluctuating, and must be imperfect ; it may vary with the intellectual and moral culture of the nation or the individual ; and in its highest human representation it must fall far short of the reality. But it is present in all mankind, as a basis of moral obligation and an inducement to moral progress ; it is present in the universal consciousness of sin—in the conviction that we are offenders against God. However degrading may be the practices into which men have fallen, under systems of false religion, it may be safely asserted that no man, and no nation of men, ever consciously deified vice as such. The voluptuous deities of the pagan mythology were deified as regards their enjoyments, not as regards their vices : their acts were contemplated as divine, not because they were breaches of morality, but because the worshipper falsely conceived them to be ingredients of happiness. The god of a nation of savage warriors may delight in revenge and bloodshed ; but the supposed

and of Müller, *Christian Doctrine of Sin*, vol. i. p. 95. God did not create morality by his will : it is inherent in his nature, and coeternal with Himself ; nor can He be conceived as capable of reversing it. But God did in one sense create human morality, when He created the moral constitution of man, and placed him in certain circumstances, such as those of mortality, of property, of sexual relation, etc., through which the eternal principles of morality are manifested in relation to this present life. On the foundation of morality in the nature of God, see Cudworth, *Treatise Concerning Eternal and Immutable Morality*, b. i. ch. iii. ; b. iv. ch. iv. v. vi.

divinity of his acts does not consist in their cruelty : they are attributed to him because their infliction is an evidence of superiority ; perhaps, also, because their endurance is a test of heroism. Even the worship of an evil principle is a worship of power, not of vice. He causes vice in man, but he is not himself vicious ; for he transgresses no higher obligation of his own nature. He is worshipped, not as a moral governor to be obeyed, but as a malignant influence to be appeased ; and thus he is not, in the proper sense of the term, God ; for his worship implies no duty of imitation or service.* The Deity, however falsely conceived, still represents a moral standard in the minds of his worshippers : the idea of the perfect goodness of God, as implied in the imperfect goodness of man, may be corrupted and degraded, but is never wholly extinguished. The consciousness of right and wrong, of duty and disobedience, even in its most perverted form, involves the consciousness of a Being to whom duty and obedience are due ; whose nature, however imperfectly represented, is necessarily conceived as moral ; and whose commands, emanating from that nature, are manifested in the authority which they communicate to the moral principle in man.

But though we have thus the direct testimony of consciousness to the existence of a supreme Being, on whom our life and welfare depend, and from whom our

* Compare Hegel, *Philosophie der Religion* (*Werke*, xii. p. 173).

moral obligations emanate, the Being thus manifested does not yet realise the full idea of the Deity. For neither in dependence nor in moral obligation can we have an immediate intuition of the Infinite. The dependent is not absorbed in that on which it depends : the consciousness of our personal existence is not annihilated when we feel its relation to a higher power. Self and not-self still divide the universe of existence between them ; and neither can be regarded as exhausting it.* But that which coexists with the finite cannot be

---

* Schleiermacher (*Der Christliche Glaube*, secs. 4, 5) maintains a different view. He resolves the religious consciousness into a feeling of *absolute dependence*, in which the consciousness of our own individuality and activity in relation to a distinct object of consciousness disappears in that of a passive relation to the infinite God. In this view he is followed by Mr. Morell, who says that man, "in the presence of that which is self-existent, infinite and eternal, may feel the sense of freedom utterly pass away, and become absorbed in the sense of absolute dependence" (*Philosophy of Religion*, p. 75). Without dwelling on the difficulties and apparent contradictions involved in the notion of an absolute dependence which is, at the same time, a relative consciousness, this theory appears to be open to one fatal objection ; namely, that it makes our moral and religious consciousness subversive of each other, and reduces us to the dilemma that either our faith or our practice must be founded on a delusion. The actual relation of man to God is the same, in whatever degree man may be conscious of it. If man's dependence upon God is really not destructive of his personal freedom, the religious consciousness, in denying that freedom, is a false consciousness. If, on the contrary, man is in reality passively dependent upon God, the consciousness of moral responsibility, which bears witness to his free agency, is a lying witness. When Schleiermacher assumes the existence of three degrees of consciousness—1. That of the infant, in which there is no conscious distinction of the subject from its object ; 2. The middle state

itself positively conceived as infinite ; otherwise the infinite and the finite together must be conceived as greater than the infinite.   Nor yet can the finite be conceived as merged in the infinite ; for this would be to conceive myself as existing and not existing at the same time. In like manner, it is impossible to conceive an infinite moral nature : for each moral attribute, as coexisting with others, limits and is limited by the rest ; and the very conception of morality implies law, and law is itself a limitation.   Yet, on the other hand, we cannot escape from the conviction that the infinite does in some manner exist, and exists, though we know not how, along with the finite ; and though we can form no positive conception of its nature, we cannot regard the limits of our conception as the limits of all possible existence.   We know that, unless we admit the existence of the infinite, the existence of the finite is inexplicable and self-contradictory ; and yet we know that the

of distinct relation between self and not-self ; and 3. The highest or religious consciousness, in which the relation again disappears—he overlooks the fact that the second and third are not successive stages in the mental development, but must alternate with each other during a man's whole life ; the one presiding over his moral duties, and the other over his religious feelings.   On what ground is one of these states to be regarded as higher than the other, except in so far as it more truly reveals to us our actual state in the sight of God, as free or absolutely dependent ?   And as this state must be always the same, whether we are conscious of it or not, it follows, that in proportion as one of these states reveals to us the truth, the other must be regarded as testifying to a falsehood.

conception of the infinite itself appears to involve contradictions not less inexplicable. In this impotence of reason we are compelled to take refuge in faith, and to believe that an infinite being exists, though we know not how, and that he is the same with that being who is represented in consciousness as our sustainer and our lawgiver. For the contradictions involved in the denial of the infinite are positive, and definitely self-destructive ; as we directly conceive the universe as limited, and yet as limited by nothing beyond itself ; whereas the contradictions involved in the assumption that the infinite exists are merely negative, and might be soluble in a higher state of intelligence ; as they arise merely from the impotence of thought, striving to reduce under the conditions of conceivability that which is beyond its grasp. Thus they are not contradictions manifested in the infinite itself, but only limitations in our power of comprehension. We are compelled, therefore, by reason as well as by faith, to acknowledge that the infinite must exist ; though how it exists, reason strives in vain to fathom, and faith rests content with the duty of believing what we cannot comprehend.

Hence we are compelled to admit that Theology as well as Cosmology, viewed as a branch of philosophy, is not a true Ontology, but only a higher kind of Phenomenology. We believe in the existence of an infinite God ; and we know also that we cannot conceive Him *as* infinite. Our highest conception of the Deity is still bounded by the conditions which bound all human thinking, and therefore cannot represent the Deity as He is, but only as He appears to us. Such a representation, though sufficient for all the practical purposes of religion, is unable to satisfy in full the demands of a philosophical curiosity. But a sounder and more sober philosophy will tell us why those demands cannot be satisfied;—why the highest problems of speculative theology must and ought to be abandoned as insoluble. It tells us that our whole consciousness is relative, and therefore cannot comprehend the absolute; that our whole consciousness is limited, and therefore cannot comprehend the infinite. It tells us that a comprehended infinite could be no infinite at all; for comprehension itself is a limitation; and the unlimited must necessarily be the incomprehensible. To know God as He is, man must himself *be* God. The pantheist accepts this position, and identifies the Divine mind with the universal consciousness of mankind. The theist accepts it also, and is content to worship where he cannot understand.

If this limitation of philosophical theology be admitted, the ground of many a controversy, and the root of many a heresy, is cut from under it at the very commencement of inquiry. In acknowledging the existence, and at the same time the incomprehensibility, of the infinite, we at once confess that we have sufficient grounds for belief, but not for theory. If we have no conception of the infinite attributes of God as such, we may not so interpret those attributes as to place them in antagonism, either to the direct testimony of consciousness, or to the plain language of Scripture; nor yet, on the other hand, can we distinctly shew their compatibility with either, though we are bound to believe it. How, for example, can we reconcile man's free-will with God's foreknowledge? Rather, why should we attempt to do so, when in the attempt we must needs substitute our limited conception of the Divine nature for that nature as it is? We know not how an infinite intelligence contemplates succession in time; we know not whether his consciousness is subject to the law of succession at all. Eternity, in relation to the Divine mind, may be, as the schoolmen said, a *nunc stans*, in which there is no distinction of past, present, and future. Foreknowledge may be merely a means of accommodating the representation of Divine Omniscience to human faculties. To speculate in any direction—to adopt a theory of *scientia media* on the one hand, or of absolute predestination on the other—is to deify our own ignorance; to make the human conception the measure of the Divine reality. Why, again, cannot we conceive infinite power as undoing that which is already done. If the sun has risen this morning, why can we not conceive that even Omnipotence can now cause that it shall not have risen? Simply because we cannot conceive infinite power at all ;—the limitation is not of omnipotence in itself, but of all power as the object of human thought. How, again, can we reconcile the exercise of two Divine attributes with each other? How can infinite mercy pardon every sin, and yet infinite justice exact the utmost penalty? How can we tell, when we can conceive justice and mercy only in their finite forms, as they are capable of existing in human consciousness? It is obvious how the same principles may be applied to controversies concerning those deeper mysteries of the Christian faith which rest on the evidence of revelation only. But into this sacred ground it would be foreign to our present argument to enter.

OF THE REAL IN MORALITY.

The Ontology of Morals is subject to the same limitations with that of Religion. If the standard of perfect and immutable morality is to be found only in the eternal nature of God, it follows that those conditions which prevent man from attaining to a knowledge of the infinite as such, must also prevent him from attaining to more than a relative and phenomenal conception of morality. And, in truth, man's moral, like his religious consciousness, will vary according to his state of mental and moral culture : he may have higher or lower ideas of duty, as he may have higher or lower ideas of God. But it does not therefore follow, as was maintained by the sophists of old, that each man is the measure of all things to himself, and that morality is nothing more than the law which any man or nation chooses to enact for a certain time within a certain sphere.* The very expressions a *higher* and a *lower* standard, imply that there are degrees of right and wrong, even in relative and limitedmorality ;—that one human conception of duty may be more perfect than another, even if none can attain to absolute perfection. There is such a thing as an enlightened and an unenlightened conscience ; though no man may presume to say that his own conscience has attained to the greatest amount of enlightenment of which even human nature is capable. It is a

---

* So far from it, that the above ground is constantly taken by the antagonists of the sophistical doctrine, for the express purpose of refuting it. Thus Plato, in the Dialogue especially devoted to the refutation of the dogma of Protagoras, that " man is the measure of all things," asserts that some portion of evil must needs exist in our mortal nature, and that we must endeavour to escape from it by an imitation, according to our power, of the Divine justice and holiness (*Theatetus*, p. 176). And Aristotle, after stating, as opposed to his own view, the sophistical position that all justice is conventional and variable, remarks—καίτοι παρά γε τοῖς θεοῖς ἴσως οὐδαμῶς (*Eth. Nic.* v. 7). Even the comic poet, in his Dialogue between the Unjust and the Just Discourse, representing respectively the sophists and their antagonists, puts into the mouth of the latter the same argument :—

ΑΔ. οὐδὲ γὰρ εἶναι πάνυ φημὶ δίκην.
ΔΙ. οὐκ εἶναι φῇς; ΑΔ. φέρε γὰρ, ποῦ 'στιν;
ΛΙ. παρὰ τοῖσι θεοῖς. (Aristoph. *Nubes*, 902.)

mark of the progressive character of natural morality and religion, that no new advance in knowledge contradicts the *principles* which have previously been acknowledged by the conscience, however much it may modify the particular acts by which those principles are to be carried out.   To be zealous in God's service is a principle of religious duty common to Saul the persecutor and to Paul the apostle ; though its result in action is at one time to destroy the faith, and at another to preach it. And it is a mark of the same character, that each fresh advance in moral and religious knowledge carries with it the immediate evidence of its own superiority, and takes its place in the mind, not as a question to be supported by argument, but as an axiom to be intuitively admitted. Each principle of this kind recommends itself to the minds of all who are capable of reflecting upon it, as true and irreversible so far as it goes ; though it may represent but a limited portion of the truth, and be hereafter merged in some higher and more comprehensive formula.   The principles, for example, that virtue, relatively to the human constitution, consists in observing a mean between two extremes, or in promoting the good of others, or in a reasonable self-love, all represent views containing a portion of truth ; though none can be considered as exhausting the whole truth. While human nature is complex in itself, and susceptible of various relations and various duties arising out of those relations, it is not to be expected that all human virtue should be reducible to a single attribute, or capable of expression in a single formula. Yet its general character is not therefore doubtful because it admits of being viewed in various special aspects. Two men who differ in their definition of virtue will yet generally be agreed as to who is the virtuous man. "Let me die the death of the righteous, and let my last end be like his," expresses the conviction of one who, though far from righteous himself, was yet compelled to acknowledge the existence of a higher human standard than his own rule of conduct.* "As much as it has been disputed," says Bishop Butler, "wherein virtue consists, or whatever ground for doubt there may be about particulars; yet in general there is in reality an universally acknowledged standard of it. It is that which all ages and all countries have made profession of in public: it is that which every man you meet puts on the show of: it is that which the primary and fundamental laws of all civil constitutions over the face of the earth make it their business and endeavour to enforce the practice of upon mankind :—namely, justice, veracity, and regard to common good."†

Nevertheless, there is an useful lesson to be drawn from the frequent fluctuations of men's moral theories

---

* See Bishop Butler's *Sermon on the Character of Balaam.*
† *Dissertation on the Nature of Virtue.*

as well as from the general agreement of their practical confessions. It is not unusual for philosophers to reason as if they were possessed of an absolute, and not merely of a relative standard of morals ;—as if they had attained to the conception of eternal morality, as it exists in the nature of God, instead of to that temporal manifestation of it which is adapted to a particular state of the constitution, and stage of the progress, of man. The works in which Kant and Fichte have attempted to construct an à priori criticism of revelation, upon moral grounds, are remarkable instances of this departure from the limits of all sound philosophy.* Both assume that the sole purpose of revelation must be to teach them morality ; and both assume that the morality thus taught must be identical to the minutest particular with the system attained by human philosophy ;—which last is supposed to be absolutely infallible. Hence Kant maintains that the revealed commands of God have no religious value, except in so far as they are approved by the moral reason of man ; and Fichte lays down, among the criteria of a possibly true revelation, that it must contain no intimation of future reward or punishment, and must enjoin no moral rules which cannot be deduced from the principles of the practical reason. Whereas, in truth, the principles of the practical reason are susceptible of

---

* See Kant's *Religion innerhalb der Grenzen der blossen Vernunft,* and Fichte's *Versuch einer Kritik aller Offenbarung.*

additional enlightenment with every stage of man's progress in this life (and it may be also with every stage of
his progress in the life to come), and revelation, in two
sentences, has conveyed to us a principle of human
morals, which the philosophy of ages had toiled after in
vain, and which the philosophy of a later day has been
content to borrow without acknowledgment, and to pervert in attempting to improve :—" Thou shalt love the
Lord thy God with all thy heart, and with all thy soul,
and with all thy strength, and with all thy mind ; and
thy neighbour as thyself." *

OF THE REAL IN THE PHILOSOPHY OF TASTE.

With the Ontology of Morals is not unfrequently associated that of Taste.   The good and the beautiful were
in the Greek language often expressed by the same word ;
and are by many regarded as alike expressing absolute
and immutable principles, equally independent of human
opinion, and equally objects of philosophical inquiry.†
But, in truth, the object of the so-called Philosophy of
Æsthetics appears, even in its highest form, to have far

* See Kant's criticism and attempted explanation of these precepts,
Kritik der praktischen Vernunft, B. i. Hauptst. iii. (p. 209, ed Rosenkranz).

† See especially M. Cousin's Lectures, *Du Vrai, du Beau, et du
Bien*, where absolute beauty is referred to the same Divine standard with
absolute goodness and absolute truth : and so Hutcheson entitles his
treatise *An Inquiry into the Original of our Ideas of Beauty and Virtue.*

less of an absolute and immutable character than belongs to the objects of Metaphysical inquiry, even within the limits to which they have been confined in the preceding pages. The beauty of an object appears to depend, not so much on the character of the object itself, as on the feeling of pleasure which it excites in the spectator; and this, again, on the accidents of his present constitution.* This appears to be the case even with the moral beauty of an action, when that quality is viewed apart from the other ingredients of its moral character. The consciousness that a certain action is morally pleasing to me is not necessarily connected with that of its moral rectitude; though the two have frequently been confounded together in the various theories concerning the moral sense.† But it is easy to conceive that moral obligation might remain undiminished, even if no gratification were derivable from the observance of it; while, on the contrary, it seems impossible to conceive the existence of an obligation to be pleased apart from the apprehension of the moral character of the act. The beauty of sensible objects appears to ex-

* See Kant, *Kritik der Urtheilskraft*, secs. 1, 6, 15 (*Werke*, iv. pp. 46, 56, 76). The sublime, as well as the beautiful, is admitted by Kant to be not a quality of things, but a feeling of our superiority over nature (*Ibid.* sec. 28, p. 122). Some masterly remarks on the nature and origin of our feelings of pleasure, in relation to the beautiful and the sublime, will be found in Sir W. Hamilton's *Lectures on Metaphysics*, Lect. xlvi.

† See above, p. 163.

hibit still more fully the marks of a merely phenomenal and relative character. A slight change in the shape and refractive power of the eye would alter all our perceptions of the form and colour of objects, and, with them, the impressions of beauty and deformity derived from this source. And if the senses themselves are confined to the apprehension of phenomena, how can the beauty of the objects of sense lay claim to a higher character? Can we then assert that sensible beauty is a reflection and imitation of ideal beauty, in the same manner and degree in which our perceptions of moral duty aim at and imply a divine standard of right and wrong? Even the fluctuation in the opinions of various individuals and nations, though far from being a decisive criterion in any case, appears to be acknowledged by the general sense of mankind to be a test more conclusive in questions of taste than in those of truth or rectitude. The very name *taste* seems to imply something subjective, and, to a considerable extent, arbitrary. The maxim, "*De gustibus non disputandum est*," may be the exaggerated expression of a popular conviction ; but, at any rate, it carries no such shock to the natural feelings of mankind as does the sophistical assertion that the distinctions between truth and falsehood, virtue and vice, are based on convention, and not on nature. Nor is it difficult to detect the foundation of truth which underlies the exaggeration. The maxim is

true, in so far as it virtually asserts that beauty is subjective, not objective ; an affection of the person who is
conscious of it, existing only in and by that consciousness, not a permanent quality existing in things, and
capable of being expressed by a general notion.* But
it is exaggerated, in so far as it apparently denies the
existence of a common sense of beauty, among men of
cultivated minds, by virtue of which similar affections
will be produced in different minds by the same object.†
But this admission, while it saves the standard of taste
from the charge of arbitrariness and instability, at the
same time removes the philosophy of taste from the
province of Ontology, and limits it to a Psychological
investigation of those relations between the imagination
and the understanding which give rise to the consciousness of beauty in an object actually present.‡

* See Kant, *Kritik der Urtheilskraft*, sec. 17 (*Werke*, iv. p. 81).

† See Kant, *Kritik der Urtheilskraft*, secs. 6, 22. Kant resolves
the feeling of beauty into an indefinite consciousness of *fitness with reference to an end* (Zweckmässigkeit), but without the representation of
any definite end. He admits, however, that this consciousness is merely
subjective, and that there can be no objective rule, capable of determining beauty by conceptions. Similarly Jouffroy, in his *Cours d'Esthe-
tique*, regards the feeling of beauty as a sympathy with the expression
of active force (as distinguished from inert matter) developing itself in
conformity with its end. Here, again, the action of the force is not
perceived in the object, but supplied by the imagination of the spectator.

‡ See Kant, *Kritik der Urtheilskraft*, sec. 34.

CONCLUSION.

We have thus indicated, rather than discussed, some of the manifold aspects of the great fundamental problem, which, various in its external forms, but one in its real import, has stimulated the researches of thoughtful men in all ages, under the names, used for the most part synonymously, of First Philosophy, Ontology, or Metaphysics :—the problem, namely, to distinguish *that which is* from *that which seems to be.* Whether we look to its earliest definite statement, in the dogma of Parmenides, that Being is one and unchangeable, and that variety exists only in the fancy of men ; or to the boast of Zeno, that he would explain all things, if there were only given to him the One ;—whether we examine Plato's conception of the science of Dialectic, as that which contemplates real existence by the aid of the pure intellect, illuminated by the brightness emanating from the essential form of good ; or ask the question which the same philosopher describes as embracing at once the deepest mysteries of philosophy and the pettiest quibbles of sophistry, How can the one be many or the many one ;—whether we adopt Aristotle's definition of the First Philosophy, as the science which contemplates being as being, and the attributes which belong to it as such ; or, with Descartes, assume the fact of our own personal existence, manifested in consciousness, as the one primary and indubitable truth ;—whether, with Leibnitz, we regard the sensible world as composed of an aggregate of unextended monads or metaphysical points ; or, with Kant, divide objects into noumena and phenomena, things as they are in themselves and things as they are related to human faculties ; or, with Fichte, postulate the existence of an absolute self, implied by, though not given in consciousness, or, with Schelling, attempt by intellectual intuition to reach the point of indifference in which the relations of subject and object are merged in the identity of both ; or, with Hegel, found a philosophy on the hypothesis of an absolute thought, identical with absolute being, and susceptible of development into the various modes of personal and impersonal finite existence ; or, with Herbart, find a common object of all metaphysical inquiries in the solution of the contradictions which present themselves in experience ; in all these, and other different statements, we recognise only verbal varieties of one and the same fundamental distinction ;—a distinction which, however perverted in artificial systems, must have a natural origin in the human mind ; which must be given in one mode of consciousness, or else it could not have been invented in any.

We have endeavoured to ascertain the primary and presentative fact of consciousness in which this distinction is given,—a fact upon which all the secondary and representative varieties of it must be based ; and thus to fix the limits within which a Science of Being is possible and beyond which it cannot be carried. This fact seems to be discoverable in the relation between a permanent self and its successive modifications, which forms the condition of all human consciousness. If this be admitted, Ontology, in the highest sense of the term, becomes identified with Psychology ; and the future task of the metaphysician will consist in exhibiting the conditions involved in the idea of personal existence, and solving the difficulties to which that idea appears to give rise. To attempt to accomplish this task in detail would require a far greater space, and a more minute examination, than is possible within the reasonable limits of a work like the present. We must content ourselves with having pointed out the fact that such problems exist, and stated the reasons for believing that they are not to be abandoned as insoluble.

Beyond the range of personal existence we have no positive conception of real being, save in the form of those more permanent phenomena which constitute our general conceptions of certain objects, as distinguished from the transitory phenomena with which those conceptions are at certain times associated. Here Ontology is but a higher kind of Phenomenology : its object is not a thing in itself, but a thing as we are compelled to conceive it : and to attempt to give to this branch of philosophy a more absolute character is to substitute negative ideas for positive—to desert thoughts, and to take refuge in words which have no real meaning, save in relation to a different mode of consciousness. We do not, therefore, attempt to solve the higher problems of Cosmology and Theology, nor even to indicate the conditions under which they might be solved. But we have attempted to shew why they are insoluble, and what is the origin of that delusion which has led men in various ages to fancy their solution possible, and to devise systems for accomplishing it. The failures of great minds are often not less instructive than their successes ; and the time that is spent in wandering among the mazes of Metaphysical speculation will not be wholly lost, if it teach us that knowledge which it is the end and aim of all sound philosophy to inculcate,—the knowledge of ourselves and of our faculties ; of what we may and what we may not hope to accomplish ; of the laws and limits of Reason ; and, by consequence, of the just claims of Faith.

INDEX.

THE END.